What Others Are Saying About This Book

"This fascinating, insightful book is more than technique; it has very practical suggestions on 100+ common issues most parents and educators face. It breathes a sound philosophy and way of thinking that empowers us, instead of our constantly looking to others for solutions."

Stephen R. Covey, Ph.D.
Author of *The 7 Habits of Highly Effective People*

"This book delivers! It will dramatically improve the quality of your own life and make an astounding difference in your relationships with others."

John Gray, Ph.D.
Author of *Men Are from Mars, Women Are from Venus*

"Marvin Marshall's insights, innovative ideas, and ingenuity provide a clear plan for raising responsible children. The benefits to schools and families are enormous."

Gene Bedley, National Educator of the Year
Author of *Character Lessons for Life*

"This comprehensive book is an excellent resource that should be made priority reading."

Martin Lubetsky, M.D.
Chief, Child and Adolescent Psychiatry Services
University of Pittsburgh School of Medicine

"The strategies that Dr. Marshall describes for developing humane, responsive, and responsible classrooms are grounded in research AND good practice. They link classroom management concerns to the more fundamental issues of how teachers can create powerful curriculum, teaching, learning, and lasting motivation. I recommend this book to anyone who wants to create a 'right to learn' in all classrooms."

Linda Darling-Hammond, Ed.D., Professor of Education
Stanford University
Author of *The Right to Learn*
Director, National Commission on Teaching and
America's Future

"Dr. Marshall is renowned for his expertise in teaching, parenting, discipline, and motivation. This book proves how well he also knows this new generation as his timeless principles are remarkably effective in the new millennium."

Eric Chester, President and Founder
Generation Why, Inc.

"As a parent, teacher, guidance counselor, speaker, trainer, and author, I can confidently say this book is a dream come true! Dr. Marshall addresses problem areas in each of my roles. I am fascinated by his revolutionary approach to rewards, punishments, and responsibility. I am eager to integrate his ideas into my own philosophies and behaviors and to recommend this treasure to others in my training sessions."

Barbara-Lynn Taylor, M.Ed.
Author and Co-Producer of *Successful Parenting*

"Several years ago, I had the opportunity to do a lengthy interview with B.F. Skinner. I concluded that I do not subscribe to much of what he taught—for example, his rejection of all inferred states such as attitudes and motivation . . . . Dr. Marvin Marshall's book addresses a fundamental problem that every society must solve: how to produce individuals who will take responsibility for doing the important tasks that need to get done. He focuses on what is the essence of good citizenship in the home, school, and nation. Using some of the latest findings of social science, Dr. Marshall has developed an approach that enables parents and teachers to help young people grow into responsible citizens and live satisfying and rewarding inner-directed lives."

Gene Griessman, Ph.D.
Author of *The Words Lincoln Lived By*

"Dr. Marshall has provided both new and experienced teachers with a comprehensive and thought-provoking resource—one sure to be used with great frequency. The breadth of information covered might prove daunting were it not for the practical and concise nature with which it is delivered. This text should prove to be an invaluable tool for educators."

Marti Pogonowski, Staff Development Specialist
Anne Arundel County Public School, Gambrills, MD

"I can't wait to recommend Marvin Marshall's book at my parenting classes and seminars. He gives practical knowledge that inspires us to think in new effective ways. I'm already using his principles in my personal relationships."

Kathy Collard Miller
Author of *When Counting to Ten Isn't Enough*

"This brilliant work should be required reading for every parent and teacher. If everyone applied these practical techniques, we could build a truly wonderful future for our society."

Steve Kaye, Ph.D.
Presentations on *The Human Side of Business*

"Marv Marshall makes a compelling argument that stress, punishment, and rewards are counterproductive in raising or teaching children. At best they merely create temporary compliance. More likely, they corrode relationships, deter risk-taking, overlook the underlying causes of behavior, and subvert the learning process. Marshall points the way to successful strategies such as reframing perceptions and initiating specific intervention techniques. Parents, teachers, and principals should read this book—and rush to do so."

Elaine Haglund, Ph.D., Professor
Education, Administration, & Counseling
California State University, Long Beach, CA

"For those teachers and school leaders who want to get serious about improving student achievement, this book will be very helpful. Its attention to classroom management skills, motivating students, and establishing a positive relationship with students are key ingredients to ensuring that students aspire to great things starting with academic accomplishment."

Gordon Cawelti, Senior Research Associate
Educational Research Service
Former Executive Director
Association for Supervision and Curriculum Development
(ASCD)

"This timely work is on the mark in providing rich, practical tools for every reader. Each chapter opens doors to fresh insights and pragmatic roadmaps."

Robert Danzig, Former President
Hearst Newspapers

"Discipline is not easy in our culture. Our Puritanical past has led to many wrong assumptions about how to channel behavior. In this book, Marvin Marshall shows us how to overcome these counterproductive patterns while promoting responsibility and growth in young people. It is an important work, and I highly recommend it."

Jim Cathcart
Author of *The Acorn Principle: Know Yourself—Grow Yourself*

"As parents and educators, we need all the assistance we can get. Marv Marshall helps us reduce our stress and increase our potential success by giving us many helpful ideas. You will find this book filled with insights and proven strategies that can be applied to all age levels."

Nancy K. Utterback, Ph.D., Professor
Education & Character Education, Walsh University, OH

"This book has great payoffs. It shows how to raise responsibility—a basic desire and need of our society. The quality of family life and school life will improve as the principles of this book are put into practice. School and workplace leaders will make many applications to management practices as well."

Steve Barkley, Executive Vice President
Performance Learning Systems

"This book is excellent for teachers dealing with the pressures of curriculum, parents, and students. Relationships are a key, and the book is a great source for building them."

Cindy Moilanen, 5th Grade Teacher
Centennial Elementary, South Lyon, MI

"This is the most comprehensive book I have ever seen complementing Choice Theory (William Glasser). It clearly explains practical ways to use internal motivation and noncoercive approaches. I heartily endorse and recommend it."

Wayne O'Brien, Earth Science Teacher
Campbell/Savona Central School District, Campbell, NY

"This is an important, highly readable book for beginning teachers struggling to find techniques that work—as well as for experienced teachers and administrators tired of maladaptive educational practices. Coupling solid research with countless practical examples, Dr. Marshall has made a valuable contribution to the literature. I highly recommend this book for everyone's professional library."

Larry Litwack, Ed.D., Professor
Counseling and Applied Educational Psychology
Northeastern University
Editor-in-Chief
International Journal of Reality Therapy

"This book is a potent contribution to the field of child service. Not only has Dr. Marshall shown us a philosophy that works, he makes it easy to understand and implement. Everyone wins—especially our young people."

James Sutton, Ed.D., Child Psychologist
Author of *If My Kid's So Nice...Why's He Driving ME Crazy?*

"*Education* comes from the Latin, *educare*, to bring forth. This book is a masterful guide to bring out the best in yourself and others."

Robert Gedaliah, Former New York City High School Teacher
President, *Speaking for Results*®

"This book is a pleasure to read. It has a wealth of insights and illustrations to reduce classroom frustrations and improve educational performance. The strategy for raising conscious awareness gives increased understanding of how to improve relationships. Any reader will be impressed with the depth and breadth of the topics covered."
Al Mintzer, Principal
AIM Center for Ethical Critical Thinking and Decision Making

"Self-directed people are resourceful. They engage in cause-effect thinking, spend energy on tasks, set challenging goals, persevere, are optimistic, feel good about themselves, and control anxiety. To achieve this human potential, the focus of education needs to shift. Both teachers and students must become internally-driven learners: self-analyzing and self-modifying. Marvin Marshall's book provides the science, structures, and strategies that further this cause."
Arthur Costa, Ed.D., Professor Emeritus
California State University, Sacramento
Co-Founder, Institute for Intelligent Behavior

"If every teacher, at the beginning of the school year, would share this book with students for just 10 minutes a day, by October, teaching and learning problems would be reduced to a miniscule portion of the day."
Linda McKay, Director, CHARACTERplus
Cooperating School Districts, St. Louis, MO

"Character can be measured by what we do when we are sure no one else is watching. And this book gives specific suggestions to anyone interested in the growth of young people to help ensure that they develop responsible character and behavior."
Margaret Connery, Corporate Trainer and Former Teacher

"Marv Marshall's book covers a broad spectrum of ideas and information guaranteed to help promote responsibility. His approach to internal motivation and *The Raise Responsibility System* are right on target. As a mother of a four-year-old, it was valuable information for me."
Jodi Walker, Speaker and Trainer
Author of *Exceptional Accomplishment*

"This book provides a wonderful opportunity to put parents and teachers on the same page! It describes effective strategies to help parents and teachers work together toward a positive and encouraging environment for the children they care for."
Adria Manary
Author of *Mommy Magic: 450 Ways to Nurture Your Child*

"This book should be required reading for student as well as credentialed teachers."
Dr. Don Brann, Superintendent
Wiseburn School District, Hawthorne, CA
Co-Founder, California Small School Districts Association

"The practical and useful strategies presented in this book make it a must for teachers—beginning as well as veteran. The chapter on teaching will improve every teacher's skill. The suggestions for reducing anonymity are on the mark, especially for our large high schools. Several suggestions implement the recommendations of the National Association of Secondary School Principals report *Breaking Ranks: Changing an American Institution.*"
Anthony Avina, Ed.D., Superintendent
Whittier Union High School District, Whittier, CA

"This book is a quick and enjoyable read, a sound contribution to education, and an excellent investment to every reader. Wise and timeless concepts, along with good sense and practical wisdom, are woven throughout the book in a logical sequence. Dr. Marshall's book deserves to be read by every teacher and administrator."
Steve Hammond, Superintendent of Catholic Schools
Diocese of Nashville, TN

"Dr. Marshall's book addresses many concerns voiced by new and continuing teachers. This book can serve as a powerful and practical resource for educators and parents alike."
Martha Evans, Ed.D., Assistant Superintendent
West Covina Unified School District
Senior Adjunct Professor
University of La Verne, La Verne, CA

"This book provides the tools to create an enriched learning environment. It provides practical applications, thoughtful suggestions, and excellent insights to improve teaching and learning in any classroom."
Al Katz, Classmeeting Program
William Glasser Institute

"This comprehensive book brims with life-enhancing ideas. At a time when student behaviors are at the forefront of American consciousness, this book actualizes theory and provides educators with ideas, skills, and techniques that are eminently practical."
Robert Wubbolding, Ed.D., Professor
Counseling Department, Xavier University, Cincinnati, OH

What People Say About
The Raise Responsibility System

District

"Since we have employed your system, our students not only exhibit an immense turnaround in how they act in school, they also work with others at their respective peer level to create a positive learning environment."

—Clair R. Garrick, Superintendent
Elgin School District, Elgin, OR

"We have tried dozens of strategies to improve classroom discipline, all with limited or no success until we tried Dr. Marshall's program. I believe his program, "Discipline without Stress, Punishments, or Rewards," is the best hope public schools have for dealing with discipline issues. We are planning to implement his strategies in all eighteen of our schools."

—Robert E. Beck, Ed.D., Associate Superintendent
Richmond County Schools, Hamlet, NC

"I am so impressed with Dr. Marshall's strategies and the simplicity of the program."

—Sarah Crippen, Education Specialist
Education Service Center Region XV, San Angelo, TX

"Teachers, administrators, social workers, and psychologists were able to begin immediately applying the concepts and implementing many of the strategies you taught us."

—Barbara McFadden, EH/SED Program Resources
Brevard District Schools, Viera, FL

Primary School

"Your ideas about what motivates us have had a profound impact creating a positive environment for our children."

—Pamela Blood, Child Care
Murrieta Valley Unified School District, CA

"Since your presentation, I have already seen your ideas implemented with very positive results throughout our K–3 school."

—Kathryn Parsons, Principal
Burchfield Primary School, Colusa, CA

"Your ideas on rewards and punishments, extrinsic/intrinsic motivation, social responsibility, and strategies for effective discipline were valuable information and very relevant for my teachers in grappling over their discipline problems."

—Patricia Murakami, Principal
Arco Iris Primary Center, Los Angeles Unified School District, CA

"We use your program to accurately evaluate the school's hallways, cafeteria, transition times, and recesses. My students are incredibly empowered at the young age of five."

—Veronica Rideaux, Kindergarten Teacher and New Teacher Mentor
Verde Elementary School, Richmond, CA

"I am so pleased with the program because children take responsibility for themselves. I returned to public education this year and was horrified by the stickers, tickets, etc., that most teachers were using. It's demeaning to children."

—Megan Fettig, Pre-kindergarten Teacher
Austin Independent School District, Austin, TX

"All of my students can now recognize their own level of behavior and label it appropriately. They know almost instantly when they need to make a better choice. This takes much less time away from instruction and keeps the classroom climate stress-free and positive."

—Dianne Capell, Primary Music Teacher
Ikego Elementary School, Zushi, Japan

"The kindergarten teachers were not convinced their students would understand the terminology, but by the end of the week even their kids were using it successfully. The older students picked it up even more quickly. I was walking through the lunch area the first day of school and overheard a fifth-grade boy saying,"I'm going to behave on level C and D all year long."

—Kaye Ragland, Assistant Head of School
Hollywood Schoolhouse, Hollywood, CA

Elementary School

"I now have a way to put a stop to bullying."

—Valerie Mefford, Teacher
Frankfort Independent Schools, Frankfort, KY

"This is the best year I have had in my 25 years of being a principal. Behavior has not been a problem this year. Our students are learning to solve their problems in a positive way. We find that with the proper instruction, students can monitor their own behavior and make responsible choices without the use of punishments or rewards."

—Phelps Wilkins, Principal
Eisenhower Elementary School, Mesa, AZ

"Our staff has been working hard to eliminate coercive practices from our interactions with students. Your strategies help us move closer to our goal."

—Ruth Foster, Principal
Winans Elementary School, Lansing, MI

"We especially liked the fact that the teachers were no longer punishing students, but were instead guiding them to self-analyze. We have begun using authority in a non-adversarial manner in order to establish and maintain a caring classroom environment."

—Pamela Marton, Principal
Community School, Los Angeles Unified School District, CA

"This is the most human approach ever presented in moving children to intrinsically internalize responsibility."

—Faye Anderson, Principal, 21st Century Academy
San Francisco Unified School District, CA

"The 'positivity' that this provides for teachers, administrators, and parents, but, most importantly, for children, changes the lives of all involved."

—Charlene Norris, Principal
Northfield Elementary School, Murfreesboro, TN

"Despite our high student transiency and teacher turnover, the discipline program still has set a tone on our campus that has improved ever since your presentation. Discipline problems have been minimized because students know that misbehavior is not tolerated and that they will still be treated with respect."

—Peter Cole, Principal
San Marino School, Buena Park, CA

"Thank you for coming to Jupiter to share your humanistic approach to maintain classroom discipline. In less than a week's time, teachers have used and have already found success with specific ideas and procedures you shared and modeled."

—Lynn Spadaccini, Principal
Jupiter Elementary School, Palm Bay, FL

"I like the positive emphasis, the way to de-stress, how to get children to take responsibility for their choices, and the systematic approach."

—Lynn Howard, Assistant Principal
Alyce Taylor Elementary School, Sparks, NV

"As a counselor, there are several reasons why I like the system. The main reason is that it is teaching our students the highest levels of social behavior. A second reason is that it is leading our students to use positive, intrinsically motivated behaviors. I always wanted to get students to that level of behavior, but I didn't know how. With your system we are seeing students operate from intrinsic motivation to do the right thing without being told or reminded. The third reason I like the system is that it is a very compassionate way to deal with students, especially when the students make mistakes in their behavior."

—Peggy Morris, Elementary School Counselor
Mesa Public Schools, Mesa, AZ

"Dr. Marshall has an incredible method for increasing good behavior in the classroom."

—Michelle Austin, 2nd Grade Teacher
Fairview Heights School, Hamlet, NC

"I really love the idea of internal motivation—but didn't know it could be taught or learned. I enjoyed becoming aware that the real root of the problems facing us today is the lack of social responsibility—and we can develop it in our students. Pretty doggone exciting!"

—Joy Schmidt, Teacher
McDowell School, Chicago, IL

"This should be a required course of study in every collegiate education major curriculum."

—Al Herring, Principal
Plain Dealing Elementary School, Plain Dealing, LA

"I really liked your philosophy on how students learn. I wanted a way to intrinsically motivate. I have read and read that this is how to do it—intrinsic vs. extrinsic—but never got the how to. Thanks. You gave me that."

—Deneen Zimmerman, Teacher
McDonnell School, Flatwoods, KY

"You have truly given us one of the greatest gifts possible—hope."
—Tom Amato, 6th Grade Teacher
Foothills Adventist Elementary School, St. Helena, CA

"Thank you so much. I am truly inspired!"
—Helen Mahoney
Salisbury Central School, Lakeville, CT

"Thank you for coming up with a program that incorporates growth in the area of social responsibility. We desperately need it."
—Cecille Veloria, Teacher
El Dorado School, Stockton, CA

Middle School

"Dr. Marshall's program was not only well researched and thought out, but it had great success with our at-risk students."
—Antonia Issa Lahera, Principal
George Washington Middle School, Long Beach, CA

"Your one-day seminar laid the foundation for the best year by far ever since the demographic shift of the '80s. We followed up your seminar with some soul-searching discussions and came away from our 'charge' with unity of how discipline should be handled."
—Raymond Hill, Principal
Thomas Jefferson Middle School, Indio, CA

"More important than the reduction in referrals is the understanding of our students that behavior is their responsibility. They have come to understand that they have choices they can make when faced with real-life situations. Our staff now feels they can spend more time on teaching and less time on discipline issues."
—Alfredo Reyes, Vice-Principal
Sierra Vista Middle School, La Puente, CA

"We now have a discipline process that underpins the academic success we are aiming for."

—Barbara Aguilar, Principal
Sierra Vista Middle School, La Puente, CA

"What a great day this has been for both students and faculty. I cannot tell you how much we appreciate what you have taught us."

—Mollie Hicks, Teacher and Coordinator
Martin Luther King Middle School, Monroe, LA

"I am empowered again as a teacher."

—Kathryn Johnson, English Teacher
Cole Camp Junior High School, Cole Camp, MO

"The materials presented were your experience in classroom situations, which made them realistic, not theoretical. You have given me the opportunity to immediately incorporate this into my classroom."

—Stephen Dent, 7th Grade Science Teacher
Henry County Middle School, New Castle, KY

"It reduces stress, one of the greatest problems in teaching today."

—William Roll, 6–8 Computers and History Teacher
Blythe Middle School, Blythe, CA

"The program's use of intrinsic motivation makes the responsibility of classroom behavior fall on the individual student, not on the teacher. It is such a relief to see my students reminding their peers of the responsibility to the class, instead of having to reach a confrontation where punishment was necessary."

—Heather Hawley, English Teacher
Lexington Junior High School, Anaheim, CA

"Everything can be used immediately—not only with students but with anyone I come in contact with. I am empowered."

—Leslie Bezich, English Teacher
Dana Middle School, Los Angeles, CA

High School

"The positive rather than the punitive approach works."

—Nancy Nuesseler, Teacher
Leuzinger High School, Hawthorne, CA

"For the first time in many years, we had advice we could walk back into the classroom and actually use the next day. You helped us realize the importance of using discipline as a learning tool rather than as a purely punitive measure, and that true change in behavior comes from within."

—Gretchen J. Fleming, Ph.D., Principal
Pattonville High School, Maryland Heights, MO

"If punishments worked, our prisons would be empty. If rewards worked, all employees would be productive."

—Mike Gilman, Principal
Palo Verde High School, Blythe, CA

"I am now a better teacher and, indeed, a better person. The insights offered into what motivates us had a profound effect on me. It got me thinking about who I am as a teacher, a husband, and a father. I am stunned and grateful."

—Robert Boyd, English Teacher
Scripps Ranch High School, San Diego, CA

"The entire concept is so easily administered. I am going to recommend we address the topic of social irresponsibility as our state debate topic for next year."

—Donna Ringland, English Teacher and Debate Coach
Laredo, TX

"I was anxious to use the program. I was weary from being in an adversarial relationship with a few disruptive students who drain the energy I need to teach the majority of students who desire to learn."

—Marc Duvall, Teacher
Leuzinger High School, Hawthorne, CA

"I came away with information, learning, and motivation that will allow me to be more successful in the classroom for years to come."

—Robert Prentice, Ed.D., Teacher
Richland, MI

"The program is user-friendly by the step-by-step implementation."

—Gardner Reynolds, Teacher
LaVilla High School, LaVilla, TX

Universities

"You have integrated all the 'best practices' into one comprehensive reform model."

—Elaine Haglund, Ph.D., Professor
Education, Administration, and Counseling
California State University, Long Beach, CA

"We have seldom conducted a conference or workshop that received such consistently high evaluations from participants."

—Wayne A. Babchuk, Ph.D., Program Specialist
University of Nebraska, Lincoln, NE

"With a heightened awareness of the integral role discipline plays in successful schools, we were pleased to have such a hands-on program to help our teachers. A big thank you for sharing your expertise with us in Central New York."

—Scott Shablak, Assistant Dean for Professional Growth
The Study Councils at Syracuse University, Syracuse, NY

Parents

"Dr. Marshall's message is every bit as appropriate for adults as for students."

—Elane Scott, President
Granada Middle School PTA, Whittier, CA

"This opened my eyes to a whole new method. Some days I am nagging my seven-year-old son all day, and we both end up with a lot of negative feelings. You have shown me how to guide, rather than dictate. Now we both end up with positive feelings."

—Leticia Romo, Parent
Alhambra City School District, Alhambra, CA

"The mere fact that my daughter is actually thinking in a positive manner to accomplish something she wants gives me hope. Maybe there is light at the end of this tunnel after all!"

—Teela Gibbens, Parent
Buena Park, CA

Students

"Although I do not know what happened in past experiences, I do know the maturity of this class has heightened."

—Vince N.
Cypress, CA

"I think that the program is really good. It works and it's better than detentions. I think every school should have this. The class hasn't talked as much since you introduced this program. I think they should have this in every class."

—Andrew D.
Cypress, CA

"The program has paid off well. I feel that it is a better solution than detentions, referrals, and even suspension because of the fact that the teacher doesn't have to do a whole lot, but we do. It also helps us to understand what we did wrong. I feel that it's a lot better than serving a detention because we have to use our brains to come up with a solution to the problem. So, in the end, not only are we learning, but also the teachers get a break from all the keeping track of detentions."

—Chris W.
Cypress, CA

Others

"From time to time one comes across a program that impacts on the area in which we live. Such is the case with Dr. Marvin Marshall, who creates a win/win strategy. I found his ideas relevant to our own business where we must deal with improper actions on the part of employees."

—Jim Speer, Director
Rotary International, Covina, CA

"I have felt for a long time that many of the approaches to incentivizing performance and the punitive methods used for lack of performance were unenlightened. Your program gives hope for our educational system."

—Mike Rounds, President
Greater Los Angeles Chapter, National Speakers Association

Discipline
without Stress®
Punishments
or Rewards

Also by Marvin Marshall
Fostering Social Responsibility

Discipline _without_ Stress® Punishments or Rewards

How Teachers and Parents Promote Responsibility & Learning

Marvin Marshall, Ed.D.

Piper Press ◆ Los Alamitos, California

Published by Piper Press
P.O. Box 2227
Los Alamitos, CA 90720
www.PiperPress.com

ATTENTION: SCHOOLS AND ASSOCIATIONS
Substantial discounts on bulk quantities are available to corpora-
tions, professional associations, and educational or other organizations. For details and discount information, contact the special sales
department at Piper Press: 800.606.6105 ♦ 714.995.3902 fax

Publisher's Cataloging-in-Publication
(Provided by Quality Books, Inc.)

Marshall, Marvin L.
  Discipline without stress, punishments, or
rewards : How teachers and parents promote
responsibility & learning / Marvin Marshall. --
1st ed.
  p.cm.
  Includes bibliographical references and index.
  LCCN: 00-105517
  ISBN: 0-9700606-1-0

  1. Discipline of chidren. 2. Responsibility.
3. Learning. 4. Parenting. 5. Stress management.
I. Title.

LB3025.M37 2001   371.5
              QBI00-500158

Printed in the United States of America

Cover Designer: Robert Howard
Interior Designer: Pamela Terry

10 9 8 7 6 5 4 3 2 1
Second Printing

*To Evelyn, my partner for more than four decades,
and our daughter, Hillary, who has taught me so much.*

CONTENTS AT A GLANCE

TABLE OF CONTENTS

FOREWORD

"What should I do to this kid?" is the most common question I receive from the readers of my book, my monthly column on <teachers.net>, and my in-service presentations.

I answer by saying that you do not "do" things to people. Rather, you need to teach people to do things for themselves. Classroom management teaches procedures for accomplishing this.

Discipline is a distinctly different subject. Discipline deals with how people behave, whereas procedures deal with how things are done.

Marvin Marshall has created a program that challenges many current assumptions and practices used with today's young people. He clearly and concisely demonstrates how the external approaches of relying on rules, imposing consequences, rewarding students for appropriate behavior, and punishing students to make them obey are all counterproductive.

This landmark book is a must-read whether you are a starting or experienced teacher, parent, youth worker, counselor, administrator, professor of teacher education, or anyone with an interest in promoting responsibility and growth in young people. You will find each chapter full of insights and strategies that will improve your influence and effectiveness with others.

Harry K. Wong, Ed.D.
Author of *The First Days of School*
www.HarryWong.com

ABOUT THIS BOOK

Who is this book for?

If you experience stress, this book can help you diminish it. If you are a teacher or parent, this book will be especially useful.

What areas does this book include?

This book is a crossover of three areas: education, parenting, and personal growth. It offers practical solutions to real problems in each area. The following is a typical comment: A teacher approached me at a character education conference in St. Louis and said, "*I learned things from you today that I am going to use with my own teenage daughter.*"

Where can the ideas be used?

The strategies in this book can be used in any classroom, type of school, subject area, grade level, or with any youth or youth group. Most also can be used by anyone in a relationship with another person—parent with child, husband with wife, supervisor with supervised.

When can the strategies be implemented?

Every suggestion can be implemented immediately.

Why this book?

When I returned to the classroom after twenty-four years in counseling and guidance and supervision and administration, I met with an awakening. Society and youth had changed, but adults were using approaches no longer successful with so many of today's young people.

Here are three examples of what I learned: (1) If you focus on obedience you may engender resistance and even defiance—whereas focusing on responsibility brings obedience as a natural by-product. (2) Using rules places you in the position of a cop, rather than a coach. (3) Although you can *control* a person, you cannot *change* another person. People change themselves, and coercion is the least effective approach for influencing another person to change.

Many young people today do not demonstrate the level of responsibility necessary to continue our civil democracy. The program that I developed and used in my classrooms eliminated discipline problems—the bane of today's teaching.

I began sharing my approach and strategies in seminars. "Do you have a book?" became a common question. This publication is the result.

How should I read the book?

Each chapter is self-contained. The book need not be read in any particular order. For example, if your highest priority is to learn and implement the stress-reducing, noncoercive discipline program, go right to Chapter 3 and read about *The Raise Responsibility System.*

Chapter 1 shows how to reduce stress.

Three principles to practice are demonstrated: the power of positivity, the empowerment of choice, and the importance of reflection and self-evaluation. The chapter concludes with an exercise demonstrating that life is more successful and satisfying when these principles are used.

Chapter 2 is about motivating others.

People attempt to influence others based upon a theory. After an explanation of theories, the difference between external and internal motivation is explored. Then comes a discussion of rewards, punishments, and how these are two sides of the same motivational coin. The effectiveness of *telling* follows. The chapter concludes with a discussion of mindsets—those perceptions that drive motivation.

Chapter 3 focuses on fostering responsibility.

The Raise Responsibility System describes a discipline program that is noncoercive, is based on internal motivation so youth *want* to be responsible, and is easy to implement. The program has three parts: (1) Four critical concepts are presented. (2) When a student acts irresponsibly, checking for understanding is applied. (3) When a youngster continues to disrupt, authority is used without being punitive.

Chapter 4 is devoted to promoting learning.

The chapter begins with a discussion of the learning climate.

Suggestions are given for improving relationships between the teacher and the class, among students themselves, and between the teacher and individual students. Strategies are described for classroom meetings, collaboration—rather than competition—for quality learning, and reducing perfectionism. The chapter concludes with specific strategies for handling impulse and anger management, resolving conflicts, and dealing with difficult students.

Chapter 5 describes fundamentals for classroom teaching.
Topics include brain hemisphericity (including mindmapping), multiple intelligences, modalities of learning, emotions, styles, lesson planning, levels of intellect, instructional questions, group questioning strategy, choosing key words to frame questions and statements, imaging, stories, metacognition, the senses, additional suggestions for aiding recall and memory, laser learning, seminal shifts, classroom management, and home assignments.

Chapter 6 offers essential practices for parenting.
Topics include practicing positivity, offering choices, encouraging reflection, using effective questions, listening to learn, limiting lecturing and telling, checking assumptions, focusing on the important, asking for assistance, recognizing implicit messages, fostering responsibility, exhibiting personal responsibility, maintaining standards, using authority without being punitive, letting the youngster lead, teaching procedures to deal with impulses, intervening in sibling squabbles, being aware of gender differences, using acknowledgments more than praise, honoring home assignments, working smarter rather than harder, nurturing your child's nature, and reaping the joy of parenthood.

Epilogue – Argues that business is a poor model for learning.
Government, business, and even education leaders often compare schooling to business. Schools are referred to as workplaces, students as customers, and performance is measured in terms of accountability. Equating young people's learning processes with what adults do to make money is a false equation. Using a business model for learning is a practice that has been described by the comic strip character Dagwood Bumpstead, who said, "You know, that makes a lot of sense if you don't think about it."

ABOUT THE AUTHOR

Marvin Marshall is a professional speaker and staff developer who presents for leaders interested in *using internal motivation rather than external coercion* to influence people to change.

His writings on discipline, social development, human behavior, motivation, and promoting learning have been published internationally.

His professional education experiences include:

> *Classroom teaching* at the primary and upper elementary grades, every grade 7–12, and as a full-time instructor in the Division of Education at California State University, Los Angeles.

> *Counseling and guidance* experiences as a middle school counselor, high school counselor, guidance department chair, and certification in *Reality Therapy* and *Choice Theory* by the William Glasser Institute.

> *Curriculum and instruction* as a demonstration teacher, department chair, instructional coordinator, and high school assistant principal of curriculum and instruction.

> *Supervision and administration* as an elementary school principal, middle school assistant principal, high school athletic director, high school assistant principal of supervision and control, high school principal, and district director of education.

Masters thesis in business and economics at California State University, Los Angeles, on leadership and participatory management.

Doctoral Dissertation at the University of Southern California in the combined areas of curriculum, instruction, and guidance.

After 24 years of service in the above areas, Dr. Marshall returned to the classroom where he developed *The Raise Responsibility System.*

The program is now used across the entire teaching spectrum—in small childcare centers to large high schools and in rural, suburban, and urban schools. The strategy can be used in any home or youth setting.

On a personal note, he enjoys theatre and music, and occupies his spare time playing the great highland bagpipes, for which he has served as a pipe major and is certified by the College of Piping in Glasgow, Scotland.

His professional mission is influencing educators, parents, and leaders away from using coercion to using more effective and powerful approaches of *noncoercion* in order to reduce stress, improve relationships, and raise responsibility for both the young and the mature.

Contacting the Author

The author can be reached in the United States of America at
Marvin Marshall and Associates
P.O. Box 2227, Los Alamitos, CA 90720
714.220.0678 ♦ 714.220.2800 fax
Info@MarvinMarshall.com
www.MarvinMarshall.com

ACKNOWLEDGMENTS

I am indebted to many people but have a particularly deep sense of gratitude to:

—My father and mother, who imbued me with those values that perpetuate a civil society and who encouraged me in every way.

—Ivan Smith, who persuaded me to return to education from the business world.

—William Glasser, M.D., for his writings, his teaching, and his continual encouragement and support.

—Tom Chun for his technological skills, business acumen, and persistence that I write this book.

—William Hanrahan for his superb coaching and insights into new vistas.

—My students, who taught me that young people want to be responsible but that too many adults are using wrong approaches to help them.

PREFACE:
THE CALF PATH

One day, through the primeval wood,
A calf walked home, as good calves should;
But made a trail all bent askew,
A crooked trail as all calves do.

Since then two hundred years have fled,
And, I infer, the calf is dead.
But still he left behind his trail,
And thereby hangs my moral tale.

The trail was taken up next day
By a lone dog that passed that way;
And then a wise bellwether sheep
Pursued the trail o'er vale and steep,
And drew the flock behind him, too,
As good bellwethers always do.

And from that day, o'er hill and glade,
Through those old woods a path was made;
And many men wound in and out,
And dodged, and turned, and bent about
And uttered words of righteous wrath
Because 'twas such a crooked path.

But still they followed—do not laugh—
The first migrations of that calf,
And through this winding wood-way stalked,
Because he wobbled when he walked.

This forest path became a lane,
That bent, and turned, and turned again.
This crooked lane became a road,
Where many a poor horse with his load
Toiled on beneath the burning sun,
And traveled some three miles in one.
And thus a century and a half
They trod the footsteps of that calf.

The years passed on in swiftness fleet.
The road became a village street;
And thus, before men were aware,
A city's crowded thoroughfare;
And soon the central street was this
Of a renowned metropolis;
And men two centuries and a half
Trod in the footsteps of that calf.

Each day a hundred thousand rout
Followed the zigzag calf about;
And o'er his crooked journey went
The traffic of a continent.
A hundred thousand men were led
By one calf, near three centuries dead.

They followed still his crooked way,
And lost one hundred years a day;
For thus such reverence is lent
To well-established precedent.

A moral lesson this might teach,
Were I ordained and called to preach;
For men are prone to go it blind
Along the calf-paths of the mind,
And work away from sun to sun
To do what other men have done.

They follow in the beaten track,
And out and in, and forth and back,
And still their devious course pursue,
To keep the path that others do.

But how the wise old woods-gods laugh,
Who saw the first primeval calf!
Ah! Many things this tale might teach,
But I am not ordained to preach.

                              Sam Walter Foss

1
REDUCING STRESS

PRINCIPLES TO PRACTICE

You cannot coerce people into changing their minds.
–Benjamin Franklin, protesting the
Stamp Act to King George III

L ife is a conversation. Interestingly, the most influential person
we talk with all day is ourself, and what we tell ourself has a
direct bearing on our behavior, our performance, and our influence
on others. In fact, a good case can be made that our self-talk creates
our reality. Many psychologists have argued that, by thinking
negatively, we cause ourselves mental and physical stress. Stress is
related to perceiving the world as manageable or unmanageable. By
practicing the three principles below, we can reduce stress because
these principles enhance the management of our world. Practice of
the principles also improves relationships and increases our
effectiveness in influencing others to change their behaviors.

POSITIVITY, CHOICE, AND REFLECTION

The first principle to practice is *positivity*. We know that we learn
and do better when we feel good, not bad. Unfortunately, rather
than communicating in positive terms, we often communicate in
negative terms, such as by using consequences. Although consequences can be positive or negative, when we refer to them we usually
mean punishment, which is negative and coercive. A more effective
approach than consequences is the use of contingencies. Rather
than reactive and negative, contingencies are proactive and positive.
In addition, when using contingencies responsibility remains with
the person with whom we want to foster responsibility.
Communicating positively reduces stress, improves relationships,
and is more effective than negativity in influencing change in others.

The second principle to practice is the use of *choice*. Choice empowers. Many practitioners who have written about behavior maintain that choice is the *prime* principle of empowerment. These include Covey, Deci and Flaste, Deming, Ellis, Frankl, Glasser, Kohn, McGregor, Oakley and Krug, and Senge, among others. Young people learn that regardless of the situation, external stimulus, or internal impulse or urge, they still have the freedom to choose their responses.

The third principle to practice is *reflection*. Reflection is essential for effective learning and retention. In addition, reflection engenders self-evaluation—the critical component for change and an essential ingredient for happiness. The authors listed above all strongly advocate self-evaluation. Perhaps Covey put it most succinctly when he stated, "In all my experiences I have never seen lasting solutions to problems, lasting happiness and success, that came from the outside in." (Covey, p. 43)

KEY POINTS

◆ Stress is directly related to perceiving the world as being manageable or unmanageable.

◆ Practicing the three principles of positivity, choice, and reflection can reduce stress because they enhance the management of our world.

◆ Practicing positivity, choice, and reflection with ourself and with others improves quality of life.

THE POWER OF POSITIVITY

People do better when they feel better, not when they feel worse.

Positivity is a more constructive teacher than negativity. Positive messages elevate, encourage, and foster growth.

ACCENTUATE THE POSITIVE

When thoughts are guided to focus on the positive and constructive, then the self is nourished and enriched. Self-worth is intangible, and much of its cause, as well as its effect, is a matter of choosing thoughts that expand and strengthen the human psyche— rather than constrict or weaken it. A monkey is smart enough to eat only the nourishing banana and throw away the bitter peel. Yet, humans often "chew on the peel" of criticism, ridicule, embarrassment, failure, or other negatives. *It is important that teachers and parents help young people learn to throw away the peel by teaching them to focus on the positive.*

Onc salcsgirl in a candy store always had customers lined up waiting while other salesgirls stood around. The owner of the store noted her popularity and asked for her secret. "It's easy," she said. "The other girls scoop up more than a pound of candy and then start subtracting some. I always scoop up less than a pound and then add to it." People arc likc magncts. Thcy arc drawn to thc positive and are repelled by the negative. This is an important principle to understand when working with others. People who are effective in influencing other people phrase their communications in positive terms.

CONSEQUENCES VS. CONTINGENCIES

Consequences are associated with everything we do and can be positive or negative. An imposed consequence, however, only works when a person finds value in the relationship or when the person sees value in what he is being asked to do. Otherwise, an imposed consequence is perceived in negative terms.

When a consequence is imposed, it is often associated with a threat. Such is the case when the adult says, "If you continue to do that, here is what will happen to you." Telling a youngster, "You chose to do that and must now realize the consequence," is a pseudo choice and plays a mind game. It causes the young person to feel as if he punished himself. "If your work is not finished, you're not going," is also perceived in a negative sense. In this case, the adult also has added to his own workload because now the *adult* has the task of checking on the condition that has been established, namely, to check when the work is finished before giving permission. This approach transfers the responsibility away from the young person—where it belongs—to the adult.

In contrast to imposed and reactive consequences, proactive *contingencies* rely on internal motivation and are perceived in a positive way. "You can *do that as soon as you do this.*" *"If/then"* and *"as soon as"* assist in sending both a positive message and placing the responsibility on the young person—where it belongs. Notice these in the following examples: *"If your work is finished, then you can go to one of the activity centers." "Sure, you can go as soon as your work is finished."*

Although the result of a contingency is the same as that of a consequence, the *message and emotional effect are markedly different.* As already mentioned, when using a consequence the responsibility for checking is placed on the enforcer—the *adult.* When using a contingency, the responsibility is on the *youngster.* In addition, whereas a consequence implies a lack of trust, a contingency conveys a message of confidence and trust. The crucial difference can be best understood in personal terms. Which would you prefer to hear your supervisor say to you: "If you leave and are not back on time, we will have a real problem," or "Sure, you can leave as long as you are back in time"?

An example of the difference between a consequence and a contingency was illustrated on a television sitcom featuring Bill Cosby playing the role of Dr. Cliff Huxtable. He was sitting at the dinner table with Rudy, his youngest daughter. The father would not let the daughter leave the table until she had eaten all of her dinner. Rudy refused to finish her dinner. The father gave her a choice of finishing her dinner and leaving the table or remaining at the dinner table until she did finish. Still, she refused to eat, whereupon the father went on and on about this other 5-year-old who would not finish her dinner, and all her friends went to middle school, graduated from high school, and went to college, but the young girl remained at her dinner table. Rudy, apparently, was not impressed; she still would not finish her meal.

Denise, Rudy's older sister, came into the house, and Rudy could hear Denise and her friends move the living room couch, roll up the carpet, start to play music, and begin to dance. Just then, Denise came into the kitchen, and Rudy asked her older sister, "Can I dance with you and your friends?" Denise said, "Sure, as soon as you finish your dinner." Dr. Cliff Huxtable, the father, gave his daughter what amounted to a consequence: finish your dinner, or stay at the table. Denise, on the other hand, offered a contingency—whereupon Rudy ate her three Brussels sprouts, placed the plate in the sink, and went out to dance. Too often, we say to young people, "Eat your Brussels sprouts or else," and we don't understand why they are not motivated.

WHEN CONSEQUENCES ARE NECESSARY

My experiences with discipline as an elementary school principal, middle school assistant principal, high school assistant principal, and high school principal have all had a common thread: Young people need structure; they want to know where they stand. Consequences provide that security. Ironically, knowing the consequences beforehand provides many young people an invitation for mischief.

Some students will push as far as they can, in part, because they already know the amount of risk involved. Having knowledge ahead of time as to what will happen gives them security and reduces their risk. For example, the youngster is referred to the office for misconduct. The administrator inquires into the cause of the referral. The student pleads ignorance. He is told to stand against the wall for five minutes until he remembers. The student will stand against the wall for five minutes. The same scenario is repeated, except this time the administrator tells the student to stand until he remembers. The student inquires, "How long do I have to stand here?" The administrator responds, "I don't know." The youngster inquires again, "How long do I have to remain here?" The administrator says, "I don't know; I guess until you remember." The student will remember in fewer than five minutes because of the uncertainty of how long he will need to remain standing. The same principle is at work in the high school where the student is stopped in the hallway after the bell has rung. The administrator queries the student, who replies, "This is only my second tardy. I have one more to go before I get detention."

Announcing consequences ahead of time is counterproductive when dealing with young people. Uncertainty is much more effective. Knowing the consequence focuses on the consequence. It is better to have students focus and think about what is appropriate.

If a consequence is deemed necessary, rather than *impose* it, a more effective approach is to *elicit* the consequence from the young person. For example, whenever I was absent from my class, my substitute folder contained a form that requested the substitute leave the names of those students who acted inappropriately. Upon my return, I would speak to those students who had not been good hosts to the visitor in our classroom. The students understood that their behaviors were unacceptable, and I inquired of them what should be done. Having dealt with so many behavior problems at all grade levels, in urban as well as suburban schools, I learned that in the majority of cases the student chose something more effective for changing his or her behavior than I would have imposed. If what the student chose was not acceptable to me, the student would be given other opportunities until we could both agree on the consequence that would help the student to become more responsible. The key response I had ready was, "What else? What else?"

Here is another example of how *eliciting a consequence*—rather than *imposing one*—was used. The school year was almost over, and a student had done something that could not be overlooked. The eighth-grade party, the big event of the year, was fast approaching. The student understood that what he had done could not be ignored. The question was put to him, "What shall we do?" He said, "I guess I shouldn't go to the eighth-grade party." I responded that I could live with that decision. By my eliciting the consequence, ownership and responsibility remained with the student. The teacher was not the villian, and the student was not the victim.

To be effective for long-lasting results, the person must feel ownership. Lack of ownership is a prime reason why student discipline contracts do not work. A contract agreed to under duress engages little ownership from a young signer.

PROJECT POSITIVE EXPECTATIONS

Attitude is the mind's paintbrush; it can color any situation. The teacher who says, "This is a very important test. Be careful," paints a negative picture that shakes confidence. Saying, "This is a very important test and I know you can handle it and do well," paints a positive picture.

Which would you rather hear when you walk into a restaurant: "I can't seat you for thirty minutes" or "In thirty minutes I will have a wonderful table for you"? The result is the same, but the perception is different. The child who wets his bed conjures up one image when the parent says, "Don't wet your bed tonight" and a completely different picture when the youngster hears, "Let's see if you can keep the bed dry tonight." The message we convey can have a dramatic effect on young people's behavior.

The first step is awareness. To assist in becoming aware of negative statements, listen to yourself. When catching yourself saying something that paints a negative picture, take the extra step of thinking how it could be rephrased to paint a positive picture. "I'm afraid that I will forget my keys," becomes, "I'm going to remember that I placed my keys in the top drawer." Adults do not purposely set out to deprecate young people; awareness of positive language can ensure they do not. For example, rather than saying, "Did you forget again?" say, "What can you do to help yourself remember?" Rather than, "When will you grow up?" say, "As we grow older, we learn how to solve these problems from such experiences."

Positive attitudes affect teaching. Many years ago, the first day of school began on a bright note for the new teacher, who was glancing over the class roll. After each student's name was a number 118, 116, 121, and so on. "Look at these IQs," the teacher thought. "They have given me a terrific class!" As a result, the elated teacher challenged his students, raised their expectations, and communicated his confidence in them. The teacher tried innovative techniques and involved students so they became active learners. The class did much better than expected. Only later did the teacher find out that the numbers placed by students' names on new class roll sheets were locker numbers.

Here is a simple way to start off each year, especially at the elementary level. At the end of the previous year, each teacher writes one positive comment about every student that will be passed on to the student's new teacher. The comment can relate to an interest, a talent, a personal skill, an attitude, or anything else worth sharing.

The result is that the student's new teacher is equipped at the very outset with a positive viewpoint toward each student.

Students at risk often think about what they are *not* good at doing. These students are often right-hemisphere dominant, so their strengths do not lie in the left-hemisphere (logical, linguistic) areas in which schools focus after the primary grades. These students may have some hidden talent in art, psychomotor skills, leadership, or personal relations. Find one interest, talent, or skill these students possess and, in private, say something positive to them. "I see you draw well. I can tell because of the detail in your drawing." The message with students who have low self-worth needs to be repeated a number of times in different ways. Sometimes young people have to believe in someone else's belief in them until their own belief in themselves kicks in. Building on the positive gives a positive mindset. *The pictures that young people have of themselves drive their behaviors.*

We always want to refer to the behavior, never the person. If you say, "You are late all the time; you are just one of those late people," the person will work to that expectation. On the other hand, saying, "You have such great work habits in many areas, and punctuality is something that you can improve on. I know you are capable of being here on time each day," then the young person has something for which to strive. A positive picture has been created.

Also, consider the fact that mood follows action. Grandmother knew this, which is why she said to mother, "If you don't feel good, clean the stove." Similarly, doing something productive engenders positive feelings, in contrast to doing something negative or doing nothing at all. The advice is sound: *Change what you do and you change your view.*

Research has shown that optimism, whether "natural" or "learned," results in better health. People who are optimistic have a better handle on dealing with their emotions, which has an impact on the immune system, heart, and other body functions.

Positivity brings hope, which is a cousin of optimism. A series of tests on hope was given at the University of Kansas, and results were compared to the Scholastic Aptitude Test (SAT) scores, which are supposed to determine success as a college freshman. It was found that the test scores on hope were better predictors than the SAT scores. Hope and optimism are learned. They are teachable. A starting point is always to ask yourself, *"How can I say that in a positive way?"*

KEY POINTS

◆ People do better when they feel good, rather than when they feel bad.

◆ Consequences are usually imposed, which is the prime reason why they are perceived negatively and why they do not change the way a person wants to behave.

◆ Advertising consequences ahead of time is counterproductive because it focuses on consequences, rather than on expected behaviors.

◆ If a consequence is deemed necessary, rather than assign it, a more effective approach is to elicit the consequence, thus placing ownership and responsibility on the young person.

◆ Contingencies promise with the positive and place the responsibility on the young person, where it belongs, rather than on the adult.

◆ Negative comments engender negative attitudes. Positive comments engender positive attitudes.

◆ People who are most effective in influencing other people phrase their communications in positive terms.

◆ Positivity brings hope.

◆ The pictures that people have of themselves drive their behaviors.

◆ Positivity prompts feelings of being valued, enthusiastic, supported, respected, motivated, challenged, capable, and proud.

THE EMPOWERMENT OF CHOICE

They offer sufficient proof
that everything can be taken from a man but one thing
…to choose one's attitude in any given set of circumstances.
–Viktor Frankl

Teaching young people about choice-response thinking—*that they need not be victims*—may be one of the most valuable thinking patterns we can give them. Students become more responsible when they learn that in almost any *situation*, or with any *stimulus*, or with any *impulse* or *urge*, they still have freedom to choose a response.

CHOICE-RESPONSE THINKING

Situation

I was comfortably seated in an airplane ready for take-off on a flight to California. I had just started reading a book when the pilot announced there would be a two-hour delay; Los Angeles International Airport was fogged in. After a few minutes of additional reading, I gazed up from my book and discovered that I was one of the few passengers who had not deplaned. Even with a good read, adding two-hours to the three-hour flight seemed a little long to remain seated. I left my materials, already in the overhead storage compartment, and returned to the airport terminal. After a half-hour of strolling and shopping, the thought occurred to me that, if the fog in Los Angeles lifts, the plane might take off sooner than the two-hour announced time. I quickly returned to the loading area and watched my plane depart with my coat, seminar materials, and luggage.

This was a situation I could have avoided if I had not gone strolling and had stayed in the loading area. Although at that moment I could not change that situation, *I could still choose my response.* Getting angry would have been useless. I checked the departure schedule, arranged for a later flight to Los Angeles, and told an official my belongings were on the plane. Upon arrival in Los Angeles, I found my coat, materials, and luggage waiting for me. I felt pleased that I had taken a rational approach to the situation.

We all experience situations that are beyond our control, either momentarily or permanently. We are confronted with weather and other natural forces, with inconveniences, unpleasant assignments, unrewarding family or work relationships, and numerous situations that we cannot change. However, *we can choose our responses to these situations.*

Victor Frankl, the psychiatrist who survived Nazi death camps, experienced situations beyond his control. Yet, he taught that a person has the power to choose his thinking, his independence of mind, even in the most terrible conditions of psychic and physical stress. Although conditions such as lack of sleep, insufficient food, and various mental stresses suggest that the camp captives were bound to react in certain ways, in the final analysis it became clear that the sort of person the captive became was the result of an inner decision—not the result of camp influences alone. Even under such extreme circumstances, a person still has one freedom: "the last of the human freedoms—to choose one's attitude in any given set of circumstances, to choose one's own way." (Frankl, p. 104)

Stimulus

We also have the freedom to make a choice after something *stimulates* us. When a parent smiles at the infant, the infant smiles back. Such stimuli become less "automatic" with growth, as when the parent smiles at the teenager, but the teenager does not reciprocate with a like facial expression.

Assume for a moment that you are looking forward to watching a special broadcast on television. You have had your dinner, are comfortably reclining, and are engrossed in the program. The telephone rings. You can choose to answer it, or choose to let it ring, or choose to let the telephone-answering device respond to the call.

When you are driving and approach a red light in a busy inter-section, you choose to stop. Your initial response to answer a phone that is ringing or to stop at a red light are learned responses to stimuli. Neither of these stimuli *makes* a person do anything. Consciously or nonconsciously, we choose our responses to stimuli. These examples of reactions are everyday occurrences in daily living. In practical application, it doesn't make a particle of difference if these reactions are conscious or nonconscious. There is a problem, however, when we think our responses are automatically controlled by external stimuli. The harm comes when, by implication, we think that the ringing of the phone or the red light *causes* us to react—as if an outside force or person causes our behavior.

This same choice-response situation is operating when we are stuck in traffic and start to get angry. The traffic does not care; it is simply a situation that stimulates us. We allow ourselves to become angry. We could play a tape, a compact disc, or listen to the radio. We could think about past pleasant thoughts or future plans. *We can choose our responses to situations—no matter how unpleasant the situation may be.*

This was the situation during surgery when a very competent nurse was asked for a particular instrument and handed it to the surgeon a moment later than the surgeon expected it. The brilliant surgeon, who lacked people skills, turned to the nurse and berated her. Needless to say, the nurse's day was not very bright. She constantly thought throughout the day how the surgeon made her angry. She also reflected on the situation while driving home, and she then related the story to her husband at the dinner table. Her husband inquired what time the incident occurred. The wife responded that it took place around nine o'clock that morning. Her husband then inquired, "What time is it now?" She responded, "Seven o'clock." The husband then said, "You are telling me this incident took place ten hours ago and the surgeon is still making you angry." (I am indebted to Sam Horn for sharing this incident.) The nurse decided never again to give that surgeon the power to ruin her day, ride in her car, or be invited to her dinner table.

The nurse's original thinking was that the surgeon *made* her angry. This type of faulty thinking leads to an inference that one person can change another. Anyone who has lived with another person for any length of time discovers that no one can really *make* or *cause* another person to change. *People change themselves.* The environment can certainly be established where the person *wants* to change. This is the reason why very young people do things adults would like them to do. Youngsters value adults and *want* to please them. This is also true in the classroom. Young students like their teachers. Unfortunately, many teachers and parents use rewards and punishments thinking that these external manipulators *cause* young people to change.

Even after receiving a stimulus, an instant passes wherein a person can decide upon a response. Assume that Leo bullied Eddie. Young Eddie may choose to retaliate, he may choose to run away, he may choose to tell an adult, or perhaps he simply chooses to cry. We know that Eddie chooses what he does because he runs home, and only when he is in front of a parent, only then, does he begin to cry.

On the other hand, there are reflex actions that are automatic responses to nerve stimulation, like a sneeze. When the door slams, or someone shouts, or the dog barks, and you jump in response to the sudden noise, that is a reflex. All human beings inherit a certain level of reactivity to external stimuli. Some of us are highly reactive, while others can shut out certain amounts of incoming stimuli. As the brain matures, even highly reactive individuals tend to become less so. Reflexes are very important, and without them we would not function normally. The most basic reflex, the one that saves our lives—the so-called "fight or flight" reflex—is readily recognized. Think of what it was like when a friend who was watering the garden suddenly turned the hose on you. When we lived in a less protected environment, this startle reflex was caused not by the threat of a drenching, but by the possibility of a very real danger in the form of a tiger, a snake, or a spear. In order to survive against predators, we had to make an instant decision whether to stay and fight or run away. The situation engendered reflex thinking but even then involved some choice.

When confronted by a stimulus, a person needs to realize that a choice of responses exists. Imagine that in a classroom the teacher sees a student hitting another student. The teacher did not see the first student do the instigating; the teacher only saw the retaliation of the second student and calls him on it. The youngster tells the teacher, "He made me do it." Even though this student was stimulated to act, he still made the choice to hit back. No one else made the choice for him. The student had the freedom to choose a response, and he chose hitting. Students need to learn that regardless of the stimulus, each person still has some choice of responses.

Impulse

We also have the freedom to choose our response to an *impulse* or *urge*. Infants are given diapers to wear because they are not able to control their natural urges. As they grow, diapers are no longer needed. We learn to respond to our physiological urges. The same holds true for emotional impulses. When we become angry, there is a moment of awareness before the emotion takes over—before we may become "emotionally hijacked." (Goleman) As normal, healthy individuals—at that moment—we can exercise some choice of response. A response will occur, but the how, when, or where is often our choice.

Freedom to choose one's response is fundamental in a civil society. It is incumbent upon the adults of our society to teach young people that they have a choice in controlling their behaviors and that it is in young people's own best interests to choose appropriate responses.

Regardless of the situation, the stimulus, or the impulse, people choose their responses. To do otherwise means we would operate from compulsion. Jeffry Schmitt, a UCLA psychiatrist, refers to the beauty of being human, and not a rat or monkey. The difference is that we humans need not succumb to our emotions every single time. The less we succumb, the less we are bothered by tyrannical obsessions.

The following illustration summarizes choice-response thinking.

| Think: | CHOICE | > | RESPONSE |

SITUATION (Information)	>	CHOICE	>	RESPONSE
STIMULUS (from outside)	>	CHOICE	>	RESPONSE
IMPULSE (from within)	>	CHOICE	>	RESPONSE

Because we have the freedom to choose our responses, we are responsible for our own choices (behaviors). By teaching young people that they choose their own behaviors, they begin to become conscious of the fact that no one else chooses their behaviors for them. Choice-response thinking encourages self-control and responsibility. In addition, having young people become aware of choice-response thinking can have a liberating effect, especially with those who feel they are helpless or victims.

VICTIMHOOD

As a young student explains his report card to his parents, he says, "No use debating environment versus genetic causes. Either way, it's your fault." As stated in the beginning of this section, teaching young people about choice-response thinking—*that they need not be victims*—may be one of the most valuable thinking patterns we can give them.

Victim-type thinking is counterproductive to engendering responsibility. Examples of such thinking can be heard in comments such as, "He made me do it," "I couldn't control myself," "I couldn't help it," and "I had no choice." *Merely being aware that such thinking relinquishes control has an empowering effect.*

A student has a test returned. The student did not do well and concludes, "I'm not good in this subject." The student sees a flaw in himself that he believes is beyond his control and becomes pessimistic. He gives up; he stops trying. Another student, an optimist, who receives the same grade concludes, "I guess that means I should have studied more." This student sees a setback as something *over which he has control.* The critical difference between optimistic thinking and pessimistic thinking has to do with the perception of control, which, in turn, depends upon perception of choice. We feel psychologically healthy when we believe we have choices.

Research on the value of choice is solid. Our brain generates different chemicals when we feel optimistic and in control than when we feel pessimistic and without control or power.

Choice, control, and *responsibility* are so woven together that one significantly affects the others. Make a choice, and control is enhanced. Fail to choose, and control is diminished. The more responsibility that is chosen, the more control follows. Deny responsibility, and control is given up.

People who regard themselves as victims do not see themselves as in control and often see the world as unfair to them in particular. Whatever happens in their lives only happens *to* them—as if they have no choice as to their responses. Victimhood people are often angry people. People who have chosen to regard themselves as victims cannot allow themselves to be happy because being happy would challenge their perceptions as victims. Such was the case on October 1, 1997, when a 16-year-old in Pearl, Mississippi, came to his high school campus and shot two students. When chased and caught by the school's assistant principal, the teenager was asked "Why?" The shooter replied, "The world has wronged me." Lack of a feeling of control is a prime factor in young people's anti-social behavior.

Too often, socially disruptive behavior is viewed as a "condition," resulting in students' being excused for socially irresponsible behavior. Thus, viewed through the prism of special handicaps, these students are too often not held accountable for irresponsible behavior.

When these students leave school and behave in socially unacceptable ways, giving excuses such as, "I'm compulsive," and "I couldn't help it," does not impress law enforcement or society, generally. A disservice will have been done to these students because the school world in which they have grown up is unlike the greater society. All young people need to learn that they have the freedom to choose their responses and that they will be held accountable for their choices.

Language shapes our thinking, particularly when it comes to self-talk. Taking conscious control of inner chat can act like a magic wand to shift to more empowering mental states. Victimhood is the result of thinking of outside forces rather than internal responses. Common thinking patterns are: "Someone else is at fault," "Something else caused my behavior; I am not responsible for it," and "I'm a victim."

Young people can be taught to self-talk in enabling and self-empowering ways. Phrases such as "prompts me" and "stimulates me" can be substituted for the powerless "made me" and "caused me." Additional words that reduce "victimhood" thinking are references to "influence," "persuade," "arouse," "irritate," "annoy," "pique," and "provoke." These words do not give away power; they merely describe the effect on oneself.

Another strategy to reduce powerlessness is to change adjectives into verbal forms. Notice the difference between, "I am *angering*," and "I am angry." As soon as we phrase it as an action, we become immediately aware of a choice.

Also, instead of thinking, "The task is too difficult," young people can be taught to take charge by eliminating the "too" and by changing the word "difficult" to "challenging"; thus, "The task is challenging." Another, more subtle language pattern is the ill use of "try." "Try" merely conveys an attempt. Self-talk should convey commitment. A person does not get out of bed by *trying* to get out of bed or make a phone call by *trying* to call. You get out of bed and you make a call. This type of self-talk is the hallmark of success. As Henry Ford so aptly put it, "If you think you can, you can; if you think you can't, you can't. Either way you are right."

Another approach that can be used is to teach young people to ask themselves proactive questions. "What would be the best way to act in this situation?" "How can I best respond to that?" "How can I prevent that urge from directing my behavior?" These types of questions empower people and assist in fostering individual as well as social responsibility.

It is no kindness to treat people as helpless, inadequate, or victims—regardless of what has happened to them. Kindness is having faith in people and treating them in a way that encourages and empowers them to handle their situations, stimulations, and urges.

KEY POINTS

◆ People can choose their attitudes and responses to any situation, stimulus, or impulse.

◆ Teaching young people about choice-response thinking—that they need not be victims—may be one of the most valuable thinking patterns we can give them.

◆ The critical difference between optimistic thinking and pessimistic thinking has to do with the perception of control, which, in turn, depends upon perception of choice.

◆ Choice, control, and responsibility are so woven together that each significantly affects the others.

◆ Students can be taught to self-talk in enabling and self-empowering ways.

Parts of this section first appeared in EDUCATION WEEK, May 27, 1998, as *"Rethinking Our Thinking on Discipline: Empower—Rather than Overpower"* by the author.

THE IMPORTANCE OF REFLECTION
AND SELF-EVALUATION

Learning is not compulsory, but neither is survival.
–W. Edwards Deming

Reflection is a powerful teaching and learning strategy that is too often overlooked. The key to reflection is the skill of asking self-evaluative questions. It is the most effective, yet neglected, strategy both in learning and in dealing with people. Using this skill also reinforces the other two practices of positivity and choice.

REFLECTION AND LEARNING

Reflection is necessary for long-term memory reinforcement. Its absence in the learning process can be likened to chewing—but not swallowing. The food is tasted, but unless it is digested, there is no nutritional value. Before elementary students leave a subject or middle and high school students leave a classroom, teachers should lead students to reflect upon the lesson. John Dewey phrased this concept in a formula: "Experience + Reflection = Growth."

In order to create meaning from a new informational experience, we need "internalizing time." The human brain is a meaning-seeking organ. Much of what we are exposed to in learning happens so fast that we need time to process it. The brain continues to process information before and long after we are aware of it. This is the reason why many of our ideas seem to "pop out of the blue." For this reason, a teacher can either call for learners' attention to new information or have them develop meaning—but not both at the same time. This "down time" (which is not really down) is a significant step for enhancing long-term memory.

Cramming more content per minute or moving from one piece of learning to the next without reflection virtually guarantees that little will be retained. Planning time for reflection also encourages students to let the teacher know when they did not understand or did not get a point the teacher made.

A quick-check technique is for the teacher to stop every so often and say, "In case you did not understand something, you and your partner write it down and turn it into me, and I'll read it over." Often, students will ask a question about something that the teacher thought was made clear but for some students was unclear.

A good way to promote reflection at the end of a class period is for students to keep a daily learning log. Students jot down at least one thought they had as a result of the lesson and explain the significance of the thought. Helpful prompt questions are, "What did I learn today?" "What do I need to work on tomorrow?" "In what did I do well?" and "What could I have done differently?" The questions asked are often more valuable than the answers.

A "keeper journal" is another reflective approach and has the advantage of feeling more personal. Students write down one comment, thought, or learning that they would like to *keep* (remember). If such a journal were started at the beginning of a typical American school year (although the activity can be started any time), each student would accumulate 170-200 specific remembrances from a teacher.

REFLECTION AND EVALUATIVE QUESTIONS

As important as reflection is in learning new information, the practice is equally as important for self-growth. *When applied to oneself, reflection is referred to as self-evaluation.* This practice engenders self-correction—the most effective route to improvement and growth.

Asking evaluative questions such as, "What can you do to accomplish that?" and "What would you do if you knew you could not fail?" are designed to provoke deep and reflective thinking. When you use these kinds of questions, you are directing the other person's thinking in a positive way. The answers can be a gift to the person asking questions because it is a quick way to obtain and understand the other person's perception and viewpoint, crucial in a student-teacher relationship and so many other settings.

In addition, asking these kinds of *evaluative questions* empowers the other person because the ideas that people support most are ones they come up with themselves; the answers that are most important to people are their own. *Ownership is a critical component for self-evaluation and change.*

The following four questions are extremely successful *for changing behavior.*
- What do you *want*?
- What are you *choosing to do*?

- If what you are choosing is not getting you what you want, then what is your *plan?*
- What are your *procedures* to implement the plan?

Here are additional questions for specific purposes:

For Getting On Task

- Does what you are doing help you get your work done?
- If you would like to get your work done, what would be your first step?
- What do you like to do that you can apply to this task?

For Commitment

- In the realm of *all things possible,* could you have kept your commitment?
- What are you going to do to make it happen?
- On a scale of 1 to 10, how would you rank your commitment to it?

For Improving Quality

- How does that look to you?
- What would you like to have improved even more?
- If there were no limitations on what you did, what would allow you to do it even better?

For Reducing Complaining

- How long are you going to continue this?
- Is what you are doing helping you get what you want?
- What do you notice about the experience you are having?

For Starting Conversations

- What was most pleasing for you today?
- What bothered you the most today?
- What was your biggest challenge today? How did you deal with it?
- If the situation came up again, what would you do?

The quality of the answers depends on the quality of the questions. Here are some ineffective questions that increase stress because of the responses they engender. Notice how reactive and counterproductive they are to changing behavior.

- What's the problem?

- What's your problem?
- Why are you doing this?
- Who did that?
- Why did you do that?
- Don't you know better than that?

GUIDELINES

Effective questions require a thinking response. Such questions:
- are usually open-ended. They require more than a "yes" or "no" answer.
- focus on the present or future (as opposed to the past).
- help people learn through the process of thinking.
- help people ask questions of themselves.
- are framed to fit the situation and clarify.
- often start with "What?" or "How?"

Questions that can be answered "yes" or "no" often close conversations. However, they can be used if they lead to *self-inquiry* or *self-evaluation.* In some instances, just asking a question is sufficient. In other situations, "yes" or "no" questions can be effective if followed up with another question that calls for a solution. Here are some examples of effective closed-ended questions:
- Is what you are doing working?
- Is what you are doing helping to get your work done? How?
- Is what you are choosing to do helping you get what you want? How?
- Are you willing to do something different from what you have been doing?
- Are you taking the responsible course? How?
- If you could do better, should you?
- Are you satisfied with the results?

Questions do not need to end with a question mark. For example, "Please describe to me . . . ." is an effective clarification question.

POTHOLES

Avoid asking a "Why?" question. Many times a young person does not know the reason for a behavior. Besides, such a question gives the student an excuse not to take responsibility. This is especially the case where youngsters are labeled. Even though the classification is meant to help, the label becomes a justification. "I can't help it. I have poor attention," is an example. Moreover, even if the "why" were to be known, articulating the explanation is very difficult. Most important, however, *asking a "Why?" question has little effect on changing behavior.*

"Why?" questions have an accusatory overtone. If you are really curious, ask a nonjudgmental question: "Out of curiosity, why did you choose this rather than that?" Change the structure of the question to eliminate any negative inference. A negative implication can be implied in other than "why" questions, such as, "When are you going to stop doing that?" Notice the unspoken demand and negative undertone. In contrast, asking, "How long will you be continuing that?" is inquisitive when asked in a non-accusatory tone. Of course, the tone of the voice is crucial. The adage, "What you are doing speaks so loudly that I can't hear what you are saying" rings true here.

QUESTIONS AS STRESS REDUCERS

Stress is reduced when we ask reflective, self-evaluative questions. The reduction of stress comes about because of the position in which we place ourselves. When influencing someone, only a *noncoercive* approach is effective. With this awareness, the first act is mental positioning. When practicing any skill, putting yourself in position always precedes the action. This is as true when asking evaluative-type questions as it is when holding a golf club before the swing, holding a baseball bat before the pitch arrives, shooting a basketball, holding a tennis racquet, or playing any musical instrument. The first step is placing yourself in a mental stance to employ noncoercion. You do not shout a question. The tone of voice communicates at least as much as the words. Even a horse understands this, as was reported by the trainer of Seattle Slew, the 1977 Triple Crown Winner. "Slew's a show horse. Thousands of people visit him each year. He's tough but kind, and he will do anything you ask him to do as long as you pose it as a question. If you give him an order, you are going to have a fight on your hands. And you're going to lose." (*Time*, April 28, 1997, p. 27)

THE SKILL

Asking evaluative questions is a skill. As with any skill, you will feel awkward at first, but the more you practice asking self-evaluative questions, the more comfortable you become, the more confidence you develop, and the more effective you are. In addition, regardless of how often the strategy is used with a person, it is still effective because the strategy is noncoercive and empowering.

Practice is the mother of skill. Thinking about a skill is not practicing it. Thinking is necessary for focus, but only the *actual asking of self-evaluative questions* will give you the skill. With this in mind, the question is asked, "How do you develop the skill?" Answered the sage, "With experience." "But," asked the disciple, "How do you get the experience?" Came the answer, "By asking poor questions." Remember: *you cannot learn a skill and be perfect at the same time.* Each question asked is a learning experience, and if the desired result is not obtained, it should be thought of as feedback, not as failure.

A final note: Some people have a talent and can naturally use a velvet-covered hammer. But most people need a technique. When you use a technique and understand the mechanism, your skill improves and you will have more success than relying on a talent.

KEY POINTS

◆ Reflection is a powerful teaching and learning strategy that is too often overlooked.

◆ When applied to oneself, reflection is self-evaluation, which engenders self-correction—the most effective route to change and growth.

◆ The key to fostering reflection is the skill of asking evaluative questions—the most effective, yet neglected, strategy both in learning and in dealing with people.

◆ Asking evaluative questions is a skill and is developed and becomes easy only through practice.

◆ Asking self-evaluative questions reduces stress.

SUMMARY

We are just about as happy in life as we decide to be.
–Abraham Lincoln

Practicing the principles of positivity, choice, and reflection reduces stress. These three principles also improve relationships and increase effectiveness in influencing others to change their behaviors.

Negative comments engender negative attitudes. Consequences are usually perceived negatively, and they do not change the way a person *wants* to behave. Announcing consequences ahead of time is often counterproductive with young people because it focuses on the consequences, rather than on the desired behaviors. In addition, such information encourages certain types of students to push until the limit is reached. If a consequence is necessary, a more effective approach is to elicit the consequence.

Positive comments engender positive attitudes. People who are effective in influencing others to positive actions phrase their communications in positive terms. Contingencies promise with the positive and place the responsibility on the young person, where it belongs. Positivity brings hope, which is a cousin of optimism. In addition, positivity results in fostering others to feel valued, enthusiastic, supported, respected, motivated, challenged, capable, and proud.

Either consciously or nonconsciously, people choose their attitudes and responses to any situation, stimulus, or impulse. Teaching young people about choice-response thinking—*that they need not be victims*—may be one of the most valuable thinking patterns we can give them. This type of thinking teaches the difference between optimistic thinking and pessimistic thinking. Control depends upon one's perception of choice. Choice, control, and responsibility are so woven together that each significantly affects the others.

Reflection is a powerful teaching and learning strategy. It is also the most effective approach for bringing about change because reflection engenders self-evaluation, which is both noncoercive and empowering. The key to fostering reflection is the skill of asking evaluative questions, and, as this is a skill, it is only developed and improved through practice.

POSITIVITY, CHOICE, AND REFLECTION
EXERCISE FOR STUDENTS

Gratitude is not only the greatest of all the virtues,
but the parent of all the others.
–Cicero

We think about what we lack more often than we think about what we have. The following exercise combines *positivity, choice,* and *reflection.* Hal Urban has conducted this exercise with his classes for twenty years with amazing results.

Inform your students to conduct themselves for the next twenty-four hours *without complaining.*

- Tell them not to stop the experiment even if they do complain. Just have them see how few complaints they can make in one day.

- Give each student a blank card. This makes it convenient to note each time a complaint comes forth and each time they catch themselves *about* to complain.

The next day, ask:

- What was the purpose of the assignment?

- What did you learn from doing it?

Students will have discovered the frequency and smallness of their complaints.

Then, have students label a paper, *"I am thankful for,"* and make three columns:

Column 1	<u>Things</u>	(They list all the material things they are glad they have.)
Column 2	<u>People</u>	(They list all the people they appreciate.)
Column 3	<u>Other</u>	(What will emerge will be things such as freedom, opportunity, friendship, love, intelligence, abilities, health, talents, peace, faith, God, security, learning, experiences, beauty, kindness, and the list continues.)

Instruct students to review the list four times within the next twenty-four hours:

- In the afternoon

- After dinner

- Before going to sleep

- Before school the next morning

When attention is given to the *positive*, when the option of *choice* is recognized, and when *reflection* is used, life is conducted more successfully and with greater pleasure.

2
MOTIVATING

THEORIES WE USE

We can control other people,
but we cannot change them.
People change themselves.

The beliefs and theories we hold direct our thoughts. Our thoughts direct our actions.

THEORY X AND THEORY Y

In 1960, Douglas McGregor, the late Sloan Professor of Management at the Massachusetts Institute of Technology, published *The Human Side of Enterprise.* His book was a major influence in promoting the application of behavioral science to improve productivity in organizations.

McGregor examined the reasons underlying ways people attempt to influence human activity. He studied various approaches to managing people, not only in industrial organizations but also in schools, services, and public agencies. He concluded that managerial approaches could be understood from the assumptions managers make about people. McGregor concluded that the thinking and activity of people in authority is based on two very different sets of assumptions. He referred to these assumptions as Theory X and Theory Y.

Theory X

McGregor labeled the assumptions upon which the top-down, authoritarian style is based as "Theory X." He concluded that this style is inadequate for full development of human potential. Theory X is based on the following beliefs:

1. The average person has an inherent dislike for work and will avoid it if possible.

2. Because of this human characteristic of dislike for work, most people must be coerced, controlled, directed, or threatened with punishment to get them to put forth adequate effort toward the achievement of goals and objectives.

3. The average person prefers to be directed, wishes to avoid responsibility, has relatively little ambition, and wants security above all.

These assumptions are not necessarily stated in any record, but one can see them in an organization's structure, policies, procedures, work rules, management methods, and actions. Responsibilities are delineated, goals are imposed, and decisions are made without involving individuals or requesting their consent. Rewards are contingent upon conforming to the system, and punishments are the consequence of deviation from the established rules.

Theory X styles vary from "hard" to "soft." A drill instructor uses a "hard" approach. A "soft" approach is used in less coercive strategies, such as coaxing and rewarding.

Theory Y

Theory Y assumptions are more consistent with current research and knowledge, and they lead to higher motivation and greater realization of goals for both the individual and the organization. The central principle of Theory Y is that of integration: the creation of conditions whereby members of the organization can achieve their own goals best by directing their efforts toward the organization's success. This integration is most effectively achieved using *collaboration* rather than *coercion*.

The assumptions of Theory Y are:

1. The expenditure of physical and mental effort is as natural in work as it is in play. The average person does not inherently dislike work. Depending upon controllable conditions, work may be a source of satisfaction and will be voluntarily performed, or it can be a source of punishment and will be avoided.

2. People will exercise self-direction and self-control toward objectives to which they are committed.

3. Commitment to objectives depends on the rewards associated with achieving them. *The most significant of such rewards is the internal reward of self-satisfaction.*

4. The average person learns, under proper conditions, not only to accept responsibility but also to seek it. Avoidance of responsibility is a general consequence of experiences. It is not an inherent human characteristic.

5. The capacity to exercise a relatively high degree of imagination, ingenuity, and creativity in the solution of problems is widely, not narrowly, distributed in the population.

6. Under the conditions of modern life, the intellectual potentialities of the average person are only partially utilized.

Theory Y encourages growth and development. It stresses the necessity for selective adaptation rather than for a single, absolute form of control. Above all, Theory Y points up the fact that the limits of human collaboration are not limits of human nature but of the authority figures' ingenuity and skill in discovering how to realize the potential of the people with whom they work.

Theory Y is not a soft approach to managing. It can be a very demanding style. It sets up realistic expectations and expects people to achieve them. It is more challenging to the participants—the teacher, the student, and the administrator.

Although McGregor's book is primarily about business management, he was an educator. He fully understood that these theories applied to education. While a growing number of people in education and family relations use Theory Y, many schools and households tend toward Theory X. People use external approaches in attempts to change behavior, especially when disciplining someone. They believe their own goals will be achieved by using coercion rather than by collaboration, or they are simply not familiar with Theory Y approaches. *A prime purpose of this book is to share strategies to implement Theory Y.*

Theory Y can be threatening to teachers, parents, administrators, and others in authority who are accustomed to using the power of their position. People who use Theory X rely on external motivators to influence, manipulate, and change others. The Theory Y person uses collaboration and realizes that improvement comes through desire, rather than control. In using Theory Y, for example, errors are viewed as feedback because it is the key characteristic for promoting growth and continual improvement. This is what Jerome Bruner meant when he said that the goal should be to help students experience success and failure—not as rewards and punishments—but as information. (Bruner, 1973)

The traditional model for attempting to change people has been authoritarian and aligned with Theory X. People have always submitted to a higher authority. The 1960s altered the effectiveness of the "submission" model. In the last number of years, society's model has been that nobody needs to be submissive to anyone else. Everyone has rights. Authority and expected submissiveness are out. *Everyone is equal.* Notice how often you are called by your surname preceded by a title. Not very! Using given names is much more equalizing.

The information revolution is a major reason why Theory X is not effective today. Information has always been a prime source of power and control. Only those in positions of authority possessed it, and they used it to their advantage. Not so today! Information is open to everyone, so individuals are on a more equal footing with their superiors. Restricting young people's information and access to it in today's electronically connected world is most difficult, if not impossible.

An old story dramatizes the effects of continuing to use Theory X. An expedition of scientists went on a mission to capture a Tonkin snub-nosed monkey. Only an estimated 100-200 of this particular species exists, and they reside only in the jungles of Vietnam. The objective was to capture one of the monkeys alive and unharmed.

Using their knowledge of monkeys, the scientists devised a trap consisting of a small bottle with a long narrow neck. A handful of nuts was placed in it, and the bottle was staked out and secured by a thin wire attached to a tree. Sure enough, one of the desired monkeys scented the nuts in the bottle, thrust an arm into the long neck, and grabbed a fistful. But when the monkey tried to withdraw the prize, his fist, now made larger by its contents, would not pass through the narrow neck of the bottle. He was trapped, anchored in the bottle, unable to escape with his booty, and yet unwilling to let go. The monkey was easily captured.

We may smile at such foolishness, but in some respects we operate in the same manner. We cling to the very things that hold us back, remaining captive through sheer unwillingness to let go. Peter Drucker, perhaps the dean of management theory and practice, has said that people fail because of what they will not give up. They cling to what has always worked, clearly after it has stopped working.

The person who holds on to coercion, in all its various forms, will remain captive like the monkey. In a sense, the person loses freedom. A person becomes liberated when willing to let go of the coercion and manipulation of Theory X with its stress, resistance, and poor relationships. The use of the collaboration and empowerment of Theory Y reduces stress, improves relationships, and is much more powerful in effecting change in others.

KEY POINTS

◆ How a person attempts to motivate others depends upon how the person views others.

◆ Theory X relies on control through direction and manipulation. This traditional top-down authoritarian style is inadequate in its approach in today's society.

◆ Theory Y encourages people to experience a sense of accomplishment and personal growth and relies on collaboration, rather than coercion, to engender higher motivation.

◆ The use of collaboration and empowerment reduces stress, improves relationships, and is much more powerful in effecting change in others.

EXTERNAL AND INTERNAL MOTIVATION

If you want to build a ship, don't drum up people together to collect wood and don't assign them tasks and work, but rather teach them to long for the endless immensity of the sea.
−Walt Disney

The previous discussion of Theory X and Theory Y explained approaches people use to *influence others.* This section deals with two ways that people *become influenced* that have an effect on their motivation. The case can be made that no one really motivates another; people motivate themselves. Although this is technically true, motivation can occur in more than one way. When the legendary football coach, Vince Lombardi, started his half-time charge to the Green Bay Packers with, "Girls, let's have a talk," one would have a bit of a challenge convincing the players that they motivated themselves. Lombardi was a great motivator.*

EXPLANATION OF TERMS

The usual terms employed when discussing motivation are "extrinsic" and "intrinsic." Extrinsic motivation applies when the aim of the performance is to gain approval, to receive a reward, or to avoid punishment. The motivating force comes from outside the person. Intrinsic motivation applies when people perform for inner satisfaction or connotes something that emanates from within.

When referring to motivation, this book intentionally employs the terms *external* and *internal*, rather than "extrinsic" and "intrinsic." The reason is that this book is devoted to raising responsibility in young people, and responsibility is not a characteristic that we associate with "intrinsic" motivation. Acting responsibly may not be satisfying in the same sense as intrinsic motivation. The motivation to be responsible is more cognitive and rooted in ethics and values, in contrast to the emotion or feeling that is associated with the word "intrinsic."

The term *external* is used to connote something that comes from outside the youngster. Since motivation of the young is significantly influenced from outside, the term *external* makes the concept and

---

* Lombardi *stimulated* his players, but we do not refer to humans as stimulators.

power of peer pressure more effectively understood. The powerful pressure of peers significantly affects young people's behavior, and an awareness of this external motivation is the first step in analyzing it and determining when to accept the pressure and when to resist it.

Although humans operate from both external and internal motivation, the motivation itself often cannot be discerned by a person's actions. For example, if a youngster makes up her own bed because asked to by a parent (external motivation) or does so because she wants to (internal motivation), the action is the same; the bed has been made up.

EXTERNAL MOTIVATION

There is no discounting the significance that external motivation has in the "shaping" of the young. The modeling that parents and other role models display for youth is an essential part of their upbringing. This is evidenced by the first language babies learn, youngsters' experiences in forming and maintaining relationships, and their first lessons in appropriate—or inappropriate—behavior. Yankee wisdom referred to external influence on the young this way: "A young twig is easier twisted than an old tree."

Early in the 20th century, the concept of adolescence was developed and has had a profound change on young people's upbringing. In recent years, the emphasis on youth as a culture of its own is especially exemplified by the entertainment and fashion industries. The violence and lightning-speed actions of many videos, films, and television programs are aimed at the adolescent market. A look at almost any fashion advertisement on billboards, in newspapers, and in magazines attests to the focus on the young. A parent's purchase of the "wrong brand" of clothing is ample evidence of the strong desire of youth to "fit in" with what is popular with their peer group.

James Coleman's classic study, *The Adolescent Society: The Social Life of the Teenager and Its Impact on Education*, clearly showed that the age of adolescence could be thought of as its own ethnic group. Adolescents have their own language, their own uniforms, and they have a strong tendency to conform to their peers. Judith Rich Harris has since made the cogent point that when the age of adolescence is reached the traditional beliefs and discussions of *nature vs. nurture* are replaced by the reality of *peer pressure.*

External motivation plays an important part in people's lives. The behaviorist school of psychology is based on the principle that external motivation is pre-eminent in influencing a person's behavior. This approach can be seen in the strategy of rewarding young people when they do something good and punishing them when they do something bad. Notice that the responsibility here is on the person in authority initiating the action. The fundamental characteristic of this approach is that another person is necessary to change someone else's behavior. The responsibility rests with the other person, rather than with the one to be influenced.

It is also important to note that when teachers and parents employ external approaches, the aim is usually to have the young person do what the elder wants. This is basically teaching toward obedience. A major dilemma here is that obedience too often begets resistance. Even on the "positive" side, when an external motivator such as a reward is used, the motivation becomes not the desired prize of appropriate behavior but obtaining the reward. This is because the reward, not the desired behavior, drives the motivation.

Punishments are obviously external in nature. Their fundamental source of energy is fear. The power of fear underlies negative visions and can produce extraordinary changes—but only for short periods. William Glasser noted that attempts to apply external pressure upon students to try to motivate them generally fail. Direct motivation can be produced only with a "gun" or some other forceful method.

> But guns, force, threats, shame, or punishment are historically poor motivators and work (if we continue the gun example) only as long as they are pointed and as long as the person is afraid. If he loses fear, or if the gun is put down, the motivation ceases. (Glasser, 1969, p. 18)

INTERNAL MOTIVATION

Abraham Maslow stated the concept of internal motivation clearly:

> Human life will never be understood unless its highest aspirations are taken into account. Growth, self-actualization, the striving toward health, the quest for identity and autonomy, the yearning for

excellence (and other ways of phrasing the striving "upward") must now be accepted beyond question as a widespread and perhaps universal tendency. (Maslow, p. *xx*)

W. Edwards Deming believed that internal motivation (desire), performance, productivity, and quality work cannot be legislated or manipulated. He believed that all human beings are born with internal motivation—an inner drive to learn, to take pride in their work, to experiment, and to improve.

Thomas Armstrong writes that even when working with students labeled with Attention Deficit Disorder (ADD) and Attention Deficit Hyperactivity Disorder (ADHD), it may be far better to use behavioral strategies that *internally empower* them rather than those that externally control them. (Armstrong, 1999, p. 97)

In their explanatory book, *Why We Do What We Do: Understanding Self-Motivation,* Edward Deci and Richard Flaste show that internal, rather than external, motivation is at the heart of creativity, responsibility, healthy behavior, and lasting change. Internal motivation is the key to learning and educational success. The point was stated well in the perceptive Calvin and Hobbs cartoon where Calvin said to his teacher, "You can give me the information, but you can't make me learn." Calvin is correct; no one can make another person learn. However, a student can certainly be influenced to learn. With today's youngsters, the most effective approach for learning and changing behavior is to influence without coercion—in short, using Theory Y.

Imagine, for a moment, that you are Calvin in a classroom and are presented with the questions below. The italicized concept following each question describes the principles used in this book—most of which are rooted in internal motivation.

- You walk into your math classroom. The initial activity is to do 10 problems. Which assignment would you prefer to hear?

  A. Do the 10 problems on the board.

  B. Your choice: Do the 10 problems on the board or the 10 problems on Page 12.

  Choice empowers.

- You disrupt the class. Which would have greater, more lasting impact?

  A. The teacher tells you that what you did was wrong.

  B. You realize that what you did was wrong—without the teacher's saying anything.

  Self-evaluation is essential for lasting improvement.

- You throw a wad of paper across the room. The teacher *sees it leave your hand.*

  Which would be more successful for controlling yourself in the future?

  A. The teacher tells you to pick it up.

  B. The teacher doesn't say anything—and you pick it up.

  Self-correction is the most successful approach for changing behavior.

- You walk into a classroom and notice the wastepaper basket on its side.

  Which would give you more satisfaction?

  A. Having the teacher suggest you turn it upright.

  B. Turning it upright without the teacher's saying anything.

  Acting responsibly is more satisfying through internal motivation.

- You enjoy one of the learning centers in the classroom and would like to go to it.

  Which would you rather hear?

  A. No, you cannot go to the center until your assignment is completed.

  B. Of course you can go to the center—as soon as your assignment is completed.

  Positivity is a more constructive teacher than negativity.

- You have disrupted the classroom again.

  Which would have the greater effect in changing your future behavior?

A. The teacher says, "You will serve detention tomorrow afternoon."

B. The teacher says, "With the assistance of your learning buddy, describe your behavior on this form."

Growth is greater when authority is used without punishment.

- The student sitting next to you hits you. You hit back.

Who caused your behavior?

A. The other student.

B. You.

People choose their own behaviors.

Most people choose answer "B" to these questions because this choice uses two dynamic motivators, both of which are internal. The first is integrity and a sense of fair play. The second is an appeal to pride. Neither of these indicates a sense of the external approach, which often carries with it a sense of control. Enthusiasm quickly evaporates in the face of being controlled. In this sense, internal motivation is closely related to choice. Deprive people of choice and you have likely deprived them of motivation. As one student said, "Being able to make choices leads to learning rather than just remembering."

People who are successful in relationships understand the differences between external and internal motivation. We can try to motivate others by advising, cajoling, exhorting, rewarding, demanding, and sometimes by punishing. However, these external approaches are far less powerful than those that tap into internal motivation. When a young person is given the choice of either being punished or of disappointing a parent, the answer universally forthcoming in my seminars is that people would rather be punished. People do not want to live with the feeling of disappointing a parent—or a teacher—whom they hold in esteem.

Aristotle concluded that an emotional outcome, like happiness, is the appropriate end of all behaviors because it is internally satisfying. (Scorseby, p. 37) Internal desire and satisfaction are far more effective in relations and in changing behaviors than are external or imposed approaches.

KEY POINTS

◆ External motivators are rooted in adult modeling and peer culture. They often influence through rewards and punishments.

◆ The term "external" motivation is used in this book, rather than "extrinsic" motivation, because the power of peer pressure is more easily conveyed.

◆ A fundamental characteristic of external motivators is that they rely on another person to stimulate a change, thereby placing responsibility on that person.

◆ The term "internal" motivation is used in this book because responsibility is more cognitive and rooted in ethics and values, in contrast to the emotion or feeling that is associated with the usual motivation term "intrinsic."

◆ Internal motivation is closely related to choice. Deprive people of choice and they lose motivation.

◆ Internal desire and satisfaction are far more effective in changing behaviors than are external or imposed approaches.

REWARDS

Young people do not need bribes to act responsibly.

Rewards and acknowledgments can serve as great incentives. However, when used for expected standards of behavior, they can be counterproductive. Giving rewards for behaving appropriately encourages dependency, a process that is diametrically opposed to raising responsibility.

REWARDS AS INCENTIVES

Rewards serve as incentives. For example, grades are incentives and may motivate students to pay attention in class, study after class, complete home assignments, and do whatever else is necessary to receive the reward of a good grade. However, schools have great numbers of students who believe that a good grade is not an important enough reward to act as an incentive. *Rewards are effective only if the person is interested enough to work toward receiving them.*

Knowing this helps teachers and parents understand why some young people do not expend energy to improve their school grades. Rather than grades, learning should be the incentive. Jerome Bruner made the point in his classic, *The Process of Education,* in which he stated, "Ideally, interest in the material to be learned is the best stimulus to learning, rather than such external goals as grades or later competitive advantage." (Bruner, 1961, p. 14)

ACKNOWLEDGMENTS AS INCENTIVES

Acknowledgments encourage and motivate. They serve to give recognition without the disadvantages of praise. Praise has a price. It implies a lack of acceptance and worth when the youth does not behave as the adult wishes. Using a phrase that starts with, "I like…." encourages a young person to behave in order to please the adult. By contrast, acknowledgment simply *affirms* and *fosters self-satisfaction.*

Notice the difference in the following examples, first of praise followed by acknowledgment. "I am so pleased with the way you treated your brother," versus "You treated your brother with real consideration." "I like the way you are working," versus "Your working shows good effort." "I'm so proud of you for your grades," versus "Your grades show you are doing well."

Two characteristics usually determine whether the comment is one of praise or one of acknowledgment. The first is that praise often starts with a reference to oneself: *"I am so proud of you for...."* or *"I like the way...."* The second is that praise is patronizing. If you would not make the comment to an adult, then think twice before making it to a youth.

REWARDS FOR EXPECTED STANDARDS OF BEHAVIOR

When we give students rewards for expected behavior, we are sending a false message. In the world outside of school or the home, no one receives a reward for doing what is appropriate and expected. Rewards are not given for stopping at red lights or for not jaywalking.

Rewards for good behavior teach children that if they are good they will receive something in return. Young people soon learn that being good can be bargained for, can be bartered, and, in a very broad sense, has commercial worth. This can be understood in remarks like, "If I'm good, what will I get?" and "What's in it for me?"

Giving such rewards does not foster moral development. Good or bad, right or wrong, just or unjust, moral or immoral—these values are not considered. Winning the prize becomes the incentive, mitigating against questions such as, "Is this good?" "Is this a responsible thing to do?"

The message that a behavior is good because it is rewarded gives a false value: "What I am doing must be good because I am being rewarded for it." Rewarding appropriate behavior implies that such behavior is not *inherently* worthwhile. In addition, giving rewards for expected standards of behavior deprives students of the satisfaction that comes with doing what is socially responsible and right.

The effect of giving rewards also has an effect on character development. Studies at the University of Toronto, Arizona State University, and elsewhere show that external rewards or recognition for socially responsible behaviors are associated with *less* commitment for helping, caring, and sharing over the long haul. (Kohn, May 1997, p. 732)

In summary, giving *rewards for expected behavior is counterproductive* to fostering social responsibility, an expectation society has for schools. Young people do not need bribes to be cooperative or to be good. They actually want to be and do good. This is evidenced by the simple strategy of asking a young person for assistance. If the request is presented in a way that shows you genuinely need the person's assistance, rarely will the person refuse.

WHY WE USE REWARDS

Rewards are used because they create obedience. A primary teacher approaches a group of students working on task and says, "I just love boys and girls who do their work." Of course they will do their work. Boys and girls love their teachers. However, notice that another message has also been sent. "Unless you do your work, I'll abandon you; I won't like you; I won't be your friend unless you do what I want." Notice how, *inadvertently*, the comment has changed the students' motivation from the joy of the task to pleasing the teacher.

Rewards are quick and easy to use. Games, movies, free time, and M&Ms manipulate young people toward good behavior. But how long do the rewards last? The answer: Until the games have been played, the movies ended, the free time used up, and the M&Ms swallowed. Attitudes and commitments remain largely untouched.

Another reason we use rewards is that *we rely too much on stimulus-response psychology to change human behavior.* This "external" psychological approach is based on the theory that human beings can be motivated by the same approaches used with animals and, like animals, humans can be trained. This concept of training is reminiscent of the man who wanted to train his young dog. The owner figured that if the dog had an accident on the rug, the owner would take the dog and shove his nose in it, then pound him on the butt with a newspaper, and then push the dog out the little kitchen door into the backyard, where the dog was supposed to do his job. Sure enough, you can guess what happened. After three days, the dog would poop on the floor, and then run out the little kitchen door into the backyard. The dog did not learn what the master intended, but the little animal knew to clear out of the area.

We also use rewards because *we have come to believe they are necessary.* Carolyn Early, a teacher near Houston, Texas, told me about a parent whose seventh-grader was in her class. The father insisted that his son needed a positive note when he didn't make disruptive noises such as singing in class. A belief that a stimulus-response approach is necessary to change behavior is not unique to this parent. It is prevalent among many parents—and teachers.

Another reason rewards are used is *the desire to increase student self-esteem.* Yet, the self-esteem movement, as it is often practiced, has had disappointing returns on its investment. The fatal flaw in the self-esteem movement lies in the very belief that one person can change another's self-esteem through *external* motivators.

Praise is a prime strategy used to increase the self-esteem of young people, as can be witnessed when children sit in circles and compliment one another. Flattery may prompt us to feel good, but these feelings are transitory; they do not significantly change our self-perceptions. Our self-perceptions relate to our own thoughts of our capabilities. If a sense of worth is not *forthcoming from within the student,* even a positive external message may be interpreted as superficial.

Young people are very sensitive to our motives, even when we may not be clear about them ourselves. Even very young children can detect insincerity and manipulation, as when the kindergarten student crumpled up a paper the teacher had just gushed over. The teacher winced when she heard a neighbor say to the complimented youngster, "She just says that to get you to be good." The teacher's good intentions become counterproductive.

When rewards are given on a regular basis, as is often the practice in attempts to raise self-esteem, they become competitive. Young students compare and count stickers and compliments. This competition is counterproductive to raising self-esteem because of the measuring aspect. Measuring always connotes a purpose or goal—whether it is physical, emotional, or mental, and whether or not the goal is good for the person. Striving for self-esteem through measuring almost always leads to self-downing and self-deprecation because there is always a chance that the goal will not be achieved. This is the case when the person has not met with success or believes that someone else is superior. Even if self-esteem is raised, and the person feels good momentarily, the feeling is conditional because in order to maintain it, the individual must keep attaining the goals, which requires constant effort.

In addition, measuring oneself is disadvantageous because it tends to lead to anxiety. Measuring may result in the person's feeling less successful than desired and may produce a pessimistic belief of the inability to change or to improve. This, in turn, causes the person to try even less, resulting in even lower achievement. Here is a prime reason why self-esteeming is utterly deadly for those who are weak, slow, inadequate, or untalented. Unfortunately, these are some of the very people at whom the self-esteem movement is aimed.

An unspoken purpose of measuring is to be superior. Yet, self-esteeming and self-measuring may inadvertently lead to alienation from others and ruin relationships because they lead to self-absorption. The need for achievement increases while relationships with other humans diminish. When self-esteeming leads to bad feelings because the goal has not been accomplished, or when good feelings don't result, others may begin to disrespect the person because of the resulting self-downing. This, in turn, leads to the loss of respect, friendship, or love.

Unconditional self-acceptance, rather than self-esteem, should be the aim. "Non self-acceptance" really means that the person chooses to condemn herself, to feel undeserving. Unconditional self-acceptance is far more successfully accomplished when the *action*, rather than the person, is acknowledged. *It is the achievement itself that brings self-acceptance and self-satisfaction.* Unconditional self-acceptance laps over to others by accepting them, which, in turn, leads to better relations.

As Oseola McCarty, the Mississippi washerwoman who gained fame by donating $150,000 to the University of Southern Mississippi, said, "If you want to be proud of yourself, you have got to do things you can be proud of." Self-esteem is always the result of thoughts and actions emanating from within.

ADDITIONAL CONSIDERATIONS ABOUT REWARDS

Rewards punish. When a teacher rewards student "A" with praise while student "B" is not praised for the same behavior, this oral reward is counterproductive. "I really like the way Wallace is sitting in his seat," is not doing Wallace a service. In fact, the exact opposite occurs. Not only can children see the attempt to manipulate behavior, but also Wallace is not endeared to his fellow classmates. He feels punished by the teacher's comments, especially if he is the type of student who is embarrassed by the public recognition. In this regard, it is not uncommon for a teacher to compliment a student whose behavior has improved, only to have the student immediately misbehave again. Some students simply do not like to be pointed out, or the comment contradicts the self-image of the child, who then attempts to reinforce his own self-perception by acting out his usual behavior pattern.

Rewards change motivation. This is the prime principle to remember about the use of rewards. Teachers of upper elementary grades through high school know this by the most common questions students ask: "Will the material be on the test?" and "Will this count on the grade?" Rather than being motivated by curiosity, the challenge, or the enjoyment of learning, the students' motivation turns toward the external reward—the grade. The motivation is to do well for the teacher's evaluation, rather than for the learning itself. In addition, and this is rather obvious, the more emphasis placed upon the external reward of the grade, the more students look for the easiest way to obtain it.

Here is a paradox. Many studies have shown that the more we reward people for doing something for which they are not internally motivated, the more likely they are to lose interest in whatever they had to do to get the reward. (Kohn, February 1997, p. 430) In other words, the more emphasis we place upon the external motivator, the more students lose interest in what they are doing. Deci phrased it, "Stop the pay, and stop the play." (Ruenzel, p. 26) Rewarding students for reading is a typical example. When students read for pay or for some prize, their long-term interest in reading declines. They will be motivated to read in order to obtain the prize, but they read less after receiving the booty.

Creativity declines when more emphasis is placed upon grades. You can prove this to yourself with any group of students. Give them an assignment and let them know that you are very interested in seeing what they can do with it. Be clear that you will not assign a grade. Then give a similar assignment and inform the students that the activity will be graded. See for yourself the decline in creativity.

Another characteristic is that rewards *foster competition.* This concept is examined further in Chapter 4 in the section *Collaboration—Rather than Competition—for Quality Learning.* The important point to note here is that a person wins a reward at the expense of others. Everyone cannot be the winner. But even more important is the realization that cooperation is essential for the establishment and maintenance of a learning community. In "*Musings in the Wake of Columbine: What Can Schools Do?"* the authors conclude, "Until we make schools engaging learning communities whose members value those communities and feel welcome within them, we are right to think that the next Columbine could happen anywhere." (Raywid and Oshiyama, p. 449) Giving external rewards inevitably leads to competition, rather than cooperation and collaboration—two critical factors in establishing a learning community.

KEY POINTS

◆ A reward can serve as an effective incentive only if the person is interested in the reward.

◆ Acknowledgment is more effective as an incentive than is praise.

◆ The prime principle to remember about the use of rewards is that they change motivation. Winning the prize becomes the incentive.

◆ Rewards for good behavior teach children that if they are good they will receive something in return. This is a false message. Society does not give rewards for expected standards of behavior.

◆ Giving rewards for appropriate behavior is counterproductive to fostering internal motivation for raising responsibility.

PUNISHMENTS

People pressured against their will remain of the same opinion still.

Punishments in the form of penalties, retribution, isolation, and incarceration are traditional ways society attempts to achieve fairness and justice. *No argument is presented here against such societal practices for adults who have been convicted of socially harmful behavior.* If you believe that a youngster is an adult, then it may seem natural to treat a young person with the same approaches used to break socially harmful adult behavior patterns. However, if you believe that *young people are not adults,* then the use of *imposed* punishments to raise responsibility must be examined.

THEORY AND PROBLEMS WITH PUNISHMENTS

Punishment and threats of punishment have been our chief tools for dealing with irresponsible behavior. This is especially the case when it comes to disruptive classroom behavior. The rationale is that something must be done *to* the student. What is done usually involves some type of pain or threat of pain (not physical pain, of course). *Punishment operates on the theory that young people must experience pain in order to grow into responsibility.*

One reason we keep thinking punishment works is that sometimes the behavior stops. This may be the case with very young children if the behavior is caught early so that it has not become an established habit and if the punishment itself is a novel experience. However, we must also consider whether or not the subject understands which action is being punished.

Punishment may also be effective with the person who feels *connected* to the punisher. This is especially the case with young people who want to learn and do well. *They experience punishment as a reminder, not as an attempt to hurt them.* (Glasser, 2000, p. 154)

Punishment *is ineffective with far too many young people.* A testament to punishment's ineffectiveness is its escalation. When punishment fails to work, inevitably more punishment is prescribed, and the cycle perpetuates itself. By the time some students reach the secondary level, they have been talked to, lectured at, sent out of class, kept after school, referred to the office, referred to Saturday school, and suspended from school—and they simply no longer care.

Punishment is temporary and transitory. Fear and force only produce changes in the short run. Once the punishment is over, the student has "served his time" and is "free and clear" from further responsibility. A coercive approach that works in the short run does not mean it is effective in the long run. Threatening a youngster with punishment may force compliance—but only so long as the threat is present. Needless to say, it does not change behavior when the coercion is gone.

Punishment is teacher-dependent, rather than student self-dependent. The threat of punishment may coerce a student to act appropriately in one class but have no effect on the way she interacts with others outside of that class. In addition, because punishment is teacher-dependent, its use is inconsistently applied. What is a punishable offense by one teacher is not by another.

Punishment has little effect on fostering desired long-term changes because it deprives young people of taking responsibility for their own actions. It moves ownership of a problem from the student to the teacher, at the expense of engendering self-evaluation. The oft-punished child obtains few experiences in self-evaluation and in making sound judgments, a pattern of deficit that carries through to adulthood. In addition, when a youngster is punished, from his vantage-point the failure is no longer his fault. He becomes the victim and blames the adult for his predicament.

Punishment is based on avoidance, a negative response. Punishment stirs primal feelings of fear, fleeing, or fighting. Such emotions are counterproductive to the learning process. In addition, its use automatically puts the student and teacher in adversarial roles, which usually has predictable results: (1) the student tests the teacher to see what he can get away with and/or (2) it diminishes the person's motivation to learn. Punishment kills the very thing we are attempting to do—motivate the student to learn what the teacher desires. In addition, very sensitive young people retreat into feelings of low self-esteem where they begin thinking they are truly bad.

Punishment or the threat of it does not help the young person learn how to modify the behavior involved. What the young person learns—if the behavior is so strongly motivated that he or she continues it—is not to get caught the next time. Making excuses and covering one's tracks become the focus. Evasiveness increases rapidly under punishment, a sad situation in any class or family setting. Also, repeated or severe punishment has some very nasty side effects: fears, anger, resentment, resistance, revenge, even hate in the punished one—and sometimes in the punisher, too.

None of these mental states is conducive to learning. As educators, our goal should be to build self-reliant, responsible citizens. We want to foster the kinds of characteristics that emanate from a personality with an ethical self-image and a healthy sense of self-worth. Shaming, humiliating, and hurting students are counterproductive to both good teaching and to the ultimate objective, which is to encourage students to become responsible, cooperative, and motivated in socially healthy directions.

Not too many of us remember that the horse that pulled the buggy was urged on by a flick of the whip, and information was pounded into students by the cane, the strap, or fear of them. But since then, we have found better ways to teach; yet we are still using the horse and buggy approach to foster social responsibility in an era when both society and the nature of youth have dramatically changed.

An interviewer once related the following to me after a discussion of how society and youth have changed in recent generations:

> The other day, my teenage daughter, who is really a lovely child, was eating in a rather slovenly manner, and I *lightly* tapped her on the wrist and said, "Darling, please don't eat that way."
> My daughter replied, "Mother, don't abuse me."

The mother had grown up in the 1960s and volunteered the point that her generation tested authority but really was afraid to step out of bounds. She reiterated that her daughter was a good child and added, "*But the kids today not only disrespect authority, they have no fear of it.*"

When students are not afraid, punishment loses its efficacy. Yet, we often resort to punishment as a strategy for motivation. For example, students who are assigned detention and who fail to serve it are punished with more detention. Yet, in the hundreds of seminars I have conducted around the world, teachers who use detention rarely suggest that it is effective in changing behavior. If detention were effective, the same students would not be consistently assigned to it. The reason detention is ineffective is that it is punishment-based—a negative, coercive approach. The fact of the matter is that *people learn and act better when they feel better, not when they feel worse.*

The negative and stressful effects of using coercion take their toll on the coercer, as well. Education has been referred to as the "*profession that eats its young.*" "Thirty percent of teachers leave in the first five years and the exodus is even greater in some school districts." (Halford) In my home state of California, the rate has reached fifty percent. (Fuetsch) The Phi Delta Kappa/Gallup Polls of both teachers and the public consistently list disciplinary problems as a major cause of concern. *A prime reason—both for teachers' leaving the profession and the concern for discipline—is the clinging to coercive approaches as a strategy for motivating students to behave appropriately.*

If coercion were effective in reducing inappropriate behavior, discipline problems in schools would be a footnote in history. The irony of coercion is that the more you use it in an attempt to control others' behaviors, the less real influence is exerted over them. The reason is that coercion breeds resentment. In addition, if students behave because they are forced to behave, the teacher has not really succeeded. Little of the teacher as a positive influence will remain. Students should behave responsibly because they *want* to—not because they *have* to.

PUNISHMENT SATISFIES THE PUNISHER

In practice, coercive approaches such as punishment serve to benefit the punisher more than the punished. A cartoon demonstrates the point. It shows a father running after his son, strap in hand. The mother calls to her husband, "Give him another chance." The father retorts, "But what if he doesn't do it again?" *If the child does not do it again, then who is the punishment for?*

Punishment is reinforcing for the *punisher* because it demonstrates and helps to maintain dominance. Until the day when a child is big enough to retaliate, the adult is the dominant one. This, unknowingly, may be the main motivation behind our tendency to punish. The punisher may be primarily interested, not in behavior, but rather in proving higher status. In essence, the parties are engaged in a power struggle. The paradox of this situation is that the youngster knows which "button" to push to stimulate anger in the more powerful. When anger is demonstrated, the power desires of the vanquished become satisfied.

In all my school experiences, I observed more situations than I care to recall where the intent of the person referring a student to the office was focused on receiving satisfaction, basically revenge. I would like to think that the desire was to have the student become more responsible. It was not. Satisfaction for the punisher was the goal.

We are expecting students whom we "intentionally hurt" to act constructively. But can you recall the last time you felt bad and did something good? *You cannot think positively with negative feelings.* We do "good" when we feel good. *Coercion can force compliance but never commitment.* Have you ever seen anyone punished into commitment? Punishment kills the very thing we are attempting to do, viz., to change behavior into something that is positive and socially appropriate.

When a punishment does effectively halt a behavior, then the sequence of events becomes reinforcing for the punisher. The punisher tends to confidently punish again. This may be the prime reason why so many continue to use it, thinking that it is effective, even though other approaches can achieve better results without using punishment at all.

THE POWER OF NOT USING IMPOSED PUNISHMENTS

Self-punishment is the worst type and the most severe. Punishment is too often used for those who don't need it. These students will respond without punitive action. Kahlil Gibran makes the point when he asks, "And how shall you punish those whose remorse is already greater than their misdeeds?" (Gibran, p. 43)

All too often, the assumption is made that punishment is the only successful course of action to immediately halt inappropriate behavior. The paradox is that noncoercion can be far more effective than coercion. This point is brought home when we expect punishment but do not receive it. In such cases, we often remember the experience more than if we had been punished.

A friend of mine related a childhood incident. He and his brother expected some dire consequence when their father found out they had turned off the lights in the local restaurant as they ran out the door. Rather than meting out punishment, their father—knowing that his sons knew that he knew what they had done—did not resort to punishment. To this day, my friend remembers his own inappropriate behavior and the impact of his father's knowing of it and not punishing him. The fact that the father was disappointed by my friend's action was much more powerful than a transitory punishment would have been.

A fellow passenger on a flight told me an incident about this very point. Here is the story as Eric McDermott later wrote it to me.

> Though I haven't seen her in almost 20 years, my second-grade teacher has left a positive impression on me that has since, and will always, shape the way I treat people. It is with great affection for her creative direction that I share with you just one seemingly modest example of how a teacher's creativity can transform a young child's vision.
>
> I have always had a lot of energy, and second grade was no exception. In quiet period one morning, I was drawing a picture on a piece of paper. I was so excited about my drawing, I wanted to share it with my friend on the other side of the room. Knowing that I dare not get up to walk over to him, I transformed my piece of paper into a paper airplane. Waiting for just the right moment, I threw it to him.
>
> Having seen my launching from her desk, my teacher broke the quiet and said in a stern voice, "Eric, come over here right now, and bring that piece of paper with you."
>
> I walked over to her giant desk, terrified.
>
> "Hand me that piece of paper," she said gazing into my eyes.
>
> She inspected the paper airplane for several seconds as I awaited my sentence.
>
> "Hmm...," she said, never breaking her stern facade, "This is a very good paper airplane. I want you to go to the front of class and teach us all how to fold this kind of paper airplane. Afterwards, we'll all go outside and see whose flies the farthest."
>
> She handed paper out to everyone, and being the big ham that I was, I took great delight in teaching the class how to make it.
>
> At the time, I was in awe. Until that point, I had

always been punished by my teachers for what they viewed as undisciplined disturbances. Instead of scolding me, she had transformed my misbehavior into a learning opportunity. I loved her for what she had done.

While the class learned how to make paper airplanes, an essential skill in second grade, I learned the importance of using one's creativity to bring out the creativity in others.

I share this anecdote with all of my friends who have gone on to be teachers, and remember it even when I teach at my local Sunday school.

We moved away from Knoxville, Tennessee, in my third grade year and I now live in California. I went back to Knoxville just recently for the first time in 16 years. With great excitement I visited my Cedar Bluff Elementary School, but my teacher had retired just four years earlier and I never got to see her.

I don't know how she's doing, but according to the staff I spoke with when I visited, she is still residing in Knoxville. My second grade teacher, though she may not know it, and I may never get to see her and tell her so, will forever be in my thoughts and serve as an inspiration to make a difference in the lives of others.

Eric told me that if he were punished, he didn't think he would ever remember the incident. However, to this day he remembers how his second-grade teacher used the incident to teach him a lesson in a positive way by building on an incident that could very well have resulted in punishment.

These stories are but a sampling of those where the perpetrators still remember how a skillful adult used the opportunity to teach, rather than to punish.

KEY POINTS

◆ Punishment operates on the theory that young people must be "harmed" when they behave inappropriately in order to grow into responsibility.

◆ Punishment is temporary and transitory.

◆ Punishment has little effect on fostering desired long-term changes because it deprives young people of taking responsibility for their own actions.

◆ Punishment kills the very thing we are attempting to do— motivate students in positive ways.

◆ A prime reason for teachers' leaving the profession is the use of coercive approaches as a strategy for motivating students to behave appropriately.

◆ Coercive approaches such as punishment serve to benefit the punisher more than the punished.

◆ Coercion can force compliance—but never commitment.

◆ Self-punishment is the worst type and the most severe.

_____

REWARDS AND PUNISHMENTS:
TWO SIDES OF THE SAME COIN

The greater thing in this world is not so much where we stand
as in what direction we are going.

–Oliver Wendell Holmes

Bribing youngsters with rewards to behave appropriately and punishing them when they do not are two sides of the same motivational coin. Both are external approaches used to influence behavior.

WHERE WE STAND

Rewards and punishments can be likened to the use of the carrot in front of the mule and the stick behind it. The carrot only works with a hungry mule. If the mule is fed first, he has no interest in the carrot. When the mule becomes so hungry that it is worth the effort to get the carrot, then he will move. So, if the mule has been fed and a carrot is placed in front of him and he moves, we think the carrot motivates him. However, what really motivates the mule is the beating. The reason is that once you beat him hard enough, it is less uncomfortable for the mule to walk than to be hit. The response is to ease the pain of the discomfort, rather than to eat the carrot.

The Swiss psychologist, Jean Piaget, believed that adults undermine the development of autonomy in children when they rely on the use of rewards and punishments to influence their behavior. Punishment, according to Piaget, is an externally controlled behavior-management technique that often leads to blind conformity, deceit, or revolt in those being controlled. Children who choose to become conformists need not make decisions; all they need to do is obey. Other children practice deceit to avoid punishment. When parents or teachers say, "Don't let me catch you doing that again!" children respond by exerting every effort not to get caught—rather than focusing on appropriate behavior.

Kurt Lewin, the first to write in the area of social psychology, intentionally used the word "manipulation" when referring to these external approaches. Rewards and punishments amount to just that. The adult plays a game of power and control in which only the adult wins. The reason is that they are unilaterally imposed. The long-term use of this manipulative tactic requires raising the stakes. The teacher must keep these incentives ever present because children learn to depend upon these types of motivators. More and more treats must be offered or more threats or sanctions must be used to induce people to continue acting in the way the manipulator desires. They become self-perpetuating and need to be intensified to remain effective.

Not only does this reward-punishment approach become progressively more objectionable the older the person becomes, but it works only up to a certain point, up to a certain age. Anyone who works with adolescents and teens knows it gets tougher and tougher—because teenagers have shifted their reference group. Their desire for approval no longer comes from their parents and teachers. It now comes from their peers.

By using rewards and punishments, we give children the easy way out—at the expense of their development and maturation. Rather than empowering them with responsibility, they quickly learn that temporary compliance will get them off the hook, cither in the form of accepting a loss of privileges or writing apology notes that will right all wrongs. Many children would rather take the pain of punishment than take the time to make difficult decisions and exert self-control.

When we use rewards and punishments as motivational strategies, we are teaching kids to make their decisions based on someone else's reaction. We reinforce the practice of people making their decisions based on how the other person is going to respond. The message tells people, "It's not what is best for you but how the *other person* is going to react." Teachers and parents are not around when peer pressure encourages young people to take up tobacco, get high on drugs, or do something that is destructive to themselves or society. The *ultimate* goal is not to obey and keep adults happy. The ultimate goal is for young people to act in a responsible way because it *pays off for them—because responsible behavior is in their own best interests.* If you have this vision—of what is good for *them*—it is going to reduce your stress in your relationships with them because it doesn't box you into manipulative and punitive modes.

The case bears repeating. In order for a person to take responsibility, the person must *want* to. *Obedience does not create desire.* Desire only comes through internal motivation, through *commit-*

ment—not compliance. Responsible behavior is a chosen behavior. It cannot be given; it can only be taken.

Rewards and punishments, then, are counterproductive to fostering self-discipline. The paradox here is interesting. Our goal is to assist students to become responsible, self-disciplined, self-reliant, independent problem solvers. Yet, giving rewards and using punishments for expected behavior set up students to be dependent upon an external agent. They set the person up to receive, rather than to give, *but it is in the giving that responsibility is developed.*

An inquiry into how external motivators affect behavior when no one is around reinforces the point. Here is the critical question: *How effective are rewards and punishments when no one is looking?*

WHERE ARE WE GOING?

There is an old Greek myth about a gentleman who was looking for Mt. Olympus. On his journey, he passed an elderly man and asked him for directions. The elderly man turned out to be Socrates. When the traveler asked him how to get to Mt. Olympus, the old sage responded in his reflective tradition: "Be sure every step you take is in that direction."

Rewards and punishments do not take us in the direction that fosters responsibility. Rather than doing things *to* young people, the most effective way to raise responsibility is to use noncoercive approaches by working and collaborating *with* young people.

KEY POINTS

◆ Rewards and punishments create obedience, but the problem is that they do not encourage responsible thinking.

◆ Rewards and punishments set the person up to receive, rather than to give, but it is in the giving that responsibility is developed.

◆ Rewards and punishments stimulate, but they do not encourage reflective thought such as, "Is this good for me?"

◆ Doing things *to* young people is not nearly so effective in changing long-term behavior as doing things *with* them.

TELLING

*When I was a boy of fourteen, my father was so ignorant
I could hardly stand to have him around.
But when I got to be twenty-one, I was astonished
at how much he had learned in seven years.*
                                                    –Mark Twain

Telling and mini-lecturing are generally ineffective with young
adolescents, who are trying to assert their own independence.

TELLING OTHERS

The parent wants to save the adolescent from the consequence of
what the parent sees as a negative experience, so the parent begins
to lecture. After a few minutes, the glaze comes over the young
person's eyes. The parent has been tuned out. The adolescent is
thinking, "I'm being lectured again," or "Just because you tell me
what to do, doesn't mean I'm going to do it." The intentions of
giving guidance and counsel are good, but the young person who
is attempting to assert independence perceives the advice as an
attempt to control. People don't mind controlling, but they usually
dislike *being* controlled.

Whenever we tell people to do something differently, we convey a
message that the way they have been performing is wrong or not
good enough. Telling implies that something has to be changed,
but people tend to resist change that is thrust upon them. This
often creates defensiveness and a tendency to resist.

I recall a friend sharing with me how he hated having his mother
tell him to do something. Even though it was something he wanted
to do, such as playing outside, because she *told* him to do it, he
found an excuse not to do it. Just for a moment, think of a situation
where someone told you that you *had to do something*. When someone
tells us what we should do, most of us think, "Don't tell *me!*"

When a teacher tells a student what to do, the student perceives
this as coercion, and it is often resented. Some teachers even keep
a record of how many times a student is told—and often on the
board for the entire class to see. The ineffectiveness of this approach
can be verified simply by looking at names on a board in a classroom
at the beginning of the year, and then revisiting the classroom again

at the end of the year. The same—and additional—names appear with checkmarks.

By bringing to mind the all too familiar expression, "If I have told you once, I have told you a...." we see how ineffective telling is in changing behavior. If telling were successful, we would not have to repeat ourselves.

The ineffectiveness of telling, in contrast to the more effective approach of asking self-evaluative questions, is well illustrated by the classic story of people who started selling life insurance. These people went through the company's training program, and they were very successful for about a year and a half. After this period, sales dropped off.

The company made quite an intensive investigation as to the reasons, and they found that the people followed the prescribed sales approach for about eighteen months. The training approach taught by the company showed how to ask specific kinds of questions, which fostered a bonding with clients because the sales people not only learned about the clients' financial situations and future plans, but also something about the people as individuals.

However, after about eighteen months, the salespeople had learned so much that they thought to save time. They began asking fewer questions and talking more. Sales dropped because the salespeople did not bond with the prospective customers. When sales plummeted, the salespeople began talking even more. They soon began focusing on the fear of losing sales, became discouraged, and the downward spiral of performance went into full gear. The time that telling saved came at the expense of success.

TELLING OURSELVES

Telling a person what to do is not nearly so effective as a person's deciding for oneself. Asking reflective and self-evaluative questions engenders this. If we stop and reflect, we realize that when we are successful in obtaining something we really want from someone, *we don't tell*; we ask. If you are now or ever have been married, ask yourself whether the proposal was *asked* or *told* you. Chances are that the proposal was asked.

Simply stated, telling does not engender the *desire* in people to do what you would like them to do.

KEY POINTS

◆ Even though the intent of telling a youngster is worthwhile, the actual telling is perceived as an attempt to control, and people do not want to be controlled.

◆ Telling creates defensiveness and a tendency to resist.

◆ Telling does not engender desire.

———————————————

MINDSETS

"How do I make Johnny learn?" is a question
that has plagued all teachers since the beginning of time.
The answer is simple. It can't be done!
No one can make a child or anyone else learn.
                        –Madeline Hunter

Mindsets are attitudes, dispositions, intentions, and inclinations. If Johnny's mindset is one of little or no interest in learning (and this includes learning appropriate behavior), Johnny will not learn much. Therefore, *a major task of adults working with young people is to promote mindsets that promote learning and appropriate behavior.*

James Sutton is a psychologist in Pleasanton, Texas, who trains child service professionals. Jim emphasizes how perceptions are as important as reality. If a child is afraid, behaviors will reflect that fear, regardless of whether there is anything to be afraid of or not. Jim's experiences have led him to conclude that there are youngsters who are damaged more by their perceptions of their lives than by the realities of their lives.

Roger was a perfect example. He had undergone the successful removal of a brain tumor (benign, fortunately). Following the surgery, Roger began to fall apart in academics and in social relationships. Dr. Sutton was consulted. As best as he could determine from hospital and surgical records, there was no medical reason why this boy should have trouble after the surgery. In fact, it was expected that he would improve. While working with the young boy, Dr. Sutton asked a question that was not on his usual interview list.

> "Roger, do you think that when the surgeon removed the tumor he also took out part of your brain?"
>
> "No, sir," the boy replied softly. "I thought he took all of it."
>
> Good grief! No wonder this boy was having trouble. He thought he had to function with no brain at all. Jim explained the surgery to Roger and assured him that he still had all of his brain and the ability to use it.
>
> "Really?" he asked with an obvious sense of relief

in his voice. His young face broke into the first smile
Jim had seen from him.

"Absolutely!"

Over the next few days and weeks Roger improved, and he kept on improving in both his academic and social relationships.

All people visualize, and these *visualizations play a large role in determining mindsets.* A noted example of this is the saga of James Nesmeth, an average golfer who shot in the 90's. For seven years, he completely left the game; he did not touch a golf club nor set foot on a fairway. Major Nesmeth spent those seven years imprisoned in a small cell as a prisoner of war in North Vietnam. During almost the entire time he was imprisoned, he was isolated. He believed that he could keep himself sane in his tiny cell under hideous conditions by occupying his mind. He decided to practice his golf game. He was in no hurry. He had no place to go. He imagined that he was at his favorite golf course playing a full round of golf. Every day he experienced each detail. He saw himself dressed in his golf clothes. He smelled the fragrance of the trees and the freshly trimmed grass. In his mind's eye, he experienced different weather conditions—windy spring days, overcast winter days, and sunny summer mornings. He visualized every single step, from how he positioned himself before each swing to the follow-through afterwards. Starting at the first tee, he looked down and saw the little ball. He visualized addressing it, the feel of the grip of the club, and the position of his stance. He instructed himself as he practiced smoothing out his downswing and the follow-through on his shot. Then he watched the ball arc down the exact center of the fairway, bounce a couple of times and roll to the precise spot he had selected. Not once did he ever miss a shot, never took a hook or a slice, never missed a putt. Day after day he played a full 18 holes of golf. When he was liberated, one of the first things he did was to go to the golf course and play a round of golf. The first time out, without touching a golf club in seven years, he shot a 74, knocking 20 strokes off his game. That is the power of visualization!

Because mindsets are partly at an unconscious level, they often need assistance to be changed. Teachers and parents can assist by the pictures they help young people create in their minds. This motivational approach is the foundation of the program to raise responsibility and is described in the following chapter.

KEY POINTS

◆ Mindsets drive our behavior.

◆ Perceptions of self-efficacy, or the lack thereof, are critical to motivation.

◆ Adults can assist young people by the pictures they help create for them.

SUMMARY AND CONCLUSION

I skate where the puck is going to be,
not where it has been.

–Wayne Gretsky

External motivators are used in attempts to change behavior. Significant and long-lasting behavior is changed through desire, rather than through manipulation and coercion.

SUMMARY

How a person attempts to motivate others depends upon how the person views others. Generally, these views can be categorized by Theory X and Theory Y. The former relies on control through direction and manipulation. Theory Y, in contrast, encourages people to experience a sense of accomplishment and personal growth and relies on collaboration and empowerment to engender motivation. Theory X relies on external motivation. Theory Y is based on internal motivation. Theory Y's use of collaboration and empowerment reduces stress, improves relationships, and is much more powerful in effecting change in others.

Internal motivation is closely related to choice. Deprive people of choice and they lose motivation.

A reward can serve as an effective incentive only if the person is interested in the reward. The principle to remember about the use of rewards is that they change motivation. Winning the prize becomes the incentive. Rewards for good behavior teach children they will receive something in return. This is a false message. Society does not give rewards for expected standards of behavior. Giving rewards for appropriate behavior is counterproductive to fostering internal motivation for raising responsibility.

Coercive approaches such as punishment serve to benefit the punisher more than the punished. The punisher receives satisfaction, but the punished has relinquished responsibility and often feels victimized. Punishment is temporary and transitory. It has little effect on fostering desired long-term changes because it deprives young people of taking responsibility for their own actions. In addition, punishment kills the very thing we are attempting to do—motivate students in positive ways.

A prime reason for teachers' leaving the profession is the use of coercive approaches as a strategy for motivating students. Coercion can force compliance but never commitment, and coercion disheartens teachers.

Even though the intent of telling a youngster is worthwhile, the actual telling is perceived as an attempt to control. Telling creates defensiveness and a tendency to resist and does not engender desire.

Mindsets drive our behaviors. These perceptions of efficacy, or the lack thereof, are critical to motivation. Adults can help young people by the pictures they help create.

CONCLUSION

Language shapes our thoughts. George Orwell pointed out that without having a word such as "freedom," the concept of freedom would be difficult to conceive. Also, the use of language shapes the meanings of both words and concepts. For example, when we say, "He is making me so angry," we perpetuate the concept that the other person is shaping our anger. Actually, how much we allow others to stimulate us depends on *our* choices—consciously or nonconsciously. Although people are easily stimulated, we technically motivate ourselves.

The only way that you can "motivate" another person—whether spouse or partner, child, friend, or employee—is to provide an environment by which that person *wants* to change. This is especially the case when it comes to a *lasting* change in behavior. Reflect on the story that originated during World War II. A young lieutenant explained the new GI insurance program to thousands of troops who were to be sent overseas. After a lengthy presentation, the young lieutenant asked for a showing of hands of those who were interested. No hands were raised. The lieutenant was rejected until an old sergeant raised his hand and asked permission to say a few words to the troops. The lieutenant nodded affirmatively.

The sergeant took the microphone and announced that within the week, they all would be sent overseas. Some of them would be sent to the front lines, and, unfortunately, some of them would not be coming back.

He went on to say, "As the lieutenant has already explained, for those of you who enroll in this new GI insurance plan and who are killed, the U. S. Government will be obligated to send your families a check for $10,000. But for those who do not enroll in this new GI insurance and are killed, the U.S. Government will not be obligated to send your families one single dime."

The old sergeant paused and then inquired, "Do you believe the U.S. Government will be sending to the front lines those of you who are enrolled in the new GI insurance and the U.S. Government will be obligated to send your families a check for $10,000, or those who are not enrolled and the U.S. Government will not be obligated to send your families one single dime?"

Outside situations and stimulations have powerful effects on us, but they do not motivate us. Technically, motivation comes from within.

Rewards, punishments, and telling are external in their approaches. As such, their usefulness in effecting long-term behavioral change and raising responsibility is limited. A more effective approach is to use an internal approach, which is the basis of *The Raise Responsibility System.*

3
RAISING RESPONSIBILITY

DISCIPLINE

The best discipline is the kind nobody notices—
not even the one being disciplined.

W hen teachers and parents discipline with stress, they are
deprived of joy in relationships. Discipline, however, can be
an opportunity, rather than a problem. As the French sociologist
Emile Durkheim observed, discipline provides the moral code that
makes it possible for the small society of the classroom to function.

DISCIPLINE AS OPPORTUNITY

Discipline is a tool for teaching responsibility. The ultimate goal
of discipline is self-discipline—the kind of self-control that underlies
voluntary compliance with expected standards. This is the discipline
that is a mark of mature character and that a civilized society expects
of its citizens. John Goodlad, one of my former professors, said that
the first public purpose of schooling is to develop civility in the
young. Civility can only be achieved with self-discipline.

Discipline is derived from the Latin word *disciplina*, which means
instruction. The original meaning of the word connotes the self-
discipline necessary to master a task. This is the self-discipline of
the competitive athlete, of the professional musician, of the master
craftsman, of the expert in any field.

Another meaning of discipline refers to our nature. We may have
little control over the thoughts that spring into our minds and little
control over our initial emotions. But consciously or nonconsciously
(habitually), we *choose our responses* to both our thoughts and our
emotions. This is the discipline to which Durkheim referred that is
so necessary for a civil community.

In order for a society or classroom to be civil, discipline needs to
be fostered. Yet, according to Richard E. Clark, Chair of the Division

of Educational Psychology at the University of Southern California:

> Discipline is understood in a very limited way by most
> educators—"How do we get these children to
> behave?"—rather than, "How do we support the
> people in our charge as they learn to channel and
> direct their positive energy in ways that accomplish
> their goals and those of their community?" (Clark)

This limited understanding of discipline to which Dr. Clark refers
is reminiscent of the teacher standing in front of the class who states,
"I expect you all to be independent, innovative, critical thinkers
who will do exactly as I say." As humorous as this statement is, many
teachers operate with a focus on obedience rather than on self-
discipline. If a child does not obey, punishment seems in order.

Lee Salk, the famous child psychologist, emphatically states, "What
discipline is *not* is punishment." (Salk, p. 47) The National Congress
of Parents and Teachers agrees:

> To many people, discipline means punishment. But,
> actually, *to discipline means to teach.* Rather than
> punishment, discipline should be a positive way of
> helping and guiding children to achieve self-control.
> (National P.T.A.)

In her book *The Caring Teacher's Guide to Discipline: Helping Young
Students Learn Self-Control, Responsibility, and Respect,* Marilyn Gootman
writes that discipline is teaching self-control, not controlling or
managing students. (Gootman, p. 17)

As Richard Sagor notes, an effective discipline program requires
three particular, vital educational functions:

- The maintenance of order
- The development of internal locus of control
- The promotion of prosocial behavior (Sagor, p. 150)

All three are accomplished in an approach where the *student*
acknowledges ownership of behavior, where the *student* self-
evaluates, and where the *student* develops a plan. In the process, the
student grows by becoming more self-regulated. As Sagor notes,
the locus of control is *internal.*

This is in contrast to an *external* control approach where the *teacher*
takes possession of the problem, where the *teacher* presents the

student with a plan, and where there is overpowerment of some kind—usually in the form of punishment—which often results in enmity against the adult.

Teachers who largely rely on external methods of control may succeed in getting students to toe the line under their supervision, but what happens when the teacher is not around? As one teacher who uses external controls said, "My children are very good for *me*, but they can be holy terrors when I'm not around." Research points to the same conclusion: Children subjected extensively to discipline based on external controls develop low internal commitment to good behavior. *The real power, the real influence of teachers, is not what students do when the teacher is with them; it's what students do when the teacher is not.*

Self-development is most effective if the person is committed, rather than just complying to someone else's desires. Commitment comes through *internal* motivation. Internal motivation is fostered in a *positive learning environment* where people feel they will not be harmed, where they are given *choices* that encourage ownership and empowerment, *where self-evaluation and self-correction* are the dominant avenues to growth, and where people learn that appropriate, responsible behavior is in *their own* best interests. *The Raise Responsibility System* makes full use of these approaches.

KEY POINTS

◆ Discipline means both to teach and to learn.

◆ Discipline is a tool for teaching responsibility.

◆ A good discipline program requires the maintenance of order, the development of an internal locus of control, and the promotion of social behaviors.

◆ The real influence of teachers is reflected by what students do when the teacher is not with them.

Parts of *The Raise Responsibility System* first appeared in Phi Delta Kappa's publication *Fostering Social Responsibility* by the author.

THE RAISE RESPONSIBILITY SYSTEM

Young people want to be responsible,
but we are using wrong approaches to help them.

The Raise Responsibility System handles disruptive behavior simply and easily. In the process, the system builds self-discipline, respect for self and others, and both individual and social responsibility. It also reduces stress for both adults and young people. The three phases of the system are: *Teaching the Concepts, Checking for Understanding,* and *Guided Choices.*

TEACHING THE CONCEPTS

IMAGING THE CONCEPTS

   Since learning is retained best from experiential activities, you will gain greater insight if you participate in a simple recursive activity—one that will teach you how to teach it by actually doing the activity yourself. It will take only a few minutes and is a worthwhile investment because the instructions are given in the manner in which you can teach the concepts.

   You will need a blank sheet of paper. Standard computer printer or loose-leaf-size paper is preferable because that size is large enough to complete the exercise. (Young children may use larger paper and would not do the short writing phase.)

   Fold the paper horizontally as in a hamburger shape (rather than vertically as in the shape of a hot dog).

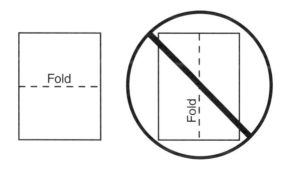

```
┌─────────────────┐
│ Anarchy         │
│                 │
│      Fold       │
│ ─ ─ ─ ─ ─ ─ ─ ─ │
│                 │
│                 │
│                 │
│                 │
└─────────────────┘
```

On the upper half of one side of the paper, print the word "Anarchy."

Explain that "anarchy" is behavior in which there is no law or order, and anyone can do anything he or she wants to do without consideration for anyone else.

Now *draw* any scene that comes to mind representing *anarchy*—any situation anywhere that shows a lack of law or order. Stick figures will do. The drawing is to cover only the top half of the page. After making the drawing, describe what you drew on the same upper half of the paper.

When finished, you are ready to make another drawing on the bottom half of the same side of the page.

Below the fold, separating the top half of the page from the bottom half,

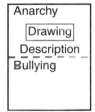

print the word "Bullying."

Now *draw* a picture that shows someone bullying someone else.

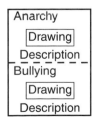

After making the drawing, describe what you drew.

When finished, turn your paper over. *Label* the top half of this second side "Conformity." On the top half of this side, *draw* something that conjures up people *behaving in an expected manner*—any scene where people are conforming or doing what is expected of them. After making the drawing, describe what you drew.

One more drawing needs to be made. *Label* the bottom half of this side "Democracy." *Draw* a picture of whatever you think connotes the idea of someone taking responsibility without being told to do so. After making the drawing, describe what you drew.

If this activity were to be used to introduce the four concepts in a classroom, each student would take turns describing the drawings or explaining their concepts to a partner.

ANALYSIS OF THE ACTIVITY

Processing the Concepts

Five learning activities were used. First, a scene was *visualized* for each of the four concepts. Second, a scene was *drawn* for each concept. Third, a description was *written* for each concept. Fourth, the scene for each concept was *orally* described to someone else. Fifth, each student *listened* to someone else's descriptions of the concepts.

Ownership

You were actively engaged in making the four concepts meaningful because *you* created them. What we do ourselves is remembered longer than what is presented to us. The principle of ownership is a prerequisite for growth and is a fundamental characteristic of *The Raise Responsibility System.*

Meaningfulness

Learning the four concepts through the foregoing exercise is brain-compatible. The brain is hard-wired to remember images more so than words or text. This explains why it is easier to remember faces more than names. It is for this same reason that we remember stories. We make mental images as we read stories or as they are told to us. Similarly, when students create examples for each of the four concepts, the images conjured up in the mind assist in both meaning and memory. It is for this reason that the four vocabulary words were introduced as concepts and examples rather than as definitions. *Because examples bring real understanding, the concepts can be taught to any person, at any grade level, in any subject area, and to any class.* With this in mind, we can proceed to explain and refine an understanding of the concepts.

EXPLANATION OF THE LEVELS

Level A – Anarchy

Anarchy is the lowest level of behavior. The word comes from Greek and literally means "without rule." This level refers to absence of government, aimlessness, and chaos. Alan Bennett summarized the concept well:

> We started off trying to set up a small anarchist community, but people wouldn't obey the rules.

Shortly after my presenting *The Raise Responsibility System* to an elementary school, the counselor called me and shared what she experienced. She had walked into a primary classroom and heard the teacher give the assignment to the first-grade students. The teacher announced that when the assignment was completed the students could go to one of the learning centers. A few minutes later, the noise level began to grow substantially louder. One of the first graders stood up and called out, "Anarchy! This is anarchy!" The noise level immediately subsided. The teacher had not said a word. The students controlled their own learning environment. An *awareness* of the concept of anarchy facilitated self-management.

Level B – Bully*ing*

Bully<u>ing</u> is the level of behavior above anarchy. (Young people have no problem with the term "bullying," but some teachers do. "Bothering" is an alternate choice for these teachers.) A student behaving at this level violates the courtesies of class operations and accepted standards. The bully attempts to become the ruler by making the rules and standards. Bullies boss others by violating others' rights.

Accommodating a bully only encourages bullying behavior. We make our biggest mistake in not understanding the nature of a bully. If a bully prevails, irresponsible and provocative behavior will be repeated. The sooner a person stands up to bullying, the easier it will be to handle and the sooner the bullying behavior will stop.

Though it can be scary for a very young child to confront a bully, most people are surprised at how quickly bullies back off when someone stands up to them.

Leonard Eron, professor of psychiatry at the Institute of Social Research at the University of Michigan, conducted a 26-year study that tracked eight-year-old aggressive boys. He reported:

> If a child is the tormentor not the tormented, don't dismiss his bullying as a phase. The earlier you intervene, the better. Studies show that aggressive kids tend to grow into, not out of, their behavior. (Jameson, p. 3E)

Classroom bullying is more prevalent than many educators think, and experts say it should no longer be tolerated as part of growing up.

> Because bullying is so often an underlying cause of school violence, the National School Safety Center now calls it "the most enduring and underrated problem in American Schools." (Mulrine, p. 24)

The research suggests that teachers and principals underestimate the amount of bullying that takes place under their noses—on playgrounds, in hallways, even in classrooms—and that too many educators are reluctant to get involved. Charol Shakeshaft, a professor at Hofstra University in Hempstead, New York, reported, "When we talked to teachers, they said they didn't think it was acceptable and they didn't like the adolescent climate at all. But they didn't know how to stop it." (Viadero, p. 21) What was surprising in the studies was that students were picked on quite often in classrooms. While boys are more often the perpetrators and victims of direct bullying, girls tend to bully in more indirect ways. They manipulate friendships, ostracize classmates from a group, or spread malicious rumors. Researchers who have studied the issue say that bullying starts in elementary school and peaks in middle school. It is too pervasive and too damaging to ignore, according to John Hoover, an associate professor of teaching and learning at the University of North Dakota. He asserts that ten to twelve percent of kids are miserable in school because of bullying. (Ibid., p. 20) Assuming the lower figure of ten percent, that means in a school of 600, sixty students are coming to school fearful for their well being.

Not much learning takes place when students are in constant fear because of being bullied.

Only this level uses the gerund or verb form, "bullying," instead of the noun form of "bully." This reduces any tendency to refer directly to a youngster as a "bully." Reference is always made to the *level of behavior*, never to the person. Also, the verbal form emphasizes that a student chooses his own level of behavior.

In a classroom, when a student disrupts the class, he is making his own standards. He is bullying the teacher by interrupting instruction and bullying the students by interrupting their learning. When this concept of bullying is first introduced to students, they register surprise because they had not thought of irresponsible behavior as bullying others—especially the teacher.

> **Some key points to remember: First, the teacher *never* labels or calls a student a "bully." Second, the *level* of behavior is identified, not the behavior itself. Third, as we shall see later, the responsibility for acknowledgment is the *student's*— not the teacher's.**

Level C – Conformity

Conformity is the next level of behavior and is as essential for classroom decorum as it is for a civil society. No society can exist without some measure of conformity. The term means to comply and cooperate with expected standards. *The term does not mean or connote regimentation.* Rather, it means to be connected and involved with others. It refers to the accommodations people make when they are naturally inclined to accept the values and mores of their immediate group and society.

The need for conformity on the part of young people brings to mind the newspaper cartoon showing a group of girls dressed in school uniforms. All of their blouses, skirts, socks, and shoes are identical. The girls are talking with a group of boys who attend a different school that does not require school uniforms. However, the boys are wearing identical caps, shirts, pants, and shoes. One boy says to the girls, "At our school, we don't have to wear uniforms." However, the boys are wearing uniforms—of their group. Their dress is motivated by peer pressure to conform.

So compelling is the pressure to fit in that many young people lack the strength of character to resist. This pressure affects student achievement. It is largely because of peer pressure that some students do not want to show they can do well in school. Being smart does not fit into some student subcultures. The *Washington Post* profiled a girl who allowed her grades to drop from A's and B's to C's and D's in order to win back her friends. (Chase, 1999, p. 37) The president of the National Education Association even reported that he personally knows a teacher who resorts to a ruse in order to protect her high-achieving students from peer retribution. The teacher writes an F on the students' test papers with the note, "See me after class"—at which time she confidentially reveals their real grades of A's or B's. (Ibid.)

Gardner Reynolds, of Loredo, Texas, shared some thoughts on peer pressure at the middle and high school levels.

> Peer pressure: now here is a force most pernicious and most powerful in the lives of teenagers. It can make a youngster who is friendly and cooperative in a "one-on-one" with a teacher turn into a complete hellion when he has a group of his classmates to impress with his "cool." A student who does try to accomplish something worthwhile in class is immediately labeled a "teacher's pet" or a "nerd" by the "cool" students.
>
> This is a rather "topsy-turvy" view of things: good is bad and bad is good. Try to work within the system and achieve something and you are an outsider from the "in-crowd"—a nerd or a dork or whatever the current colloquialism is. Rebel against authority, exhibit disrespect and insolence to teachers and administrators and you are a "cool dude" worthy of respect and emulation by your peers. Fail your classes, get sent to the office on a repeated basis and you are "with it." (Reynolds)

As pointed out by James Coleman in the section on *External Motivation* in Chapter 2, adolescents have a strong tendency to conform. In *The Nurture Assumption: Why Children Turn Out the Way They Do,* Judith Rich Harris concluded that the peer group in today's society often displaces the family's influence when youngsters reach middle-school age.

It is important to keep in mind the power that peer pressure has on this age group. It does not matter that the adult is asking for legitimate behavior. If the youth believes that his or her peers will perceive the request as disrespectful, the youth will react negatively, even if he likes the adult. If dignity is at stake, consideration of how peers will react takes precedence over the consideration for the adult.

The key concept of level C is that the *motivation is external.* Once young people become aware that external forces are manipulating them, they begin to feel liberated. Such awareness and subsequent articulation assists adolescents to resist group temptations of an "anti-learning subculture." Understanding peer pressure helps young people to become more autonomous and to decide against engaging in socially irresponsible acts, both inside and outside of school.

Level D – Democracy

Level D is the highest level of behavior. At this level, the motivation to be responsible is *internal.* The person has integrated the regulation of important behaviors. Dr. Edward Deci, professor of psychology at the University of Rochester, who has studied motivation extensively, refers to behavior undertaken or carried out without outside pressure as "autonomous."

> Autonomous functioning requires that an internalized regulation be accepted as your own; the regulation must become a part of who you are. It must be integrated with your self. Through integration, people become willing to accept responsibility for activities that are important but not (necessarily) interesting—activities that are not intrinsically motivating. (Deci, p. 94)

Behavior at this level is manifested by qualities of character that individuals habitually recognize as the right thing. The four classical virtues of *prudence, temperance, justice,* and *fortitude*—as old as Aristotle—are just as compelling today. *Prudence* is practical wisdom—recognizing and making the right choices. *Temperance* involves much more than moderation in all things. It is the control of human passions and emotions, especially anger and frustration. *Fortitude* is courage in pursuit of the right path, despite the risks. It is the strength of mind and courage to persevere in the face of adversity. *Justice*, in the classical sense, includes fairness, honesty, and keeping promises.

My own state of California has joined the growing character education movement and refers to these attributes as follows:

- *Caring*: To be compassionate, considerate, helpful, and understanding of others

- *Civic Virtue & Citizenship*: To hold to the values and principles basic to American constitutional democracy; to accept the rights and duties of citizenship; to act for the common good

- *Justice & Fairness*: To be considerate, unbiased, and equitable

- *Respect*: To show regard for self, others, property, and the environment

- *Responsibility*: To be answerable; to be accountable for one's actions

- *Trustworthiness*: To be worthy of trust and confidence; to be reliable and honest (California State Department of Education, 1999)

Whether classical or current, the characteristics depend upon self-discipline—level D behavior. Clearly, this, the democratic level, is the level to which we hope our youth will aspire. *Responsibility and democracy are inseparable.* In teaching this level, a critical point is communicated, namely, that young people are not only capable of behavior at this level, but this is the level of *expected* behavior. John F. Kennedy, 35th President of the United States, articulated the point in his Pulitzer Prize winning book, *Profiles in Courage:*

> For, in a democracy, every citizen, regardless of his interest in politics, "holds office"; every one of us is in a position of responsibility; and, in the final analysis, the kind of government we get depends upon how we fulfill those responsibilities.
>
> (Kennedy, p. 255)

The teacher communicates that "every citizen" includes young people. The hierarchy not only offers an inherent motivation for students to act on level D, but the teacher communicates that this is the level of expected behavior. As "location, location, and location" are the three prime factors for success in real estate, so "expectation,

expectation, and expectation" are the prime factors to be communicated to young people.

The difference between levels C and D is fundamentally in the motivation, rather than the action. The motivation on level C is *external,* but the motivation on level D is *internal.* Observing the difference between these two levels is often very difficult, if not impossible. For example, assume a student spotted a piece of trash on the classroom floor. If the student picked up the trash at the teacher's direction, the student was acting on level C. The student complied by implementing the teacher's request to assist in keeping the classroom clean. This is good behavior. Conforming is necessary for community. However, if the student picked up the trash without anyone's asking or telling him, the action then is at level D. The piece of trash was picked up because it was the right thing to do. The *behavior* was the same at both levels, but the *motivation* was external in the first case and internal in the second. Similarly, if a parent asks a youngster to help carry in the groceries, and the youngster complies, level C behavior is demonstrated. However, if the youngster knows that the expectation is to assist the mother and does so without being asked, level D behavior is demonstrated. These are simple explanations that young people of any age can understand. *A critical component for growth and development is for students to understand the difference between level C (external motivation) and level D (internal motivation).*

During the initial learning phase, reference is made to the name of each level: anarchy, bully*ing,* conformity, and democracy. However, after becoming familiar with the ABCD's of social development, reference is only made to their letters. Also, little time is spent in differentiating between the levels. Neither A nor B are acceptable behavior levels, while levels C and D both meet expected standards.

REVIEW OF CONCEPTS

A   Anarchy
   ◇ **Lowest level of behavior**
   - Absence of order
   - Aimless and chaotic
   - Absence of government
   Anarchy is the fundamental enemy of civilization.

B   Bully*ing*
◇ **Neither appropriate nor acceptable level of behavior**
- Bosses others
- Bothers others
- Breaks laws and makes own rules and standards
Obeys only when enforcer shows more authority.

C   Conformity
◇ **Appropriate and acceptable level of behavior**
- Complies
- Cooperates
- Conforms to expected standards
NOTE: Conformity does not mean regimentation.
The motivation is external (stimulated externally).

D   Democracy
◇ **Highest level of behavior**
- Develops self-reliance
- Displays civility and sense of community
- Does good because it is the right thing to do
- Demonstrates responsibility because it is essential for democracy
The motivation is internal.

PRIMARY POINTS

The primary points to emphasize *when teaching* the levels are:

(1) A and B are unacceptable levels of behavior.

(2) Behavior at level A or B will result in the use of authority.

(3) The motivation at level C is *ex*ternal—
to gain approval or avoid punishment.

(4) The motivation at level D is *in*ternal—
to do the right, appropriate, or responsible thing.

CONCEPT VARIATION

The concepts can be varied to meet the needs of any class. Dianne Capell has a bulletin board entitled "**Behavior Plan.**" Under this title, she has the following four posters:

A   Anarchy
- Noisy
- Out of control
- Unsafe

B   Bully*ing*/bother*ing*
- Bosses others
- Bothers others
- Breaks classroom standards

C   Conformity
- Listens
- Practices
- Cooperates

The motivation is external.

D   Democracy
- Develops self-discipline
- Shows kindness to others
- Does good because it is the right thing to do

In her letter from Japan, Dianne wrote me:

> Several other teachers have begun using the same
> language to reinforce the children's understanding,
> and some have actually started using the same plan.
> Of course, this has added a great deal to its
> effectiveness. All of my students can now recognize
> their own level of behavior and label it appropriately.
> They know almost instantly when they need to make
> better choices. This takes much less time away from
> instruction and keeps the classroom climate stress-
> free and positive. (Capell)

APPLYING AND TEACHING THE CONCEPTS

As mentioned at the outset, images are more effective in
understanding the concepts than are definitions. The images are
examples that people create themselves. The key to understanding
the concepts is to make the examples relevant to the learner. The
examples need not be limited to classroom situations only. Young
people can also create examples of situations found in their

neighborhood or in the larger societies that will exemplify each of the four levels. The point is emphasized that for optimum understanding, young people need to be actively engaged in constructing examples specific to their classroom, playground, social, or community setting. Questions are posed such as, "What would anarchy look like here? Give an example." The same questions are asked regarding levels B, C, and D. In a classroom, students share their examples in pairs, small groups, and then with the entire class.

The concepts can be taught and used with any grade level, in any class, with any subject matter, or in any situation because the examples created are what make the concepts personal, meaningful, interesting, and relevant. For example, "bullying" in the first grade will be different from "bullying" in the fourth grade, where name calling and similar activities are often more subtle.

The manner in which the concepts are taught depends upon the age of the youngsters, their maturity level, and the subject area. In the case of very young people, one concept can be introduced each day. Stories and literature are excellent ways to introduce the concepts. For example, *Miss Nelson Is Missing* illustrates level A. This story is about a primary classroom that is out of control until an authoritarian substitute takes over. After decorum is established, the regular teacher reappears. The story illustrates that when things are chaotic, authority is the most expeditious approach to establishing order. *The Three Little Pigs* can be used for level B to show how the wolf bullied the little pigs. *Snow-White and the Seven Dwarfs* can be used to illustrate level C in that the dwarfs, although all different, complied with their responsibilities by going to the ore mine to work each day. *The Hole in the Dike* can be used for level D by illustrating how the little Dutch boy put his finger in the dike and saved the town. Peter exercised self-reliance and a concern for the community. As students become more familiar with the levels, further discussions about external and internal motivation will aid the maturation process. *Ira Sleeps Over* is a good primary story that contrasts external pressure with internal desire in the decision-making process.

At the upper elementary and middle school levels, the four concepts can be introduced by the activity used at the beginning of this chapter. Students create examples to show how each level of development would look in their particular class. The Appendix contains a sample implementation procedure used in grades five to eight. At the high school level, the program can be taught in one short lesson by creating examples for the particular class. *The point is emphasized: examples, rather than definitions, bring understanding and applicability.* The critical exercise is to relate examples of specific behaviors to each concept.

At the middle and high school levels, the program even can be adopted school-wide without having the concepts taught in every classroom. For example, if all students have a social studies requirement, the concepts can be taught in these classes because the concepts particularly lend themselves to analyzing current, historical, and sociological events. Teachers in other subjects only need make the concepts pertinent to their own classes.

COGNITION AND MORAL DEVELOPMENT

Awareness of the hierarchy is the foundation of this approach to raising responsible behavior. When a young person can say that a behavior is on a level that is unacceptable, that young person has taken the first step toward moving to more responsible behavior. The reason is that *awareness comes before acknowledgment.* Teaching the concepts fosters the necessary awareness. Awareness and acknowledgment are both cognitive activities. Both are necessary to change one's own behavior. Both Piaget and Kohlberg—the Swiss and Harvard University psychologists, respectively—believed that moral and, therefore, civic responsibility depended on cognitive growth.

William Glasser, the psychiatrist and originator of Reality Therapy and Choice Theory, goes a step further. He believes that morality should be discussed in schools. The discussion should be part of a nonthreatening, nonpunitive environment so children can learn to commit themselves to living a moral life, not just paying lip service to it. "In schools without such an environment, morality and responsibility will be only words for most children." (Glasser, 1969, p. 192) An introduction of the four concepts serves as the first phase for establishing and maintaining a noncoercive, nonthreatening environment as well as an introduction to moral and ethical development.

Awareness as it relates to moral development has an emotional component. When young people perform an inappropriate action, often their only emotion is the negative feeling of getting caught. Instead, the negative feeling should be related to the inappropriate action itself. Young people need to be helped to see that the negative emotion should be the result of *what they do*, rather than the result of being found out.

ADVANTAGES TO TEACHING THE HIERARCHY

Oliver Wendell Holmes said, "The human mind, once stretched by a new idea, never regains its original dimensions." When young people become aware of levels of social development, they become conscious of social responsibility in their own behaviors and in relationships with others.

The hierarchy *serves as a means of communication.* It offers young people and adults the same conceptual vocabulary. The vocabulary brings clarity of understanding and assists communications both between teacher and student and among students themselves.

The hierarchy encourages *students themselves to maintain an environment conducive to learning,* rather than always relying on the teacher. Members of the class take on leadership roles to retain decorum. When students help each other to maintain an atmosphere conducive to learning, they are taking a major step in creating a learning community. A community is most successful when members look to themselves to solve problems.

The hierarchy *raises awareness for responsible citizenship.* Our society is based on great autonomy for its citizens. However, citizenship assumes values such as responsibility, respect, caring, fairness, and trustworthiness—the values that transcend divisions of race, creed, politics, gender, and wealth. These values are fostered in the hierarchy and are reinforced in the examples students create for level D—democracy.

The hierarchy *raises awareness for individual responsibility.* Teaching for democratic living requires more than just choosing when to conform and when not to conform. When peer pressure is so compelling as to prompt people to do something that is personally or socially irresponsible, just knowing the levels of social development can have a liberating and responsibility-producing effect. For example, a problem in many middle and high schools relates to studying and doing home assignments. Many students do not study or complete learning assignments because such work is discouraged in the peer culture. The hierarchy can be a motivator in this regard. Students begin to realize that not turning in home assignments or not studying because of peer pressure is level C behavior. After exposure to the concepts, students begin to evaluate the level of their choices. Internalizing the levels can do much to foster desired behavior and individual responsibility.

Using the hierarchy *calls attention to the fact that people are constantly making choices* and that students choose their own level of behavior, consciously or nonconsciously. Students learn that their behaviors are self-chosen, a product of their decisions. They learn that they have a choice in how they respond in a situation, to a stimulus, and even to an urge.

The hierarchy *empowers young people.* It sets the groundwork for students to analyze and correct their own behaviors. It shows students they can be in control of their lives, be agents of their own empowerment, and can resist a *victimhood* mentality.

The hierarchy *encourages students to achieve the highest level of behavior.* The very nature of a hierarchy serves as an inspiration. Young people have an internal desire to be as competent and successful as they can be. We deprive them of opportunities if we do not expose them to possibilities. Using the hierarchy fosters internal motivation so students *want* to act responsibly.

The hierarchy *encourages mature decision making.* Adolescents are looking for roles, more than goals. Exposing young people to the levels has a natural effect of encouraging them to think about long-term decisions. This is a significant consideration since so much advertising, peer pressure, and behavior of young people is aimed at instant gratification rather than at fostering character development and growth.

The hierarchy *fosters character education,* as described under the explanation of level D, without ever mentioning what some communities would consider red flags of teaching values, ethics, or morals.

The *hierarchy serves to distinguish between the inappropriate behavior and the person who acts inappropriately.* It separates the *act* from the *actor* (Kohn, 1996, p. 123), the *deed* from the *doer,* a *good person* from *bad behavior.* A fundamental advantage of the hierarchy is that it naturally accomplishes what adults talk about but have a most difficult time in accomplishing, namely, separating a person's behavior from the person himself. For example, reflect on the last time you were evaluated. Did you separate what the evaluator was telling you about your *performance* from you as a *person?* While the evaluation session was taking place, were you aware that the supervisor was not really talking about you personally, just about your on-the-job actions? My surveys with hundreds of teachers and administrators have indicated that only an extremely small number of people consciously separate themselves from their behavior during an evaluation. If the separation is difficult for adults, imagine how much more difficult it is for young people. Even though we try desperately to make it clear to a young person that we are not criticizing the student as a person—that we are just not approving of inappropriate behavior—it is extremely difficult for a young person to perceive the difference. Teaching the hierarchy makes this challenging task quite easy. We never talk about the student's behavior; we only talk about the *level* of behavior.

The hierarchy focuses on *labeling behavior, not people.* Labeling people often has negative overtones and is not conducive to building relationships. In contrast, labeling a description is far less antagonizing. One summer day on a long drive, my wife was describing a story she was writing. She was, in effect, thinking aloud. After what I thought was a somewhat lengthy pause, I turned on an audio tape cassette that was already in position to be played. After listening to it for a minute, I ejected the tape, turned to my wife, and asked, "Is everything O.K.?" She answered, "Sure, you're from Mars!" (alluding to John Gray's book *Men Are from Mars, Women Are from Venus*). We had often discussed natural differences between males and females and were familiar with John Gray's metaphors of men being from Mars (action-oriented) and women being from Venus (relations-oriented). By labeling my action as Martian, she dispersed in a matter of seconds what otherwise might have created great tension. She knew where I was coming from, and I realized my behavior was inappropriate. It was the understanding communicated by labeling the behavior that allowed us to continue on a pleasant ride. The important learning from this episode is that we had a common vocabulary; we were both familiar with the Mars and Venus metaphors. We understood that reference was made to a type of behavior, not a personal attack on the person. My wife did not tell me I was a rude person; she merely referred to my actions as being Martian. I did not feel personally attacked. Labeling the behavior was non-confrontational, aided communication, assisted understanding, and encouraged readjustment.

The hierarchy fosters understanding about *internal and external incentives.* Understanding the difference between an external incentive and an internal incentive can have a significant impact on motivation. It is common for elementary and middle school teachers to offer incentives for students to behave. When these students move on to a different teacher, they often ask what will be given to them if they behave properly. The incentive has become getting the reward, rather than commitment to appropriate behavior. In this process, students have fallen under the control of the external reward at the expense of autonomy. The paradox is that we want to assist students to become self-disciplined, independent problem solvers; yet, external incentives set up students to be dependent. Students quickly understand that external incentives are really bribes to manipulate their behavior. Although they are influenced by incentives, they learn that they can choose to be or not to be motivated by them.

The hierarchy leads to *improved self-esteem.* After students have discussed the differences between external rewards and internal satisfaction, the stage is set for understanding self-esteem. Teachers give external rewards such as certificates and praise in attempts to build self-esteem. However, according to *Toward A State of Esteem: The Final Report of the California Task Force to Promote Self-esteem and Personal and Social Responsibility:*

> The building blocks of self-esteem are skills. The more skillful a person, the more likely he or she will be able to cope in life and situations. By fostering skills of personal and social responsibility, schools can help students increase their behavioral options. (California State Department of Education, 1990, p. 64)

Self-esteem is closely related to self-satisfaction. A person who is satisfied with an accomplishment has a tendency to repeat it. The more often one completes a task successfully, the more proficient he becomes in it. This reinforcement builds feelings of competency and self-worth, critical elements of self-esteem. In short, self-esteem is the result of feelings of competency.

Students learn that their *behavior plays a role in determining how they want their teachers to relate to them.* Neither A (anarchy) nor B (bullying) is an appropriate or acceptable behavioral classroom level. Behavior at either of these levels encourages a *controlling* reaction from the teacher. When students operate on these levels, they are telling the teacher, "Use authority on us." When students understand the levels, a teacher can stop an unpleasant situation with a simple question, "Do you want me to become a level B teacher today?" Given the choice, students invariably say, "No, we will be on level C." What a simple way to resolve the situation! In addition and most important, students soon learn that when the class operates on level C or D, the atmosphere encourages autonomy and supportive behavior on the part of the teacher.

Teaching the hierarchy *fosters student self-management.* While learning the concepts, young people are also learning the underlying value system. For example, "bullying," which implies selfishness, is at a lower level of social development than "conformity." Conformity, which implies order and fairness, must prevail before democracy can exist. Democracy calls for responsibility and doing the right thing—*whether or not someone else is watching.*

The concepts are the foundation of *The Raise Responsibility System.* The next strategy, the second part of the system, is simply checking for understanding.

KEY POINTS

◆ *The Raise Responsibility System* is *proactive.* The plan is to set the stage for dealing with disruptive behaviors *before* they occur. This is in contrast to a reactive strategy of dealing with disruptive behaviors after they occur.

◆ A *deductive* approach is used. Four concepts are taught first. This is in contrast to the more common inductive approach of first teaching specifics in order to arrive at general concepts.

◆ The *person* identifies a *level* of development—separating the *behavior* from the *person*.

◆ The program uses *internal* motivation so the young person develops a *desire* to be responsible—both individually and socially.

———————————————————————

CHECKING FOR UNDERSTANDING

People need to know you mean them no harm.

This section explains how to have a young person acknowledge and take ownership of inappropriate behavior. The strategy is referred to as *Checking for Understanding*. In order to foster ownership, the youngster, not the adult, must do the talking. This approach is more than a paradigm shift. It is a *metanoia*—the Greek word meaning a profound conversion. It is a fundamental change in thinking from an external control mentality to internal control thinking. Although the strategy can be used in any school or non-school setting, it is explained here in a classroom setting.

MENTAL FRAMING

The strategy for *Checking for Understanding* starts with the teacher's own mental framing. The mental framing is essential in order to remain in control. Otherwise, when the classroom is disrupted, the disrupting student is controlling the situation. This is evidenced by the stress the teacher feels. Therefore, the teacher first establishes or reclaims a positive outlook, viewing the situation as one for guiding rather than punishing, as an opportunity to help the student readjust behavior. The positive mental reframing reduces the teacher's stress and has a significant effect on communications and relationships. The student perceives the teacher as attempting to *help*, rather than punish.

After teaching the hierarchy but before using the *Checking for Understanding* strategy, many unobtrusive techniques may first be considered. The following suggestions allow the teacher to stop a disruption by using a minimum of effort to refocus a student's behavior.

UNOBTRUSIVE TECHNIQUES

These include body language, mannerisms, posture, inflections and nuances in tone of voice, the pacing of speech, and the feelings that language evokes.

Visual

- Your face is a powerful tool of communication. Use a friendly smile.

- Change your facial expressions, such as widening your eyes or moving your eyebrow(s).

- Use a "beat beyond" eye contact by looking at the person for a second or two beyond the normal time—and then smile. This is in contrast to a stare that is often accompanied by a stern expression. Staring is aggressive and works against a noncoercive relationship.

- Lower your head or nod as you look at the student.

- Employ a group signal for attention, such as all raising hands or lowering the lights.

Verbal

- Use a pause—perhaps the least used and most effective technique.

- Change your voice inflection or reduce the volume of your voice.

- Use a release of tension, such as breathing out and then taking a deep breath.

- Make a variety of sssshhhh sounds, such as, "You ssssssshhhhhould be listening now."

- Give a subtle hint, such as, "Thank you, Sheldon," or "Please, Sandy."

- Use a friendly request, such as, "Thanks for considering others," or "Thank you for your attention."

- Ask an evaluative question, such as, "Please ask yourself if that meets the standards of our class," or "If you could do something about changing that, what would you choose?"

- Combine a need with a request, such as, "The noise you are making is disturbing us. Is there a way you can work so that we won't be distracted?"

- State your needs, such as, "I need your help in this."

Kinetic

- Move to a different location. You may even establish a special place in your classroom to where you will move when students' behaviors need changing.

- Use proximity by standing next to the student and perhaps including a gentle touch on his or her desk.

- In cases of a tapping pencil or some other tapping sound of which the student may not be aware, redirect the object to the student's thigh, or slip a tissue underneath the area on the desk so the sound will not be heard.

- Use the principle of entrainment. Entrainment is a form of communication that occurs when we "get on the same wavelength." In the case of a rhythmic sound, such as a tapping pencil, the teacher can tap a foot or stretch a rubber band at the same tempo as the student is tapping the pencil. When the teacher slows the tempo of the foot tapping or rubber band stretching, the tapping of the pencil will also slow down. Entrainment can also be used by the teacher's stretching or deeply inhaling. Students will follow the same action.

- Use a positive—rather than a negative—rapport position. Standing side-by-side or at an angle with the student is non-confrontational. This is in contrast to a head-to-head, face-to-face confrontational pose. Also, lowering your body below that of the student by stooping places the student in an empowering position. This easily diffuses unwanted situations.

- Entrainment and positive rapport can be combined. When you are speaking to a student, mirror his body posture. For example, if a student is slumped over, then the teacher slumps. When the teacher straightens up, the student will follow the new posture.

- Use your hands in an inviting posture. A palms up, open hand is an invitational position. A hand-down, finger-point position is a repelling position.

- When near a student, you can safely assume that the student is listening to you. It is often counterproductive to demand a

student look you directly in the eyes. The student may be embarrassed or is showing respect by not looking directly at you.

QUESTIONS AS INQUIRY

The Raise Responsibility System uses the simple cognitive learning
theory of teaching and then testing. The first phase is teaching the
levels. The second phase simply tests the disrupting student to
acknowledge the level of chosen behavior. The testing—*Checking
for Understanding*—is simple inquiry.

Asking questions encourages the respondent to clarify thoughts,
which in turn leads to acknowledgment of actions. This inquiring
approach also assists the inquirer in setting a positive mental frame.
One does not normally become stressed while asking questions.

When administrators and counselors use guidance techniques with
students who have acted inappropriately, the conversation takes
place on a one-on-one basis. How can a teacher establish such a
relationship in a classroom full of students? The answer lies in having
taught the hierarchy. By having this instructional base, the teacher
moves into a guidance mode when a disruption occurs. The teacher
uses a non-accusatory, noncoercive questioning approach because
the purpose is solely to inquire whether or not the student
understands the level on which the action belongs. The teacher
simply *asks* the student to identify the *level* of the behavior. Note
that the student is *not asked to describe the behavior itself*—just the
behavioral *level*.

Although it is always preferable to speak to students about
misbehavior problems on a one-to-one basis, an advantage of the
strategy is that the questioning can be done in front of the class
without alienating the disruptive student. An additional advantage
to the strategy is that instructional time is not wasted during the
short teacher-student interchange because the levels of social
development are being reinforced to the class.

A STARTER FOR EFFECTIVE QUESTIONING

The purpose of the questioning is simply to check for
understanding, to see whether the student can identify the level of
unacceptable behavior. If the student appears not to know, then the
teacher guides or coaches the student to acknowledge level B because

this is the level of making one's own standards, rather than following the standards of the class. Once the hierarchy has been learned, the questioning process is extremely short. The student knows that level B is the level of irresponsible and unacceptable behavior.

Following are some sample dialogues between a **Teacher** (**T**) and a *Student (S)*.

T: On what level is that behavior?
S: I don't know.

T: Tell me a civility or standard in our class.
S: Not to be talking when the teacher is.

T: Then you are making your own standards. What level is that?
S: B.

T: Thank you.

     *   *   *

T: On what level is that behavior?
S: He was doing it, too.

T: That was not the question. Let's try it again.
  On what level is that behavior?
S: I don't know.

T: What level is it when someone bothers others?
S: I don't know.

T: The letter comes right after A in the alphabet.
  What letter comes after A?
S: B.

T: Thank you.

     *   *   *

T: Would it be right for everyone to operate on that level?
S: No.

T: What level do we call it when someone makes his own rules
  and bothers others?
S: I don't know.

T: As capable as you are, I don't believe that.
  CLASS, can anyone help?

ASKING IS THE KEY

Notice that in the second illustration, the student was evasive. The teacher, however, persevered. This point is critical: *The person who asks the question controls the situation.* The question directs the conversation. If this type of situation occurs, continue to question. Remain in control by continuing *to ask* until an answer is satisfactory.

When first starting, a student may "test" by pleading ignorance, as in the examples. Waste no time. Just ask the class, *"What level do we call it when a person makes his own rules?"* After the level is acknowledged, the teacher immediately returns to the lesson. Nothing more is said because the objective has been met; *level B behavior has been acknowledged.*

The power of the strategy is that when a student acknowledges an inappropriate level of behavior, the misconduct not only stops but younger students often apologize. The reason is that an apology is a natural by-product of accepting responsibility. Note: An apology is *never* requested; that would be coercive.

CAUTIONS

The effectiveness of the answers depends on the effectiveness of the questions. For example, asking a disruptive student, *"What are you doing?"* will lead to a potential confrontation and frustration because the student will most likely respond, *"Nothing."* The teacher would have been better off not asking that question. The strategy is made simple, however, by always starting the questioning process with, *"On what level is that behavior?"*

Be careful when it comes to using closed-ended questions. In the above examples, open-ended questions were asked. Close-ended questions ("yes" or "no") should be used only if the question calls for self-inquiry or self-examination. Here is an example of using a well-placed closed-ended question where (**T**) **is the Teacher** and *(S) is the Student:*

T: On what level is that behavior?
S: I don't know.

T: Tell me what the other students are doing.
S: They're working together.

T: Were you doing your best to work together with them?
(Closed-ended question calling for a "yes" or "no" answer but involving reflection)
S: No.

T: What is the level when someone makes his own rules?
S: Level B

T: Thank you

SIMPLE BUT NOT EASY

Asking effective questions is a skill, not a talent. In order to be successful, the questioning needs to become a conscious, practiced strategy. Otherwise, we remain prisoners of what seems natural.

Alan Schneider grew up in New York City and drove a taxicab to put himself through Columbia University. He knew how to drive quite well. He now lives in upstate New York where one day he encountered "black ice," which cannot be seen but is felt when the car goes into a skid.

Alan was driving to work one day when he drove over some black ice, and his car started to skid to the right. The more the car skidded to the right—straight towards the trees—the more he turned the wheel desperately to the left. The car kept skidding. He related to me that it felt like experiencing slow motion. The car finally hit a tree. Fortunately, Alan was not injured, but the car had to be towed. When the tow truck came and the driver looked at the ice on the pavement, he said, "You know, you should have turned with the skid in order for the car's tires to regain traction with the road." Alan thought to himself, "I knew that." Why didn't he do what he knew? He told me, "I did what came naturally."

Alan lives by a lake, and that winter the lake was over two feet thick with ice. In order to practice, he put his car on the ice, revved his car up to 15 mph, and slammed on the brakes. Naturally, the car went into a skid and Alan turned the steering wheel in the same way he did when he had his accident. He made a second attempt and again turned the steering wheel the wrong way. Alan told me it took him three tries before he actually turned the steering wheel in the direction he knew he should—with the skid, not against it. When he turned the steering wheel in the same direction as the skid, the tires gained traction and Alan regained control of his car.

One thing is certain. When you start asking self-evaluative questions, you are going to feel slightly strange. You will be doing something that does not feel natural or comfortable. You need to be aware of this. A skill becomes comfortable and feels natural *only after practicing it.*

The most effective way to become habituated is to consciously put yourself in the proper mental position—as before hitting a golf ball or baseball, or before playing a musical instrument. Your proper mental position is that of a counselor. Using this mental framing, stress is immediately reduced and the short dialogue will be very pleasant.

TONE

Tone is an essential ingredient of communication. It doesn't matter what the verbal communication is if the tone is one of anger. The tone negates the message. It takes time and practice to speak in a nonconfrontational tone when your impulse is to display verbal anger.

TONE OF VOICE
It's not only what you say
But the manner in which you say it;
It's not only the language you use
But the tone in which you convey it.

"Come here!" I sharply said,
And the child cowered and wept.
"Come here," I said. He looked and smiled
And straight to my lap he crept.

Words may be mild and fair
But the tone may pierce like a dart;
Words may be soft as the summer air
But the tone may break my heart.

Words come from the mind
And grow by study and art—
But tone leaps from the inner self,
Revealing the state of the heart.

> For if you want behavior to change,
> Of this you must remain aware—
> More than words, *it is the tone of your voice*
> Which communicates how much you care.
>   (Author Unknown)

KINESICS

In addition to how the question is asked and the tone in a person's voice, kinesics also communicates. Kinesics is non-verbal body language. Gestures, facial expressions, movements, and posture all communicate. If a teacher is *checking for understanding* with a frowning face, arms folded, body stiff, and eyes glaring while asking, "What level is that?" a very clear coercive message is sent. However, when the same question is asked with a slight smile, arm extended with the palm up, body slightly forward, and eyes wide open, the resulting message is completely different.

PRACTICE IS THE MOTHER OF SKILL

When we first learned how to walk, we wobbled, were unsteady, and fell down. When learning to ride a bicycle or drive a car, most of us went through an awkward stage. Remember how awkward you felt the first time you stood before a class? The awkwardness leaves when we get the "hang of it." *We cannot learn a skill and be perfect at the same time.* We don't expect it of our students, and we should not expect it of ourselves. Using the strategy and expecting perfection the first time or even the first few times is unrealistic. *Give yourself permission to be a learner.*

The skill improves with use. Each question is a learning experience. After starting to ask self-evaluative questions, you will begin to ask more and more of them. You learn which ones bring desired outcomes and which do not. It helps to think of developing a skill as a direction, rather than as a destination. The story is told of two camels with riders in the desert. The rider on the first camel looked back over his shoulder to a woman and two children on the second camel, and said, "Stop asking when we are going to get there; we're nomads for crying out loud!"

With practice, the teacher develops an "ear" for effective and ineffective questions. Following are two questions attempting to get the same result, but notice the subtle differences in sound and message: "When are you going to stop doing that?" is demanding and has an "attack" overtone. "Have you planned your time for getting on track?" is inquisitive—not accusatory. The significant difference is in the direction of the questions. The first aims at stopping a negative. The second aims at the power of positive direction. Certainly, the tone of voice is crucial, but notice how the questions themselves can influence the tone.

Learning the skill is simple but not easy—until the skill is regularly practiced. As Ralph Waldo Emerson said,

> That which we persist in doing becomes easier—
> not that the nature of the task has changed,
> but our ability to do it has increased.

The simple tasks of teaching the concepts and learning the skill of effective questioning handle the great majority of socially irresponsible classroom behaviors. However, when a student has *already acknowledged level B behavior* and *again* disrupts the class, authority is used—but without being punitive. This is the third phase of the program, *Guided Choices.*

KEY POINTS

◆ The strategy starts by setting the mental frame: irresponsible behavior is viewed as a teaching opportunity for fostering responsibility.

◆ First use unobtrusive visual, verbal, or kinetic techniques to stop distractions.

◆ When handling disruptive behaviors, a *stress-reducing mode* is used. A noncoercive guidance approach is employed, rather than an authoritarian coercive approach.

◆ An *asking*—rather than a telling—approach is employed because asking is a more effective strategy for encouraging self-evaluation.

◆ A disrupting student is asked to identify the *level* of chosen behavior, not the behavior itself.

◆ If the questioning is done in front of the entire class, classroom time is not wasted. During the short interchange, the class is reinforcing the levels of development.

◆ The classroom maintains a positive learning environment at all times, even when a student demonstrates irresponsible behavior.

GUIDED CHOICES

You can be tough without being punitive.

OVERVIEW

If a student has acknowledged unacceptable behavior and continues to disrupt learning, the third phase, *Guided Choices,* is employed. *This third phase is used **only** with those who are constantly disruptive.*

Simply stated, *Guided Choices* refers to using authority without being punitive. Employment of authority is essential with youth who go beyond acceptable behavioral standards. However, the authority is used without being authoritarian because authoritarianism is coercive and shuts down any *desire* for change and growth. The disrupting student is given a choice, thereby maintaining self-respect and avoiding an adversarial relationship.

The strategy is to offer choices in the form of questions. Authority is used because *the person who asks the questions controls the situation.* However, as long as the student can make a decision, regardless of how minor it may be, dignity is preserved and confrontation is avoided. Madeline Hunter stated, "A student who loses dignity usually becomes rebellious and resistant in the situation and retaliatory to the person who caused the loss of dignity." (Hunter, 1967, p. 61) The overriding principle always to keep in mind is, *"Not losing is more important than winning."* No one really wins in a confrontational relationship. Solving a problem is much more difficult when people are in conflict because their egos interfere.

Guided Choices is a "win/win" strategy. In "I win/you lose" situations, the teacher only wins a form of satisfaction but the student is left with dejected feelings. In "lose/lose" situations, neither wins; the teacher gets aggravated and the student again takes the brunt. In "you lose/I win" situations, the student has outsmarted the teacher. By using *Guided Choices,* the teacher wins by using a non-confrontational guidance approach that avoids stress. The student wins because dignity has been left intact. In addition, the relationship wins because it is not fractured.

Guided Choices fulfills four purposes: (1) stops the disruption, (2) isolates the student from the class activity, (3) gives the disrupting student a responsibility-producing activity to encourage reflection, and (4) allows the teacher to return to the lesson promptly.

GUIDED CHOICES ACTIVITIES

In *primary grades,* activities will depend upon the teacher's style and creativity. Primary teachers are continually developing ways to isolate a disrupting student from the rest of the class. *Rather than just a time out, the activity should encourage self-evaluation.* Some examples are: having the student draw what the student did, describe the incident while talking into a tape recorder, or create a story that illustrates the type of behavior the student demonstrated. A simple approach is for the youngster to just relate the incident to another student; it is in the telling that reflection and self-evaluation start.

Primary teachers are cognizant that learning a behavior is similar to learning content or a skill in that children are not punished when they have not learned some information or mastered a skill. Similarly, developing responsibility and successful group interactions are skills. When disruptive behavior is thought of as a *learning opportunity* rather than as a punishment opportunity, everyone wins.

ESSAY

The strategies described in the rest of this chapter are for *upper elementary, middle, and high school classes.* The first activity consists of the student's completing a form referred to as an *Essay.* (See Appendix.) It is simply a self-evaluation activity that has three questions:

- What *did* I do? (Acknowledgment)
- What *can* I do to prevent it from happening again? (Choice)
- What *will* I do? (Commitment)

The form is handed to the student while asking, in a noncoercive tone, *one* of the following questions: (a) "Would you rather complete the activity in your seat *or* in the rear of the room?" (b) "Would you rather complete the activity by yourself *or* have someone help you?" (c) "Would you rather complete the activity in the classroom *or* in the office?" The specific question asked depends upon the teacher's appraisal of the student and the situation. As long as the student has a choice, then that student's power, respect, and dignity are retained. It is when a student feels powerless, feels a loss of respect and dignity, or feels cornered that confrontation usually takes place. Offering a choice avoids confrontations. An axiom to remember is to use the *A, B, C* approach: *A*lways *B*e *C*ourteous.

I had one student who, upon receiving the *Essay,* informed me that he would not complete it. I told the student that I understood. I also told him that he needed to understand that I am employed by the board of education and that they would not tolerate any student defying their authority. I then said, "If your pencil is not to the paper within a minute, you are telling me that you are defying the board of education, in which case you are not eligible to remain in the classroom. I would like you to stay, but the board of education would not approve." *I then immediately moved away.* The student picked up his pencil and completed the form—the only one that was ever needed with that student.

Any form used should meet two criteria: (1) it should foster student reflection, and (2) it should involve future planning.

The vast majority of students are capable of completing the form by themselves. However, if the disrupting student works with another person, that is perfectly acceptable. Having to relate and admit to something has a great emotional impact by itself.

Before a student leaves the classroom, a short discussion takes place. The student is first asked if he knows *why the activity was assigned.* The student is not asked to agree, but it is important for the student to understand why the activity was given. The short discussion reinforces the point that when a person makes his own standards, the use of authority is the most expedient approach to stop the behavior and enable the teacher to continue teaching. The point is also made that the teacher is solely interested in the student's impulse control, not in punishment. Second, the student is asked *whether or not the activity was assigned for personal reasons.* This second question is asked in order to reduce any ill feelings.

Using the essay form or other similar activity followed by the short discussion with students handles the vast majority of disruptive problems.

The completed form need not be kept on file. One way to show the student that the teacher is only interested in the student's growth, and not in punishing the student, is for the teacher to ask the student what should be done with the form. At this point, the form has served its purpose, namely, halting disruptive behavior by isolating the student and fostering student reflection. My approach was to tear up the form in front of the student and drop it in the nearby wastepaper basket. I wanted the student to leave my classroom (1) feeling good and (2) knowing I had no ill will.

Every day is a new day for student growth. If a student disrupts the class on a subsequent day, the teacher begins again with *Checking for Understanding*. That is, the student is always given an opportunity to acknowledge the level of behavior before *Guided Choices* are used.

SELF-DIAGNOSTIC REFERRALS

In those cases where a student continues to disrupt the lesson, a *Self-Diagnostic Referral* is used. This is different from the *Essay*, which is often discarded. Keep these completed referrals for the entire school year, not just for each quarter.

When presenting the student with this form, the student is again given a choice as to how he would like to complete it: by himself or with assistance from another student, in the student's own seat or in another seat, in the classroom or in the office. As with the essay, the *student* completes the form, remembering that it is the *student* with whom we want to foster responsible behavior. The following are examples of items on the form. (Items tailored to specific grade levels are included in the Appendix.)

- Describe the problem created that resulted in getting this assignment.

- Tell the level of behavior.

- Explain this level.

- Explain how the behavior is on this level.

- When acting on this level, on what level must the teacher act?

- Is this how you want to be treated?

- Why or why not?

- On what level should you have acted to be socially responsible?

- If you had acted on this level, how would the situation have been different?

- On the back of this *Self-Diagnostic Referral*, list three solutions to the problem you could use to act more responsibly.

Because the referral may find its way to the office or to a parent, all questions are answered completely. As with the essay, the form needs to be completed before the student rejoins the class activity. If the form is not completed to the teacher's satisfaction, a new form is given to the student.

ADDITIONAL SELF-DIAGNOSTIC REFERRALS

If a second *Self-Diagnostic Referral* form were to be used, a copy of the first as well as the second are mailed home along with a very short note explaining the recurring problem. (See *Parent Note* in the Appendix.) If a third referral were to be necessary, "Three strikes and you are out" is employed. Copies of all three self-diagnostic referrals would be mailed to the parent along with a second parent note indicating that the teacher exhausted every means to foster social responsibility and that any future disruption will be referred to an administrator.

Although the process may sound cumbersome, it rarely reaches the stage of a third referral. In addition, since the student's growth is the concern, the student is the person who expends the effort in completing any form or activity. The teacher's involvement in record keeping is minimal. The only form completed by the teacher is the brief parent note.

WHEN ALL ELSE FAILS

Some people see the light only when they feel the heat. Two seventh-grade students come to mind who already had three referrals sent home. Jason and Robert were students who will "push" as far as they can, the kind who cause a teacher to wake up in the morning with a first thought of, "I hope Jason and Robert are absent today."

I had gone as far as I could to help the boys become more socially responsible. The students understood "After three strikes, you are out." This was still the first quarter and I had expected to send the boys to the office, as all their other teachers had done. To my surprise, I never had to send either boy to the office the entire year.

Here is what I did. With the attitude that every day is a new day, the boys had one opportunity to self-correct. When they disrupted the lesson, the first step was to have them identify their behavioral level. This became their warning. Since I had already completed the standard office referral, ready to go except for the date, I placed the office referral on the student's desk right after the disruption and said, "My preference would be to have you stay in the classroom. However, if you act on level B again, you are telling me that you want to continue to make your own standards for the class. That is not acceptable. You may stay in the classroom only if your behavior is at level C or D." (Notice the use of the contingency.)

The boys could see and touch the referral. They knew they had pushed as far as would be allowed and that their staying in class was contingent upon their choosing an acceptable level of behavior.

Unfortunately, schools have students who will push to the brink. Once they are standing on the edge, however, they rarely jump. Students can control themselves and do, although authority needs to be used.

Guided Choices, then, uses a "no one loses" strategy. The class does not lose because the disrupting student is isolated from the class activity so that instruction can continue. The dignity of the student is not diminished because the approach uses authority but is not authoritarian, and the disrupting student also benefits because he is given an activity that assists reflection and leads to a plan for improvement. By using a non-stressful, non-confrontational guidance approach, the teacher resists becoming stressed—or distressed, as is so often the case.

KEY POINTS

◆ *Guided Choices* refers to using authority without being punitive. The strategy is based on offering choices.

◆ Any such activity fulfills four purposes: (1) stops a disruption, (2) isolates the student from the class activity, (3) gives the disrupting student a responsibility-producing activity to encourage reflection, and (4) allows the teacher to return to the lesson promptly.

◆ Primary students are given an activity that is similar to a time out but includes the young person's becoming engaged in a self-evaluating activity.

◆ With older students, the first activity consists of the student's completing a form referred to as an *Essay*. In cases where a student continues to disrupt the lesson, *Self-Diagnostic Referrals* are used.

◆ Authority is combined with guidance, and sending a student to an administrator becomes unnecessary.

———————————————————

SUMMARY, REVIEW, AND CONCLUSION

The real power, the real influence of parents and teachers,
is not what young people do when they are with adults;
it is what young people do when they are not.

The Raise Responsibility System activates internal motivation. The
system handles classroom disruptions simply and easily, creates a
noncoercive classroom, raises individual and social responsibility,
promotes interest in learning, increases the joy of teaching, reduces
office referrals, reduces suspensions, and reduces everyone's stress.

SUMMARY

Raising responsibility starts with teaching a hierarchy of developmental levels. Exposure to the levels encourages responsible behavior.
Students want to reach the highest level of the hierarchy because it
uses the motivating principle of challenge.

(1) Teaching the Concepts

The concepts comprise four levels of development that are made
meaningful by the examples students create for their own classroom.
The levels are:

(A)   Anarchy (Total absence of order)

(B)   Bully*ing* (Rather than following accepted standards,
      makes own rules and standards)

(C)   Conformity (External motivation—as with peer pressure)

(D)   Democracy (Internal motivation—because democracy is
      inseparable from responsibility)

Levels A and B are not acceptable levels of classroom behavior.
Although levels C and D are both appropriate classroom levels,
behavior at level D is the goal.

(2) Checking for Understanding

Disruptions are handled by *Checking for Understanding.* The purpose
is for the disrupting student to acknowledge the level of
inappropriate behavior (level B). Acknowledgment is the first step
towards accepting responsibility. *The vast majority of situations are
handled by using this basic learning theory of teaching (the concepts) and*

then testing (Checking for Understanding). Surveys across the country indicate that teachers use the second phase, *Checking for Understanding*, with fifteen to twenty percent of students. The self-evaluative questioning strategy encourages students to reflect on their level of self-chosen behavior. The effect of this procedure is, to quote one teacher, "They (students) know almost instantly when they need to make a better choice. This takes less time away from instruction and keeps the classroom climate stress-free and positive." (Capell)

(3) Guided Choices

Continued or repeated disruptions are handled by guided choices. The purpose is to stop the disruption and give the student a responsibility-producing activity. In these situations, authority is used but is not punitive. Surveys indicate that teachers need to use *Guided Choices* with only two to five percent of students.

In both *Checking for Understanding* and *Guided Choices*, the teacher is asking—not telling. By asking, the teacher controls the situation. However, as long as the student can make a decision, dignity is preserved and confrontation is avoided.

A major reason for the effectiveness of the system is that students know and feel that they will not be harmed. Students understand that the teacher's intention is for student *growth*, not punishment. In the process, students learn that taking responsibility, which comes from internal motivation, is more satisfying than being externally motivated.

REVIEW

1. When a disruptive student is sent to the office, the counselor or administrator invariably starts the conversation by asking a question. That conversation is on a one-to-one basis. But how does a teacher employ such an approach while teaching with so many other students in the classroom? The answer is a strategy that is proactive. *Teaching* the concepts is done at the outset.

2. When a student acts inappropriately, the teacher starts by asking a self-evaluative question. The question is aimed at having the student reflect by identifying the level of chosen behavior. Since a *level* is referred to, *rather than the student's*

behavior, the student feels no need to be defensive. The noncoercive approach prevents confrontations and reduces stress for both teacher and student. In addition, the disruption is viewed as a teaching opportunity to raise social responsibility.

3. The approach uses simple cognitive learning theory. First we teach; then we test. The testing is referred to as *Checking for Understanding*. Effective questions are asked to ensure that the student reflects, self-evaluates, and understands that he or she chose to act on level B.

4. After the student acknowledges the level of behavior, the teacher continues with the lesson. The questioning process takes no more than a few moments and can be done either individually or in front of the entire class.

5. Acknowledgment and ownership are the first steps in changing behavior. Students need to feel that the teacher's desire is for them to accept responsibility, rather than to be coerced or punished.

6. During the short checking for understanding interchange, responsibility is being reinforced to the class. Instructional time is not wasted.

7. The power of the strategy is that when the student acknowledges the level of behavior, the misconduct not only stops, but also the student oftentimes apologizes—a result of accepting responsibility.

8. Asking self-evaluative and reflective questions is a skill and, therefore, is developed only with practice. You will probably feel uncomfortable when first using it because adults are more habituated to telling young people, rather than asking them reflective questions. During the questioning, be aware of your tone of voice and non-verbal body language (facial expression, body stance, gestures). Be inquisitive, not coercive.

CONCLUSION: OBEDIENCE VS. RESPONSIBILITY

External motivators are used extensively in schools. This includes *telling* young people what to do, *punishing* them if they do not, and *rewarding* them if they do. These approaches teach young people obedience. The shortcomings of obedience appear when teachers and parents are not around to use these external motivators.

The Raise Responsibility System focuses on internal motivation, which builds the vision to act with responsible, autonomous behavior—whether or not anyone else is around.

If America is to continue the civil democracy that has been our heritage, we must do more than just talk about civil democracy and responsibility; we must actively foster it. We can do this in a classroom by providing opportunities for students to take responsibility and by showing them that virtuous behavior is in their own best interest.

By teaching a developmental hierarchy, by using a guidance approach when irresponsibility occurs in the classroom, and—when necessary—by using authority without being punitive, we empower students to manage themselves to be responsible. When we foster responsibility, which in the final analysis requires internal motivation, we foster the type of citizenship that will perpetuate a civil society.

4
PROMOTING LEARNING

LEARNING CLIMATE

If learning is what we value,
then we ought to value the process of learning as much as the
result of learning.

Learning is promoted in a climate where people feel safe and cared for. The adage, *"People don't care what you know until they know you care,"* is applicable. When working with one middle school, William Glasser stated,

> The teachers stopped almost all coercion—an approach that was radically different from the way most of these students had been treated since kindergarten. When we asked the students why they were no longer disruptive and why they were beginning to work in school, over and over they said, "You care about us." (Glasser, April 1997, p. 601)

The result of a caring interest in those with whom we work was documented in a classic study on human relations and became known as the "Hawthorne Effect." It came from a study that took place in 1927 at Western Electric's Hawthorne plant in Cicero, Illinois. Researchers went into the factory to see if, by increasing room lighting for a group of employees, productivity would increase. Improvements did indeed seem to boost worker output. But much to their surprise, when the researchers analyzed a comparable group with no change in the lighting, their productivity also improved. Further study and analysis of this puzzling result showed that productivity increased because the workers were delighted that management was showing some interest in them. *The workers felt that management cared about them and that they were valued.*

People have difficulty understanding that someone cares for them when coercion is used. W. Edwards Deming, the American who showed Japan in the post–World War II years how to improve quality, understood this. (His approach is further discussed in the section *Collaboration—Rather than Competition—for Quality Learning.*) One of his core principles was to *"Drive out fear."* Deming understood that motivation, performance, productivity, and quality are optimum when coercion is at a minimum and when a trusting, caring climate is at the maximum.

In a classroom where the teacher and class have a forced relationship, the student who disrupts the class becomes a hero. The reason is that a coercive climate is an adversarial one. In a climate of positive relationships, the disrupting student does not receive support from the other students.

V*oluntary* relationships are chosen as, for example, between friends. However, classroom relationships are *involuntary.* Students are mostly assigned to their classes; relationships between teachers and students and between students and students are not chosen. The approaches promoted in this chapter help turn involuntary relationships into voluntary ones.

Where learning is promoted, certain activities are unacceptable. These include ridiculing, threatening, forcing, compelling, punishing, bribing, manipulating, blaming, complaining, putting down, nagging, and badgering. We rarely use these coercive tactics with our friends. Coercion is simply not effective in influencing others while trying to keep good relationships.

The first section of this chapter deals with *relationships,* the second with *strategies,* and the third with *challenges.* Although addressed to classroom teachers, the discussions are appropriate in parenting and in other social settings.

KEY POINTS

◆ Learning is optimal when coercion is at a minimum and a trusting, caring climate is at the maximum.

◆ Involuntary relationships become voluntary when people are where they *want* to be. Learning is promoted in this climate.

RELATIONSHIPS

*Meaningful relationships establish
a genial place conducive to growth.*

Three categories of relationships that promote learning are discussed. The first is between the teacher and the class, where the negative orientation of *rules* is contrasted to the positive orientation of *expectations*. The second concerns reducing *anonymity*, both between the teacher and students and among students themselves. The third is the intimacy between the teacher and each individual student that occurs during *tutoring*.

RULES VS. EXPECTATIONS

I do not dress like a cop; nor did I become a teacher to be one.

The relationship between the teacher and the class improves as rules are reduced.

REDUCING RULES

A common practice in this country is to establish classroom rules, either by the teacher alone or by the teacher and students cooperatively. *Rules are necessary in games, but in relationships they are counterproductive.* Although the establishment of rules has good intentions, their implementation often produces deleterious effects.

When Johns Hopkins University researchers analyzed data from more than 600 schools, they found six characteristics associated with discipline problems. Notice that the first three concerned rules.

1. Rules were unclear or perceived as unfairly or inconsistently enforced.

2. Students didn't believe in the rules.

3. Teachers and administrators didn't know what the rules were or disagreed on the proper responses to student misconduct.

4. Teacher-administrator cooperation was poor or the administration was inactive.

5. Misconduct was ignored.

6. Teachers tended to have punitive attitudes. (Gaustaud, p. 18)

When a student does not follow a class rule, the tendency is to think in negative terms: "You broke the rule." The reason is simple. Rules in a classroom imply "or else." A rule that is not followed often leads to an accusatory encounter and results in some type of psychological pain, anger, or resentment for both teacher and student. The rationale is that there must be a consequence for breaking the rule—a punishment that, by its very nature, is coercive. It encourages feelings of enmity, which are not very conducive for positive relationships.

Rulemaking breeds enforcement, which promotes punitive attitudes and results in a teacher's moving from *the role of a coach to the role of a cop*, as was verified in the Number Six finding of the Johns Hopkins study.

Glasser affirms that "traditional education often produces problems that stem from poorly conceived and poorly administrated rules." (Glasser, 1969, p. 195)

> At present, in both elementary and secondary schools, we usually establish rigid rules that lead to punishment when they are broken. The rigid rules of the average central-city school cause even those who have more to gain, the intelligent, to rebel and to refuse to accept the education available. (Ibid., p. 194)

Glasser concludes that an inflexible, punitive approach works poorly especially with central-city children, "most of whom have difficulty obeying rules." (Ibid.) Classroom rules often work against the very reason for their existence: to have students self-discipline and maintain decorum. Quality schools and quality workplaces do not rely on rules. (Glasser, 1992, p. 123) Neither does citizenship education rely on rules. Citizenship education has to do with appropriate and inappropriate classroom conduct, and rules are kept to a minimum—such as "respect for one another and safety." (Farivar, p. 61) Citizenship is really little more than the conscious practice of civic etiquette—the public manners that make the places where we live workable when we practice them, and unbearable when we don't.

Neither are rules effective in teaching moral development.

> Many parents, teachers, and religious leaders find out too late that a concentrated or exclusive focus

on rules is problematic. Using rules and attempting to enforce them as the principal method of producing compliance has not been successful. In fact, it often creates defiance. Many schools, for instance, have established school-wide citizenship programs because large numbers of students are tardy, absent, or otherwise fail to comply with school policies and procedures. This program consisted of an enforcement system that required noncompliant students to participate in hours of community service or other educational programs for each failure to comply. 'Teeth' were added by announcing that failure to comply or complete the service hours would prevent students from graduating. It was not long until schools were forced to create large-scale service and educational programs that required extra record keeping because large and increasing numbers of students failed to comply. The rule system designed to decrease noncompliance actually appeared to promote it. (Scoresby, p. 28)

The mere fact that one knows a rule does not mean it will be followed, in much the same way that information that has been taught does not mean it was learned. When we discover that a teaching has not been learned, we try to assist the student. Similarly, *behavior* is learned and the student should be helped, not hurt or caused to suffer.

Rules are "left-hemisphered." They are sensible, orderly, and structured. However, students who "break the rules " often operate spontaneously and process randomly—typical "right-hemisphere" behavior. In addition, rules often engender a search for loopholes. Rather than using rules, teachers would be better served by using *expectations*.

EXPECTATIONS

The term "expectations" connotes a positive orientation. When an expectation is not met, a helping mentality is engendered, rather than an enforcement mentality. Expectations repair a major finding of the Johns Hopkins study, namely, that many students believe "rules" are mandates that adults put on students, but do not apply to adults.

Expectations engender student empowerment and are responsibility lifting. They tap into internal motivation and foster commitment, rather than compliance.

The following were the expectations posted in my classroom:
- Do my tasks
- Have materials
- Be where I belong
- Control myself
- Follow directions
- Speak considerately

MANNERS

Edmund Burke, the 18th century British statesman, said that manners are more important than laws. According to George Bernard Shaw, the Irish playwright, "Without good manners human society becomes intolerable and impossible." Manners are what make civilization civil. Hal Urban is a teacher, speaker, and author of *Life's Greatest Lessons: 20 Things I Want My Kids to Know*. He suggests holding discussions on manners.

Following are some questions that Urban suggests:
- Would a society be better if people treated each other with respect?
- How are classrooms and schools societies?
- How can good manners be one of the most important keys to success in life?
- What is the Golden Rule? How is it civilizing?
- Which impresses people more: being cool or being courteous?

The following questions promote additional reflection on the topic:
- What do you think about getting up, walking across the room, throwing something in the wastebasket, and then walking back across the room while the teacher is talking?
- What do you think about speaking to others and especially adults in a defiant manner?

- What are disadvantages of swearing in classrooms and in conversations between classes?

- What difference does it make when approaching someone with, "May I please have. . . ." in a pleasant tone versus saying, "I need. . . ." in a demanding tone?

- What are the advantages of using, "Please" and "Thank you"?

- What do you think about listening when the teacher is talking versus feeling the right to ignore the teacher and have a private conversation?

- What do you think about listening when a fellow class member asks a question?

- What do you think about demonstrating an interest in other people versus being solely concerned with yourself?

PROCEDURES

Very often, what a teacher refers to as a rule is really a *procedure*. We need look no further than to one of the first rules primary students are given. They are taught the classroom rule of raising one's hand to be recognized by the teacher before speaking out. The same rule is taught year after year. I have even seen this rule posted in eighth-grade classrooms! Simply reminding students that this is a procedure, rather than a rule, places the teacher in the position of a coach and eliminates an enforcement mentality.

We too often assume that students know what we know and what we would like them to do. This assumption is faulty. Teach procedures—such as how to enter the classroom, how to use an activity center, how to distribute supplies, or anything else that requires a mode of operation. A successful classroom has routines and procedures, which give organization and structure to learning. (See *Classroom Management* in Chapter 5 for more on this topic.)

KEY POINTS

◆ Rules are necessary in games but are counterproductive in relationships.

◆ Relationships improve as rules are reduced.

◆ Rules foster obedience rather than responsibility.

◆ Discussing manners is more effective than posting rules.

◆ The use of *expectations* accomplishes what rules purport to do, but without their disadvantages.

◆ Examine your rules. You will find that they are either expectations or procedures. When you see any that are procedures, *teach* them.

———————————————

REDUCING ANONYMITY

Anonymity must be banished.
–National Association of Secondary
School Principals

Many students feel isolated at school and are alienated from the learning process. Such feelings were captured in the school film *Cipher in the Snow.* The main character was a young student who felt as if he were a person of no importance or value; he felt like a nonentity, a cipher. Even though the student was in the midst of others, he felt alone. He felt anonymous and simply disappeared.

TEACHER AND STUDENT

The National Association of Secondary School Principals (NASSP) emphasizes the need to reduce student anonymity (Tamara). In *Breaking Ranks: Changing an American Institution,* their seminal publication for changing the American high school, NASSP lists six themes that schools must incorporate to break ranks with the status quo. On the top of their list is that better education depends on personalizing the school experience for students. (NASSP, p. 5) The report goes so far as proclaiming that anonymity must be banished. (NASSP, p. 46)

Dale Carnegie, in his best-selling book on winning friends and influencing people, states that a person's name is—to that person—the sweetest and most important sound in any language. Calling a student by the name the student *prefers* to be called not only reduces anonymity but also sends a powerful communication of interest and caring on the part of the teacher.

Chuck Glover of Richmond, Virginia, illustrates the power of showing interest in a student's name.

> During my tenure as an itinerant elementary physical education teacher, while walking down the empty school hall during a short break between classes, Sam, a second-grade student from Southeast Asia, emerged from his classroom to go to the water fountain. After getting his drink and turning back towards his classroom, he waved, and I reciprocated. I interrupted his return by squatting down as he

came by and asked him if his name really was Sam. He quickly replied that his name was Sambohem but that his parents told him to say his name was Sam because Americans have difficulty pronouncing his real name.

I reflected momentarily on what Sam had just told me, and then I asked if he minded if I called him by his real name. He smiled from ear to ear and reassured me that it would be all right. He and I practiced for a couple of minutes right there on the spot. After he felt comfortable with my pronunciation of his name, he continued on his way. But after only a step or two, he turned back towards me, tears in his eyes, gave me a hug, and said, "Thank you," then disappeared through the door of his classroom.

For the rest of that school year, whenever I would see Sambohem, he seemed to have an especial affinity for my class.

Asking a student how the student prefers a teacher address him or her sends a powerful communication.

A simple way to learn the name of every child, is to play identification. A student states his or her name. The next student repeats the first person's name and then states his or her own name. The third child does the same. This is repeated until every student is identified. A variation is to identify a hobby or something that the student enjoys doing. Including an item with the name elongates the time between repeating each name. Also, including an item with the name enhances retention. Knowing something about someone else further reduces anonymity between students.

Another simple approach to reducing students' anonymity is to request parents to write a letter of introduction about their child. These letters give quick parental insight as well as other information that the teacher might not otherwise obtain. In addition, the letters encourage parental support. Here is a sample letter of request from an elementary teacher to parents:

Dear Parents:

It will be my pleasure to be your child's teacher this school year. I look forward to having your child in my class.

Please assist me by writing a letter of introduction about my new student. The letter will help me to learn your child's interests, what you want me to pay particular attention to or lend particular assistance in, and perhaps something personal or something about your child's personality.

I encourage you to compose the letter with your child.

Thank you,

(Signed by the teacher)

A prime reason that anonymity should be reduced is that it can have a socially deleterious effect. With some people, anonymity breeds irresponsibility. Imagine yourself driving on a freeway on a Saturday morning when traffic is light and the road looks more like a ribbon of pavement rather than a slow moving parking lot. Your eyes have time to meander as you notice the azure sky, the various architectural styles, and the landscape of the area. You gaze in your rear view mirror and you notice a car so close to the rear of yours that you can almost feel its bumper against yours. At your earliest opportunity, you move to the right lane and, as the car starts to pass you, the driver begins to give you an unwarranted familiar gesture. At that moment, his eyes meet yours, and you recognize each other. Suddenly, his gesture changes into a familiar wave of his hand. Why did he change his intended gesture? He is no longer anonymous. Anonymity does interesting things to attitudes and behavior.

STUDENT AND STUDENT

One reason young students try to learn is that they love their parents and caregivers and want to please them. Similarly, young children like their teachers and try to please them. But as young people move into middle school and then high school, where teachers necessarily become less personal and less available, students lose some of the school caring that was more available in elementary grades. As young people move up the grade ladder, they turn more and more to their friends for belonging, and as they grow older, they depend still less upon teachers and even parents.

As much as we wish learning were the major attraction for students in attending school, during the adolescent years we find that relationships are often the major motivational factor. Kids want to be with other kids. According to Theodore Sizer, "Personalization is the single most important factor that keeps kids in school." (Shore, p. 1) When a student lacks a sense of belonging, when the student feels anonymous or isolated, motivation for school attendance is diminished. One reason why students drop out of school is lack of friendship.

Teachers can address this issue by planning activities where students spend some time interacting, where they can relate and get to know each other. This can be accomplished in any classroom in just a few minutes. Students share their interests, hobbies, experiences, and things they are proud of with a partner. Some students will not willingly tell a large group about themselves, but they do not mind sharing with one other person, and they don't mind if that person shares the information with a larger group. After a little sharing of personal information, one student introduces the other and states the partner's name and something of interest about the partner. Another activity is for students working in groups to tell three things about themselves that are true and one that is false. In the process of guessing for the false item, students learn three bits of information about each member of the group. Such activities need only to be done periodically for class members to feel a sense of belonging. Involving students in *occasional* activities such as these demonstrates that the teacher is aware of the importance emotions play in learning. (This topic is addressed in Chapter 5 in the section *Emotions.*)

Using activities where students get to know other students—not just as members of the class but as real people—can prevent mean-spirited behavior among students. A bully situation outside of class is stopped with the simple statement, "Leave him alone. I know him."

Trained professionals working with suicidal youngsters attempt to reduce anonymity as soon as possible. A high school named Columbine brings an immediate sense of urgency to this challenge.

KEY POINTS

◆ Reducing feelings of not belonging and anonymity plays a key part in promoting positive feelings for learning.

◆ Learning something personal about each student reduces teacher-student anonymity.

◆ Learning something personal about each other reduces student-to-student anonymity.

TUTORING

If you treat someone as he is, he will stay as he is.
But if you treat him as if he were what he could and ought to be,
he will become what he could and ought to be.
–Johann Wolfgang von Goethe

Tutoring is the easiest, quickest, and most effective way to establish relationships with students. Daily tutoring, more than any other activity, can reduce anonymity, foster a student's sense of belonging in a caring environment, and bring satisfaction and joy to the teacher.

Aside from what is learned cognitively, the impact on the affective level is significant. A few moments at eye level with the teacher gives the student a feeling that the teacher cares about him or her as an individual.

Encouragement is often a spark that ignites motivation. Tutoring affords the perfect opportunity for this type of communication. Time and again one hears that the most powerful factor in student effort is, "The teacher believed in me." Marlon Brando wrote that one of his middle school teachers, Burton Rowley, paid special attention to him. Brando reported that the attention of his teacher so dramatically boosted his self-image that he gained the courage to pursue acting. "His words of encouragement affect me to this day," Brando wrote in his autobiography. (Hicks)

Although every student cannot be tutored every day, *a few minutes can be planned for some daily tutoring.* This applies at any grade level. Especially at the middle and high school levels, too many teachers deprive themselves of working with individual students and establishing a personal relationship with them. Every teacher can afford to invest a few minutes with individual students on a daily basis. Spending time at the student's desk offers an excellent opportunity to see the student's organization and work pattern, and to observe specific skills.

In the old days in England in the city of Broadway near Bath and Nottingham, people would bring their horse and carriage to the inn and leave them with the carriage boy. Because people wanted to encourage the carriage boy to do well—because people thought the carriage boy *could* do well—the owner would give a tip *before* the carriage boy helped with the horse. When the carriage boy was given that tip—the value of his services up front—he wanted to prove his worth. Using this same approach, teachers can tip their students about their potential, give encouragement, share ideas, and foster enthusiasm.

A personal connection is the best gift that a teacher can give to those students who traditionally have not done well in school. We know that the brain is a seeker of connections. When new information is given to students, chaos in the brain may take place until a connection or hook is made. For some students, cognitive connections are not made easily. The human connection can serve as the part of what provides a hook for persistence that is so necessary for success with these students.

A teacher is an encourager. Jim Bellanca stated it succinctly: "Teaching is a strategic act of encouragement." (Bellanca, p. 659) Letting students know we care is the most important thing we can communicate, and seeing a student on a one-to-one basis offers the perfect opportunity.

Much of the success of tutoring is due to personal association and personal attention. One reason why cross-age tutoring is so successful is that the student who does poorly, when asked to help another student, begins to identify himself not as a failure, but as a success.

Ralph Waldo Emerson's idea can well be applied to the teacher and tutoring:

> It is one of the most beautiful compensations of life
> that no man can sincerely try to help another without
> helping himself.

KEY POINTS

◆ Tutoring is the easiest, quickest, and most effective way to establish relationships with students.

◆ Encouragement is often a spark that ignites motivation. Tutoring affords the perfect opportunity for this type of communication.

◆ A few minutes can be planned to do some tutoring daily.

STRATEGIES

Tell me the strategies you use to promote learning,
and I will tell you if you do.

Three strategies for promoting learning are described. The first, *classroom meetings,* establishes an environment conducive to learning, resolving conflicts, fostering empathy, and promoting community. The second strategy, *collaboration,* offers suggestions for enhancing and improving the quality of learning and is far more effective than having students compete against each other. The third strategy, *reducing perfectionism,* is included because the concern for perfection hinders and harms too many young people.

CLASSROOM MEETINGS

He drew a circle that shut me out
Heretic, rebel—a thing to flout.
But love and I had the wit to win:
We drew a circle that took him in.
    –Edwin Markham

Classroom meetings provide excellent opportunities for students to practice communication and socialization skills. They facilitate solving classroom problems and engender both improved instruction and student learning. Classroom meetings differ from usual class discussions in that, to some extent, *the process is the point.* These meetings not only give ownership of the class to the students, they also provide a venue to gain understanding of how other people think and feel—both aspects of getting along with others.

POSITIVE RELATIONSHIPS

Classroom meetings facilitate positive relationships because they provide opportunities for building trust and respect—which in turn leads to a caring environment. Such an environment of mutual respect is necessary in order for each class member to develop the confidence to make a statement or voice an opinion and feel safe doing so.

Self-empowerment is increased when opinions are listened to with respect and when it is seen that an individual's particular contribution has led to a worthwhile solution to a problem or has been of interest to other people.

Teachers who use class meetings develop a closer relationship with their students. The relaxed conversation often reveals things about students, their families, and their circumstances that teachers might never have found out otherwise. An "unmanageable class" can become a learning and caring community because meetings provide a support that calls forth students' best behaviors.

DEVELOPMENT OF SKILLS

The ability to listen attentively and with real understanding is a vital skill for students to acquire. Students soon realize that if they let their attention wander, they miss some key interesting points, lose track of the conversation, and even miss some of the fun arising from humorous contributions.

Students learn the skill of *reflective* listening. Teachers model the skills of paraphrasing and asking clarifying questions, e.g., "Harold, before you give your idea, would you please tell us what you heard Sharon's idea to be." This type of reflective dialogue also helps listening with understanding.

Students gain needed experiences in skills of reading nonverbal clues such as tone of voice, facial expressions, and gestures. Clear and concise speech is another important skill that is developed. It does not take long for students to learn that if their speech is unclear or disjointed, they will be unable to make their point of view known.

Empathy is fostered by asking questions such as, "Would you want to be treated like that?" and "Would you want all persons to act that way in a similar situation?" In fostering empathy, students learn to set aside their own desires, views, and values as they *hear* another person's. Sensitivity to others' feelings makes it less likely that students will hurt, taunt, or isolate others. As Robert Fulghum so aptly stated,

> Sticks and stones may break our bones,
> but words will break our hearts. (Fulghum, p. 20)

In addition to empathy, values basic to our democratic system such as fairness, tolerance, respect, and helpfulness are nurtured. Students learn civil and peaceful ways to deal with different points of view, that there is more than one way to deal with challenges, and that *being different is not synonymous with being wrong.*

Outside the world of school, academic information is not nearly as important as being able to succeed in human relations. Almost all of us interact with others—continually initiating, responding, and negotiating. Much work gets done by informal and formal teams of workers. Employers want employees who are team players, who can understand the culture within a group, and who can work successfully with others. The U.S. Secretary of Labor published a widely quoted report referred to as the SCANS competencies. (Secretary's Commission on Achieving Necessary Skills - Teaching the SCANS Competencies) The report lists skills and personal qualities that are identified as necessary in the workplace. High on the list were interpersonal skills: working on teams, teaching others, serving customers, leading, negotiating, and working well with people from culturally diverse backgrounds. Classroom meetings provide excellent opportunities to practice these necessary skills and gain required understandings.

Several years ago, I was in a one-person store standing in line to pay for my purchase. Six people were in front of me. Gary was the only employee in the store. He answered the phone and helped customers with their questions while at the same time operating the cash register. When I finally became first in line, he greeted me, and I complimented him on his skill in handling the stress of his job so well. Gary said, "I realized no one else was going to be hired; I'm it. We're all in this boat together." Classroom meetings convey this same message: "We are all in this classroom together."

MODELING CIVILITY

A prime reason why class meetings assist in the development of social skills is that they use procedures of civility. Put-downs, snide remarks, or untimely giggles are not appropriate or acceptable. Primary students can use cardboard slips with sad faces on them to keep students aware when a civility has not been followed. Courtesies that are used include respecting the opinions of others whether or not you agree with them, acknowledging others' positions, listening attentively, making constructive rather than destructive contributions, taking turns, and not interrupting others when they are speaking. Once these procedures have become internalized and are regularly observed, it is only necessary to mention them periodically or when there is an infringement.

PURPOSES AND OBJECTIVES

Some meetings have specific purposes such as instructional reflection, discussing pertinent items, articulating and applying the values that schools engender toward civility, character development, and solving problems.

Specific objectives for classroom meetings include the following:

- Improving communication skills of listening and speaking

- Providing opportunities for insightful, creative, and critical thinking

- Learning the process of respectful interaction and promoting teamwork

- Increasing social intelligence, such as empathy

- Fostering social skills, such as reducing shyness

- Enhancing aspects of character education, such as being trustworthy and fair

- Reducing anonymity and promoting feelings of acceptance and worthiness

- Building a trusting and caring relationship between teacher and student and among students themselves

- Creating and maintaining an open, trusting atmosphere for risk-taking in learning

- Creating a sense of community by increasing class cohesiveness

- Providing a channel for relevancy, where students talk about subjects that interest, affect, or concern them

THREE PARTS

Most meetings should have three parts in addition to rehearsing the procedures at the beginning and, on some occasions, summarizing at the end. The first part, *defining the topic,* ensures that everyone understands the issue or topic so that everyone talks about the same thing. The second part, *personalizing,* gives participants the opportunity to relate the topic to their own knowledge and experiences. The third part, *challenging*, provides an opportunity for the teacher to stretch the students' minds by applying the ideas to hypothetical questions or situations. In problem-solving meetings, this third part should be designed to lead to possible solutions to the problem.

CHALLENGING SITUATIONS

With students who tend to monopolize a discussion, after a reasonable period of time, gently intervene and/or talk to them individually outside the class meeting. Suggest that they limit themselves to three contributions per meeting. For students who create disturbances, sit next to them or directly across from them where you are easily visible. Arrange a special signal so the prearranged cue can help them refocus. Over time, changes will begin to appear in these students.

To reduce teacher intervention and obtain maximum student participation, some primary teachers use an index card or some object to pass around or across the circle to the next person who wants to speak. Another technique for very young students is to use a yarn ball, which can be tossed (underhanded) to the next speaker. For students who do not participate when a discussion is free flowing, emphasize the importance of their contribution. Encourage them to talk by saying, "For the next five minutes I'd like to hear from people who haven't had a chance to contribute yet." Invite reluctant members to contribute by saying, "Linda, what are your thoughts about this?" or "Since you have been listening attentively, you may want to share some of your ideas." Making a special effort to acknowledge, outside of the meetings, some positive things reluctant participants do will assist in their willingness to participate during the meetings.

If particular students are the cause of constant irritation either in or out of class, are friendless because of their behavior or poor social skills, or repeatedly violate expected standards, the situation can be a topic of discussion. In these situations, the student under discussion must be present to hear what is being said. When peers, in the safety of a class meeting, sensitively explain to a fellow student their specific feelings and how particular behaviors affect them, the student is more likely to internalize the message and grow in empathy than when an adult tries to say the same thing. Peers can often explain in ways that are more meaningful to their age group than can adults. It is most important that, at all times, *the discussion focuses on the action rather than on the person.* Blame is not attached because the emphasis is always on what the student can do to help improve the situation.

To discourage putting inappropriate or unnecessary problems on the agenda, some teachers use the following "Ground Rule": You can make a complaint about a problem, but you must also have a recommendation for solving it.

A cautionary note needs to be made about problem-solving meetings because their overuse may adversely affect students' attitude toward class meetings in general. This is especially the case if such meetings are used to address "people problems." It is predominantly the open-ended and evaluative types of meetings that stimulate students, are challenging and enjoyable, and are largely responsible for the development of the range of skills referred to earlier.

LENGTH, TIME, AND FREQUENCY

Plan on meetings of ten minutes for young children. The meetings can be expanded to twenty minutes with older students—depending on their age, the nature of the group, their interest level during the meeting, the complexity of the topic, and their experience with class meetings. The meetings should be planned at the same time in the schedule. Many teachers hold meetings before a mandatory dismissal time, such as before lunch, the end of the period, or the end of the day. Many middle and high school teachers begin once each week with a classroom meeting where students talk for a few minutes about how the class is going and how individual and group projects are progressing. Students discuss topics such as whether they think it makes more sense to review home assignments in teams or as a whole class. Because learning is more effective when students are part of the planning process, learning increases even though fewer minutes are devoted to formal instruction. Also, if a class is a particularly difficult one, a class meeting can set the tone for learning.

CREATING THE PHYSICAL ENVIRONMENT

A tight circle is by far the most satisfactory arrangement. Teachers who try the circle format for the first time are often surprised at the difference this face-to-face arrangement makes in the amount and quality of discussion. A circle format ensures that everyone can read the body language as well as hear the spoken word. It is easier to hear all speakers when they are facing the center. Rows can be used, but they are less effective. Rows of people usually result in some comment from the back being misheard or not heard at all. When a funny, witty, or particularly interesting remark is made during the discussion, many of the people sitting in rows will squirm around to see who was responsible for the contribution. In this situation it may be difficult to maintain concentration for the full time of the discussion.

FURNITURE

If furniture needs to be moved, practice in moving the furniture should precede any meeting. It will take students a few practices to move quickly and quietly into a circle formation. As with any procedure, explanation and practice are essential for smooth and successful implementation. Also, if chairs are used, they should all be the same height, thus making it less likely that the teacher is seen as being too overbearing. For younger grades, sitting on the floor often means less movement of furniture and less loss of time both before and after the meeting.

THE TEACHER AS FACILITATOR

The role of the teacher is to facilitate the discussion. This includes reviewing the procedures, posing some questions, monitoring participation, avoiding judgment, and concluding the session. When starting, there is often a tendency for the teacher to heavily contribute. A helpful strategy to avoid falling into this trap is to audiotape a few sessions. Listening to the ebb and flow of discussions leads to improved skills.

Another tendency is to insert judgment. By making a simple statement about one student's comment—regardless of how affirmative it may be—judgment is implied. This is especially the case if a comment is made about one student's comment and not another's. A judgmental statement may be very subtle and unintended but can have a detrimental effect on the reluctant participant who does not receive this affirmation. That student makes his own interpretation that his contribution may not have been worthwhile. Examples of judgmental statements are, "I like that," "What a good idea," or "I agree." Comments such as, "Do you think so?" or "Really?" have a negative effect and can be equally damaging. Class meetings should provide a supportive, encouraging environment that develops students' confidence to speak and make comments. Passing judgment destroys this environment. Most teachers find refraining from judgment very challenging, but it is extremely important that continuing effort be made to create a non-judgmental environment.

A mental strategy for helping in this regard is to fully concentrate on what each student is saying, rather than thinking about what to do or say next. One technique for accomplishing this is to wait a few seconds after a student is finished talking before doing or saying anything. The procedure sends the message that you care about what the student is saying—merely by the fact that your full attention is with that student. It also models good listening for the students and emphasizes the importance of reflection.

AGENDA

The agenda for meetings can be kept in a folder with easy access for both the teacher and students, since both can submit agenda items. On the primary level, the teacher can take dictation from very young students who wish to submit an item.

Primary teachers find classroom meetings not only helpful in resolving conflicts but in handling minor nuisances. Comments such as, "Someone is touching me," or "He is making fun of me," can be handled by the teacher's saying, "Put it in the classroom meeting folder." Similarly, when students raise issues for discussion about some aspect of the classroom operation, the teacher does not feel personally threatened. Merely raising the issue is a confirmation that students have developed the confidence to share because the teacher has demonstrated a willingness to listen. Similarly, the teacher can use a meeting for instructional reflection by stating, "Folks, how can we make this lesson better for the next time I teach it?"

FORMULATING QUESTIONS

The goal of the meeting needs to be clearly established in the teacher's mind in order to formulate questions that will achieve the goal. Questions should be open-ended to elicit more than one-word answers. Closed-ended questions—those which require only a one-word answer—usually bring a conversation or discussion to an abrupt halt. Unless it is a reflective-type question, closed-ended questions rarely show that any thinking has been employed in arriving at an answer. If a question requires a one-word answer, it should incorporate a second part, which starts with "Why?" or "How?"

When a discussion relates to a problem-solving situation, the best procedure is to pose it as a question. For example, "Several people have said there has been a lot of name-calling on the playground lately. Is name-calling acceptable?" "Why?" Then follow up with, "What should we do if it starts again?" This could then be followed up with a commitment question, such as, "Now that we know what *should* be done, who is willing to say he or she will do it?"

Here are some suggestions for question development and facilitation of discussions:

- Start with personalizing the question and relate it to the students' world.

- Ask questions that start with: Why? What if? Could we? Should we?

- Request clarification.

- Look for relationships.

- Encourage examination of assumptions.

- Guide discussions to encourage extension, application, and evaluation of ideas.

- Assist with the formulation of generalizations and recognition of underlying principles.

- Push questions to depth rather than skimming across the surface.

- Play the role of "devil's advocate" on occasion.

- Defer judgment, and encourage both conventional and creative answers.

- Search for unusual ways of doing or looking at something.

- Encourage students to question opinions.

- Use interesting ideas students present and follow these ideas with a new *define-personalize-challenge* sequence discussed earlier in the section *Three Parts.*

CLOSING THE MEETING

A final aspect of the teacher's role is to use reflection to bring the discussion to a positive close. Sometimes it will be necessary to summarize the discussion, draw out the consensus, or clearly state the final agreed-upon solution in a problem-solving discussion. Examples are, "The main ideas expressed today are...." "It seems that most people think...." "Have we agreed that...?" "I think we will have to disagree because there are so many different ideas."

Following are additional reflective techniques:

- Keepers - "Name one thing you want to *keep* from the meeting," or "Restate something that was said that you thought was a good point—even if you didn't agree with it." Have students share with a partner or share in the circle.

- Complete a sentence - Invite all to complete a sentence, e.g., "At the end of this meeting, I hope...."

- Silence - "Take a minute to think about an aspect of today's meeting, such as a new idea or something you will do differently as a result of our discussion. If you would like, take a moment to write it down."

- Post Mortem - Share a few comments asking, "What did you like about today's meeting?" "What made it a good discussion?" "What could or should we do differently next time?"

EVALUATION

After each class meeting, the teacher should evaluate or reflect on the meeting in order for skills (both of students and teacher) to be continually improved. Some considerations are:

- Am I becoming more comfortable and skillful at questioning and leading/facilitating discussions?

- Are the students expressing and supporting their own opinions?

- Are the students willing to challenge others' opinions?

- Is there evidence of insightful thinking?

- Are students talking with each other rather than speaking to the leader?

- Am I using class meetings for one purpose only, or am I using them for a variety of purposes, such as discussing pertinent items and for instructional reflection?

After experiencing many class meetings, further items of evaluation can be considered:

- Achievement towards the goal of each meeting

- Assessment of the level of participation, such as (a) whether everyone had an opportunity to express an opinion, (b) whether anyone dominated the meeting, and, if so, to plan for intervention approaches, and (c) whether anyone consistently avoided participation

- Whether changes from one aspect of a topic to another (the segues) were at appropriate points

SUGGESTED TOPICS AND SOURCES

Thirty topics are listed below that foster communication and socialization skills. Additional topics come from students, the teacher, or are raised from current affairs, television, radio, newspapers, and magazines. Community and social issues are also natural sources for topics.

1. Why do people come to school?

2. Why do schools have report cards?

3. What would you do if you found out at lunch time that you lost your lunch?

4. How can you tell if a person is healthy?

5. What is peer pressure?

6. What would happen if people have rights without responsibilities?

7. What would you do if you found a $5.00 bill on the playground, and why?

8. Would you rather be little again or just like you are now, and why?

9. Why do we call each other names?

10. If you could change our classroom, how would you make it different?

11. Why are people your age given chores to do at home or at school?

12. Does having a reason for doing something make it o.k. to do?

13. What is prejudice?

14. What is discrimination?

15. How do you deal with anger?

16. How do you deal with frustration?

17. What does thinking like a victim mean?

18. What does being bored mean?

19. What does honesty mean?

20. What does having fun mean? How is it different from being happy?

21. What does being grateful mean?

22. How do you deal with jealousy?

23. If you could watch only one TV program, what would it be? Why?

24. What is learning?

25. What are things that trouble people of your age?

26. Is it worth undergoing short-term *pain* for long-term *gain*? If no, why not? If yes, what are some examples?

27. What is the difference between being influenced and being made to do something?

28. How do you control your reaction to impulses and urges?

29. What is the difference between something that is appropriate and something that is acceptable?

30. What are some things that you learn at school that will be helpful to you later in life?

KEY POINTS

◆ Classroom meetings foster communication, social, and other curriculum skills.

◆ In classroom meetings, the process is as important as the content.

◆ Meetings have specific purposes: instructional stimulation and reflection, discussing pertinent school items, articulating and applying the values that schools engender toward civility and character development, and solving problems.

◆ Most meetings have three parts: defining the topic, personalizing, and challenging.

◆ Classroom meetings augment learning even though fewer minutes are devoted to more formal instruction.

◆ Elementary classrooms should hold class meetings daily. Middle and high school classes deprive themselves of the many advantages of class meetings if they do not hold them regularly.

For the reviewing of this section, the author is indebted to Al Katz of the William Glasser Institute, who has taught hundreds of New York City teachers how to conduct successful classroom meetings.

COLLABORATION
—RATHER THAN COMPETITION—
FOR QUALITY LEARNING

*Competition increases performance, but
collaboration increases learning.*

One needs to look no further than the business or sports sections of any newspaper to see how pervasive competition is in our culture. Athletic teams, bands, and other performing groups practice for hours spurred on by the competitive spirit. Fair competition is valuable and can be lots of fun. Competition in classrooms, however, is fun for the winner but is often dispiriting for the others because the same children usually win. If a student rarely finds himself in the winner's circle, competitive approaches kill his drive for learning.

COMPETITION

Teachers of early grades work with children who come to school eager to learn, but competition dulls their spirit. For example, when the kindergarten teacher says, "Boys and girls, let's see who can make the best drawing," the competitive spirit is fostered. The assumption, of course, is that this charge will spur the youngsters to do their best. Unfortunately, however, the teacher has unwittingly set up only one of the students to be the winner. Competition, by its very nature, engenders winners and losers. In band and athletic competitions, losing can build character. However, when a student is first learning a skill, *successes* build character and self-esteem.

A common example of competition is the use of ratings, where students are ranked according to their grades, accomplishments, or some other criteria. *But ratings are an incentive only for those students interested in the reward*—in this case, ranking high. And even though the incentive of ranking high may influence some students in a positive way, it does not necessarily enhance the quality of their learning. The reason is that the focus becomes whatever is necessary to achieve the ranking, which is not necessarily the same as quality learning. Competitive approaches influence students to work against each other, rather than for each other and with each other. "Serve yourself" is the theme. In addition, some people who get good ratings—especially those caught up with perfectionism—often register a paradox; they feel that they don't deserve to be ranked above some of their classmates. On the other hand, those who received low ratings often feel they have been misjudged. To put it simply, class rankings destroy team spirit and community.

It is imperative to understand that grades serve as an incentive in much the same way that rankings do. Many students are interested in achieving high grades. However, today there are thousands of young people in classrooms across America who show little interest in grades. When grades are an incentive, the focus is on this external reward, often at the expense of the internal satisfaction of quality work. In addition, there are many areas across the country where earning good grades is frowned upon by youngsters. The attitude even of some parents is illustrated by the bumper sticker, "My kid beat up your honor-roll student."

Joseph Duran taught that whenever there is a problem, 85% of the time it is with the system. Only 15% of the time will it be the fault of the people. W. Edwards Deming went further and suggested that the ratio is closer to 95-5. This is certainly the situation with cheating in schools, the product of competition. If the emphasis is on grades—rather than learning—students will do whatever it takes to get grades. The answer is not to crack down harder on cheaters and somehow enforce honesty; the answer is to change the system, or at least in a classroom to change the emphasis.

Grades change motivation. Teachers know this from the questions students ask. "Will it be on the test?" or "Will it be counted in the grade?" The focus is not on quality or learning but, rather, on the external reward of the grade. This is not the case in areas like performing arts and vocational classes. It is the excitement of the process that generates quality work. Can you imagine a surgeon or an airline pilot pleased with anything other than best effort? The same holds true with students. A student working in an auto shop is interested in having the car start all of the time, not 75 percent of the time. A person baking a cake is interested in the entire cake, not just part of it, tasting good. This same drive for quality work can be fostered in academic classes.

Grades will not disappear from the education scene, but they need not drive teaching since they do not drive quality work. Grades should be thought of as goals, which are mutually established by the class and the teacher. Rubrics, for instance, can show students how everyone willing to learn and work can earn an A or B.

JOY IN LEARNING

A reason people enter the teaching profession is that they have experienced the joy of learning, and they want to pass it on to others. Focusing on quality is a natural approach to achieving this objective. A quality experience hooks a student on learning. Mastery, of course, requires effort. However, when there is joy in learning, it does not *seem* like great effort because it feels good—as when a student spends hours on the basketball court, working up a sweat while practicing a particular shot. When a person *wants* to do something, the labor seems incidental. Quality work involves exertion, but it may even seem like fun.

When people are engaged in quality work, a few indicators can be observed. They choose to be engaged in the activity; it is meaningful to them. The effort involves some creativity and skill and involves more than a simple task; it is usually complex. The activity results in some success. Personal control is present. Self-assessment is involved. The activity may not be perceived as stressful; it may even feel relaxing.

STARTING ON THE PROCESS

Quality in learning is influenced by the quality of the process. A sense of *purpose* needs to be established. A discussion of the following questions assists in this regard:

Why are we here?

What are we trying to do?

What does it mean to do something well?

How will we know if we are doing it well together?

When students move from the child development emphasis in primary grades to that of greater accountability in upper grades, they need to evaluate their own work. Therefore, the first few sessions of the class should be devoted to a discussion of each of the following topics:

What does it mean to do quality work?

How will each student know that a quality level has been attained?

How will the teacher know that a quality level has been attained?

What does the student need to do in order to attain the level?

What can the teacher do to help students attain the level?

How will a third party be assured that the level has been attained?

The result of such discussions is that during the remainder of the semester, student enthusiasm and drive increase so that the students learn much more. Time "lost" by having these discussions is more than regained over a period of weeks.

Once students believe that the task is worth their time and effort, discussion then focuses on how the learning is to take place. This discussion revolves around such subjects as the following:

Testing: How often? What kind? How to evaluate? What is the purpose?

Home Assignments: Why? How often? When?

Evaluation: How will we know how we are doing? Against what shall we make comparisons (benchmarks)?

Class Management: How do we make ourselves most efficient?

Documentation: How shall we persuade others that we have really done a good job?

Once students have tasted the joy of learning and responsibility for quality work, they may not want to return to something inferior. Some students respond more quickly than others, but all students need to be engaged continually in discussions about quality.

TEACHING VS. LEARNING

The following story illustrates the difference between learning and teaching. The dog owner says, "Last Wednesday I taught my dog to whistle. I really did. I taught him to whistle. It was hard work. I really went at it very hard, and I taught him to whistle. Of course, he didn't learn, but I taught him."

Learning depends upon how enthusiastically the students tackle their assignments. To get students to do home assignments, teachers have employed "carrot and stick" approaches. By a combination of rewards and threats, we have tried to force students to do home assignments, often tying them to a grade. The students, in return, have done their best to outwit the teacher. To change the situation requires harnessing the internal motivation of students. Collaboration is one very powerful method for doing this.

COLLABORATION AND QUALITY

W. Edwards Deming (1986) clearly showed the advantages of collaboration over competition for improved quality of work. Using collaboration to improve quality, Dr. Deming brought Japan from producing cheap and shoddy products to being the world's leader in quality production. Deming's approach that quality can *reduce* cost went against common sense. The thinking at that time was that improved quality would cost more. Deming showed—by using collaboration—how quality of work would increase while costs simultaneously would be reduced. The underlying principle of the Deming approach is continuous worker self-inspection so that quality is built into each step of the process, rather than inspection by someone else at the end of the process. Deming understood that no one can legislate or dictate internal motivation (desire), performance, productivity, or quality. His approach was to use the power of ownership to empower the worker by encouraging self-evaluation. Deming diminished the use of exhortations, threats, prizes, and special rewards for doing what people are supposed to do. In a nutshell, Deming demonstrated that for improved quality of work, *working together is better than working competitively.*

The key to quality learning is to structure student interaction for maximum participation. For example, today's common approach is to *ask* students a question. Students compete for the teacher's attention by raising their hands. The only "winner" is the person the teacher calls upon. Instead of *asking* a question and then calling on a single person, *pose* the question. *Posing* implies open-endedness, invites students to engage in thought, and engenders dialogue. Have students collaborate in pairs or small groups for responses. When collaboration is used, *all* the students participate. Also, notice that students first grapple with the idea or concept. This approach of challenging students at the outset is the approach used so effectively in Japanese schools. Curiosity, interest, and motivation are fostered. Then the teacher facilitates solutions. When activities are structured to be primarily collaborative, learning becomes noncompetitive— an essential principle for increasing quality.

Here is another example of how collaboration improves the quality of learning. A high school student accustomed to above-average test scores was disappointed in her last two test results. The student had grasped the prime concepts but did not do well on reporting details. The teacher told the students that in order to place concepts in long-term memory details need to be remembered. The student's father suggested that as his daughter reads she should mindmap. The father explained that when the brain attempts to remember *words* alone, *semantic* pathways to memory are being used. Semantic pathways require much repetition in order to be retained. On the other hand, he explained, when the brain attempts to remember *images* or *icons*, it uses *episodic* pathways, which require fewer repetitions. Episodic pathways are contextual or spatial and always involve location. To make his point, the father asked his daughter what she had eaten for dinner the previous Saturday and requested that as she answers she relate her thinking process out loud. The daughter responded by saying, "Where was I last Saturday?" "Exactly the point! You looked for a location because we are always somewhere, and we remember through context and images," said the father. "This is the reason that episodic memory is more efficient than semantic memory. It is easier to remember illustrations and pictures than it is to remember information from textbooks and lectures, which usually involves only words."

After this explanation, the daughter suggested to two of her friends that they also mindmap their next reading assignment and share it. All three met and discussed their notes. During the discussion, each became aware of a few additional details that the others had included. Subsequently, all three students' test scores dramatically increased. The strategy of mindmapping assisted, but collaboration made the activity enjoyable and even more effective.

CONTINUOUS IMPROVEMENT

Schools generally use an old approach to evaluation, as when students submit work solely to the teacher. Before Deming showed the superiority of self-evaluation for improved quality of work, American managers hired inspectors to check the work of employees. Quality did not really improve; rather, the poor-quality work just did not get out. Costs went up because items that did not pass inspection were discarded.

> Dr. Deming told me that when he went to Western Electric in the 1920's there were 30,000 people making telephone sets and 10,000 people inspecting their work. The job of the workers was to get their product past the inspectors, and the job of the inspectors was to catch them if they did something wrong. This is no way to reduce cost. It is no way to achieve improved telephones. It is no way to work. (Tribus)

Rather than use this outdated factory model of the teacher as inspector at the end of the process, improved quality of work results if *continuous* improvement and *continuous* feedback are built into the learning process. It is learner-generated feedback that increases motivation and that is so critical to improved quality of work. When we are pleased with our efforts, especially when we see improvement, we invest more effort. Improvement comes through self-evaluation, practice, and more evaluation. The better the quality of our work, the more we are pleased and the more we engage in the activity.

COLLABORATIVE EVALUATION

Stephen Covey refers to the concept of collaboration as "synergy."
> Simply defined, it means that the whole is greater than the sum of its parts. It means that the relationship that the parts have to each other is a part in and of itself. It is not only a part, but the most catalytic, the most empowering, the most unifying, and the most exciting part. (Covey, pp. 262-263)

The brain is innately social and collaborative. Although the processing takes place in our individual brains, learning is enhanced when the environment provides opportunities to discuss our thinking and to bounce ideas off peers. The act of shared thinking, of having to put one's own views clearly to others, of finding defensible compromises and conclusions, is evaluative and, therefore, educative.

Teachers' workloads can be reduced, while simultaneously increasing the quality of student work, by applying approaches of collaborative evaluation through feedback. For example, after an essay assignment is given, but before it is started, students pair with each other and share their understanding of the assignment. Then the procedure of "*three before me*" is explained, which is that before the teacher corrects any paper, it will have been seen by one other student three times. (A variation is to have the work seen by three different people, which may include someone other than a classmate. A parent qualifies.) After the original sharing of ideas, each student writes a first draft, which is exchanged with another student. Each student gives feedback to the other. A second draft is then written, again with each giving the other feedback. The third copy undergoes the same, and then the final draft is completed and submitted to the teacher.

As a general principle for quality work, a first draft should never be considered a final draft. The story is told about Henry Kissinger, who submitted a report when he first started working for the government. His supervisor inquired whether the report was his best work. Kissinger worked on the report for an additional two days, fine-tuning it and giving the report greater clarity before resubmitting it. Again, a similar inquiry was forthcoming, "Is this the best you can do?" The report was worked on for an additional day. After further revisions, Kissinger submitted his work with some anger and confidence asserting that the report was the best he could do. His supervisor said, "Good! Then I will read it."

KEY POINTS

◆ Competition serves as an incentive to improve *performance* but often has a negative effect on *learning* when first learning a skill. If a student rarely finds himself in the winner's circle, competitive approaches kill his drive for learning.

◆ Working for quality is what hooks a student on learning.

◆ Collaboration results in improved quality of work because of continual self-assessment and feedback.

◆ Discussions about what constitutes quality improve student work.

◆ The key to quality learning is to structure student interaction for maximum participation, as in *posing* questions rather than asking them.

◆ When activities are structured to be primarily collaborative, learning becomes noncompetitive—an essential principle for increased quality.

◆ Collaborative learning strategies reduce teachers' workloads.

REDUCING PERFECTIONISM

You cannot learn and be perfect at the same time.

When young people perform *academic-type* tasks and are corrected before obtaining feelings of empowerment or success, they become candidates for discouragement.

A friend of mine related an incident that occurred at the birthday party of his young daughter. After his daughter opened a present he had just given her, my friend asked, cajoled, and finally coerced his daughter into sharing her new toy with the other children. It is hard for a child to share or open to others that which the child does not yet "own." The same principle holds true in learning. Young people need to feel some degree of ownership or success in performing a task—or have a feeling that they are capable of it— before correction becomes beneficial. Otherwise, the good intentions of correction are perceived as criticism, which leads to a dampened desire to perform the task.

Unless a student is very motivated, he normally does not like doing something for which he will be criticized. However, once possession is felt—once he feels competent—he can open himself to others.

Misguided attempts to correct before possession is taken can have unfortunate results.

> In the first grade, when I finished my picture with the sun in the sky, I brought it to my teacher. He looked at it and said that there is no such thing as a green sun. The sun is yellow. Everyone knows that. He said that my picture wasn't realistic, that I should start over. Nightfall came to me in the middle of the afternoon.
>
> The next year my second-grade teacher said to the class, "Draw something—anything you want." I stared at my paper and when the teacher came around to my desk, I could only hear the beating of my heart as he looked at my blank page. He touched my shoulder with his hand, and whispered, "How big and thick and nice is your cloud." (author unknown)

The awareness of the negative effects of criticism and the positive effects of empowerment may be one of the most distinguishing marks of superior teachers—and parents. When our daughter was first learning to speak, she made the sound of "s" in a nonstandard way. We called attention to it—only once. For the next several weeks, every time our daughter spoke any word that contained the sound of an "s," she hesitated and tried to make the sound perfect. We witnessed the first stage of stuttering. Attention was never called to her speech again, and my wife and I were greatly relieved when her natural speech pattern returned. You can prove this phenomenon by concentrating on the process of walking down a flight of stairs the next time you attempt it.

When an infant first attempts to walk, we offer encouragement because we know that learning comes by degrees. We do not expect the child to stand up and walk in one day. Similarly, we encourage an infant to speak even though the sounds are only approximately right. "Exactly right" is made up of a whole series of "approximately rights." Suppose you want an infant to say, "I want a glass of water." If you wait until the child articulates that request with a flawless, complete sentence, you will have a dehydrated, dead child.

Young children are cute, and it is easy to empower them through encouragement. But, when young children become adolescents, we treat learning differently. Should we? Whatever the age, having an orientation for participation should hold a higher priority than perfection. *Participation is the way to success. Perfection is too often a burden.*

The tendency adults have to correct should be modified by a consideration of where the child is in his stage of learning. For example, when the child is desperately struggling to express an idea or use his brain to solve a problem and is put down by constant correction, he may simply not want to continue attempting that or similar activities.

One way to look at the orientation of a classroom is to watch for both the teacher's and students' reactions to mistakes. When mistakes are welcome, learning is enhanced. The reason is that mistakes are invaluable clues to how students are thinking and that to welcome mistakes is to create a climate of safety that ultimately promotes more successful learning. A simple way to foster learning is to constantly remind students that mistakes are opportunities to learn.

A focus on perfection has opened pathways for many students to live with the idea that they have to be perfect for people to love them. The perception that if a person makes a mistake rejection will follow—the sense that she has to be perfect for people to find her acceptable—is an idea that plagues young people all too often.

Striving for perfection, *rather than for continual improvement,* leaves students reluctant to admit mistakes or apologize when in the wrong.

Another manifestation of perfectionism is that students stop learning; they simply give up. Perfectionism becomes so tyrannical that students develop anxiety attacks. This leads to the thinking pattern that they cannot perform or engage in the activity because they will not be good enough. The next stage is total paralysis.

Adults should foster *failure as feedback.* Failing is a natural outcome of trying, and it is a great teacher. That is, it *can* be if the choice is to learn from it rather than be crushed by it. The teacher's message to students, therefore, is to emphasize that experiences—including learning—should be *viewed as processes* and *as information,* not as weapons for self-punishment. This positive mindset breeds a willingness to experiment, to try, to risk. This is extremely important since improvement only comes with practice. Especially at the early stages of learning, *"Implement now; perfect later!"* should be our teaching principle.

KEY POINTS

◆ When young people perform tasks and are corrected before obtaining feelings of success, they become candidates for discouragement rather than for empowerment.

◆ The tendency of adults to correct should be modified by a consideration of where the child is in his stage of learning.

◆ Participation and practice lead to success; perfectionism is a burden.

◆ Accuracy and precision come later with a focus on continual improvement.

◆ Failure is feedback, not an end state.

◆ "Implement now; perfect later!" should be the principle when learning something new.

CHALLENGES

Decent behavior is non-negotiable.

Three challenges that can make the difference between success or frustration are discussed. The first describes a technique for making better decisions when reacting to situations, stimuli, or impulses. The second describes a simple approach to resolving conflicts. The third offers suggestions for dealing with difficult students.

IMPULSE AND ANGER MANAGEMENT

When annoyed, count to 10 before you speak;
if very annoyed, count to 100.
–Thomas Jefferson

Impulses and emotions surge within us, even though something outside of us may have prompted the stimulation. These impulses and emotions can reinforce themselves and become more frequent and even more intense. However, impulses can be diminished, both in intensity and in frequency, when we employ a conscious strategy for responding to them.

First, we must recognize that regardless of the emotion or impulse, a person still has a choice of responses. As earlier discussed in Chapter 1, we can choose our responses when stuck in traffic. We can allow ourselves to become angry or we can choose to play a tape, listen to the radio, or think of a pleasant experience. Similarly, when someone cuts in front of our car or does something that stimulates us to a state of road rage, we either can allow that emotion to direct our behavior, or we can choose to redirect our response to that surge of emotion.

Even very young people in an aggravated emotional state can change their responses. One of my favorites in this area occurred when a kindergarten teacher summoned me for assistance with a youngster having a crying fit. I reached into my bag of tricks and pulled out a stethoscope given to me by my physician and placed it around my neck. When I entered the kindergarten room, I knelt down to the child and applied the stethoscope to a few places on the child's chest. The crying immediately stopped. I then proclaimed the child healthy. The strategy of redirecting a child's attention worked every time.

This same diversionary phenomenon is often seen with teenagers. The adolescent is having an emotional argument with a parent. The phone rings; it is one of the teenager's friends. The tone of voice immediately changes; it is suddenly friendly, even sweet. Upon termination of the conversation, the previous surge of emotion reappears, proving that by redirecting their attention even teenagers can control their tempers.

Here is a strategy that anyone of any age can use to prevent becoming hijacked by his or her impulses or emotions. The strategy can be used when sitting or standing, but to realize its fullest effect, I suggest standing this time to learn (and teach) the strategy.

First, slowly and silently breathe as though you were *gasping* for a breath.

Do this a second time, and notice that your jaw drops open and your tongue goes to the bottom of your mouth.

Take a third long, slow, deep *gasp*. As you breathe in through your open mouth, notice your back expanding. This is Structural Breathing™ and is more effective in filling the lungs and oxygenating the system than the so-called diaphragmatic or abdominal breathing, which constricts the rib cage and allows only part of the lungs to expand to their fullest.

This simple procedure of taking a *gasp* of air releases the jaw and the emotional tension of the nearby nerves that otherwise would send the tension throughout the body.

In the moment that it takes to slowly *gasp* and release the tension, the mind has the opportunity to redirect thinking by considering options.

When working with young people, a traffic signal can be used to visualize and reinforce the three steps.

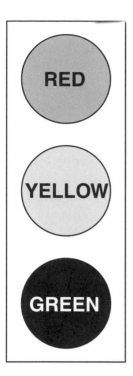

Stop
and *gasp* a long,
deep breath.

Think
of options.

Go
with your best
choice.

We should be teaching that we can recognize an impulse or emotion such as anger, that we have a choice of how to react to it, and that we can choose a constructive response.

We should also teach young people to differentiate between anger at a person and anger at a situation. When people are upset, they often misdirect their anger. Ask, "Are you angry at me or the situation?" This reflective question leads to redirection of behavior.

KEY POINTS

◆ A conscious strategy can be used to respond to impulses such as anger.

◆ Using a slow, silent, deep gasp releases the tension in the body and allows us to redirect our thoughts and behaviors.

◆ Asking, "Are you angry at me or the situation?" redirects behavior.

The author is indebted to William Hanrahan of Vocal Integration Concepts, Marina del Rey, California, for demonstrating the effectiveness of Structural Breathing™.

CONFLICT RESOLUTION:
SOLVING CIRCLES

*Changing ourselves is the most effective way
to change others.*

Solving circles is a very effective strategy for resolving conflicts between two people.

In order to understand this strategy, a simple question needs to be answered. Think of any one person with whom you have had a personal association—it may be a spouse, child, parent, fellow worker, friend, or acquaintance. Now, ask yourself whether *you* ever changed that person, and if the person did change, consider whether *you* did the changing or if the person *changed him/herself*.

The realization that no one really changes another person, but that people change themselves, is the theory behind using solving circles.

Of course, a person can control others in the sense of exercising authority over them, or directing or commanding them, as, for example, when a parent "grounds" a son or daughter or when a teacher sends a student to "time out." Temporary compliance, however, does not change how a person *wants* to behave. People are not *changed* by other people.

With this in mind, here is how solving circles works. Two interlocking circles are drawn. The first circle represents person A; the second circle represents person B. The overlapping area between the circles represents the common goal, such as solving a problem or getting along better.

In a disagreement, the usual approach is for each person to tell the other person what the other person needs to do or stop doing— basically, how the *other* person needs to change. With the realization that one does not change another person, that a person can only change him/herself, person A describes what *he* himself or *she* herself will do to reach the common goal. Person B is naturally drawn to do the same. By discussing one's *own* behavior, instead of the other person's behavior, each individual takes responsibility for his or her own actions. No additional assistance or third party is needed.

With young students, the strategy can be taught on the playground by drawing two large overlapping circles in chalk or by using two hula hoops. The teacher then asks two students to describe some problems they encounter on the playground. After a situation is chosen, role-playing is conducted by having one of the students stand in one circle and the other stand in the other circle. The conflict resolution is played out.

As long as people psychologically stay in the circle and realize that *they can change only their own behavior,* they can negotiate almost anything. Each is sending the message, "I want to improve the situation. Here is what I am willing to do."

When the parties are angry, first have a cooling-off period. With young children, have them sit down with the direction that neither can get up without the other's permission. Once they realize the situation they are in, anger dissipates, and the situation often turns humorous. With older students and adults, call a short time-out period. Leave the situation. The parties need to cool down because, when angry, the focus is rarely on a solution. When tempers have cooled, resume solving circles.

Do not recycle the past. When the focus is on the past, the misery is revisited because the past does not change. The discussion must be future-oriented since we can only plan for the future. Realizing that people can change only themselves and that the conversation is future-oriented are the reasons that solving circles resolves conflicts in a simple and effective way.

KEY POINTS

♦ We cannot change other people. We can influence them to change by what we do.

♦ Rather than talking about how the other person needs to change, each person volunteers what he or she will do to resolve the conflict.

♦ Discussion is focused on the future, rather than on the past or on the cause of the conflict.

♦ Two people can resolve their own dispute; a third person or mediator is unnecessary.

The author is indebted to William Glasser, M.D., for this strategy.

DEALING WITH DIFFICULT STUDENTS

Kids would rather be bad than stupid.
A reason they misbehave is they don't want to be failures.

The Raise Responsibility System is the foundation for handling irresponsible behavior. However, some students require special attention in order to help them become more responsible. Review the unobtrusive techniques at the beginning of the discussion on *Checking for Understanding* in Chapter 3. Additional suggestions follow.

USE POSITIVITY

When a youngster is off task or exhibiting behavior you do not like, be positive by informing him what you *want*—not what you do not want. Simply tell the student what you would like to see happen. This helps the student understand your desires and stops the student from engaging in one undesirable behavior only to engage in another non-productive one.

EMPOWER WITH CHOICES

Offering more than one activity affords choice and ownership. For a math assignment, students may be given the choice of doing assigned problems on a certain page, doing the odd-numbered problems, or doing the even-numbered problems. For an essay assignment, students can choose from among several topics. Asking students how they believe they can best learn the material is always a possibility.

ASK REFLECTIVE QUESTIONS

Work on the skill of asking reflective questions, such as, "Since you are having a challenge staying on task, what would you suggest to help?" Use an inquiring tone and a smile. Before starting an activity, ask, "What are the benefits of what we are going to do?" The discussion will take a few minutes but is worth the time to encourage "buy-in" for self-control.

COACH

Think of young people as lacking skills, rather than as being non-compliant. Few students are maliciously non-compliant. We teach young people how to swing a baseball bat, how to play a musical instrument, and how to drive a car. We do not give up on them, nor do we resort to punishment. We coach them.

GIVE START DIRECTIONS

Students with short attention spans have a difficult time getting started on a task. Give clear, concise start directions, such as, "Feet on the floor, back straight, pencil and paper in proper position." Have students complete the following to themselves, *"The first thing I see myself doing is...."* Helping a youngster set his own mental frame assists him in taking responsibility for his actions.

USE CREATIVE APPROACHES

When there are distractions, teach students to label them. One teacher used this strategy when construction was going on outside her classroom. She taught her students to label the noise "*distraction*" and that doing so would help them refocus on their task. She told me that this strategy saved her semester.

Have students count the number of times they return to their tasks. Tracking them increases the likelihood that students will stop and think about what they are doing.

ACKNOWLEDGE ON-TASK BEHAVIOR

Acknowledge *in private* when the student is on task. Do not be concerned about interrupting the student at work; the student will let you know if it is bothersome.

ENCOURAGE

Encourage students. It raises their aspirations. Robert Danzig rose from office boy to president of his company because Margaret Mahoney, his office manager, said to him, "You are full of promise." That comment prompted him to begin seeing possibilities and generated his rise from sweeping floors to becoming the president of the Hearst Newspaper Corporation. (Danzig)

Equally important is that a word of encouragement during a failure is worth more than a whole book of praise after a success. When a student has not been successful, ask, "What can we learn from this experience?"

CHANGE A SEAT

Arrange for a student who has poor self-control to be seated near the teacher's desk or at the front of a row so that the student's back will be to other students. Position the student away from distracting stimuli such as doors, high-traffic areas, and pencil sharpeners.

ASSIGN A BUDDY

Select a responsible student as a "buddy helper" to assist the student by answering questions, explaining directions, and making transitions to new activities. Periodically, rotate "buddies" to avoid burnout and to give other students the "tutor" experience.

DEVELOP SIGNALS

Develop a secret verbal or nonverbal signal or cue for redirecting a student's energy or attention to refocus. An "ahhuum" throat-clearing sound works well.

PROGRESS IS POWER

Progress is measured by improvement in oneself, not in comparison to others. Periodically, find some improvement that the youngster has made and acknowledge it. Success breeds further success.

KEY POINTS

◆ Be positive by informing students what you *want*, rather than telling them to stop doing something.

◆ Ask reflective questions, such as, "What are the benefits?" before starting an activity. This encourages "buy-in" and self-control.

◆ Think of youngsters as lacking skills, rather than as being non-compliant. This will engage you as a coach to help them.

◆ Give clear, concise start directions.

◆ Teach youngsters to label a *"distraction"* as such. It helps them refocus on their task.

◆ Encourage progress and acknowledge it.

◆ Develop a verbal or nonverbal signal to redirect students when necessary.

————————————————

SUMMARY AND CONCLUSION

The ultimate use of power should be to empower others.
That's what our Constitution is about.
–William Glasser

The most effective way to promote learning is to establish a noncoercive environment where students *want* to learn and *want* to behave appropriately.

SUMMARY

Relationships - Three types of relationships foster this type of learning climate: relationships between the teacher and the students as a class, relationships among students, and relationships between the teacher and individual students.

Relationships between the teacher and the students as a class improve as rules are reduced. Rules are necessary in games but are counterproductive in relationships because the teacher is placed in a position of being a cop, rather than a coach. This often produces adversarial relations between the teacher and class members. In addition, rules foster obedience rather than responsibility. A more effective approach is to teach procedures and to use expectations.

Student relationships improve as anonymity among students decreases. Students should not feel alone in a crowd. Having students interact and share information about themselves builds community.

Tutoring is the easiest, quickest, and most effective way for the teacher to establish relationships with individual students. It offers an excellent opportunity for learning more about each student and for giving encouragement. Encouragement is often a spark that ignites motivation. A few minutes daily can be planned to do some tutoring.

Strategies - The first strategy discusses classroom meetings—their purpose, importance, and implementation. The second is collaboration in promoting quality learning. The third focuses on reducing perfectionism.

Classroom meetings turn a classroom into a learning community. Meetings have specific purposes: instructional stimulation and reflection, discussing pertinent items, articulating and applying the values that schools engender toward civility and character development, and solving problems. Classroom meetings augment learning even though fewer minutes are devoted to more formal instruction. Elementary classes should hold class meetings daily. Middle and high school teachers should include meetings as part of their lesson plan.

Collaboration results in quality work because of continual self-assessment and feedback. Working for quality is what hooks a student on learning. The key is to structure student interactions for maximum participation, as in posing questions rather than asking them. When activities are structured to be primarily collaborative, then learning becomes noncompetitive. Collaborative learning strategies also reduce teachers' workloads.

Perfectionism interferes with learning. When young people perform academic tasks and are corrected before obtaining feelings of success, they become candidates for discouragement. The tendency of adults to correct should be modified by a consideration of where the child is in his stage of learning. Accuracy and precision come later with a focus on continual improvement. "Implement now; perfect later!" should be the principle when learning something new.

Challenges - Three challenges that teachers encounter are students' lack of impulse control, conflicts between students, and dealing with difficult students.

A conscious strategy can be taught for responding to impulses, even anger. A diversion can redirect behavior. Using a slow, silent, deep *gasp* releases the tension in the body and allows us to redirect our thoughts and behaviors.

Conflicts between two people can be resolved by the use of solving circles. Since people change themselves, rather than talking about how another person needs to change, in solving circles each person volunteers what he or she will do to resolve the conflict. Discussion is focused on the future, rather than on the past or on the cause of the conflict. Using this approach, two people can resolve their own dispute without the involvement of a third person or mediator.

When dealing with difficult students, be positive by informing them of what is wanted, rather than telling them to stop doing something. Ask reflective questions, such as, "What are the benefits?" before starting an activity. This encourages "buy-in" and promotes self-control. Think of youngsters as lacking skills, rather than as being non-compliant. Give clear, concise start directions. Teach youngsters to label a "distraction" as such. This helps them refocus on the task.

CONCLUSION

Niccolo Paganini (1782-1840) is still considered one of the greatest violinists of all time. One day, as he was about to perform before a sold-out house, he walked out on stage to a huge ovation but felt that something was terribly wrong.

Suddenly he realized that he had someone else's violin in his hand. Horrified, but knowing that his only prudent choice was to begin, he started playing.

That day, he gave the performance of his life.

After the concert, Paganini was in his dressing room speaking to a fellow musician and he reflected, "Today I learned the most important lesson of my entire career. Before today, I thought that *the music was in the violin.* Today, I learned that *the music is in me.*"

Establishing a noncoercive learning environment and implementing the suggestions of this chapter promote this kind of thinking in our students.

5

TEACHING

CURRICULUM AND INSTRUCTION

If telling were the same as teaching,
we would be such good teachers
we could hardly stand it.

Although classroom disruptions may stem from problems that students bring to school, they may also arise from curriculum, instruction, or classroom management. Curriculum and instruction are discussed in this section. The following sections offer suggestions for classroom management and home assignments.

CURRICULUM

Curriculum has to do with content or *what* is taught. Every level of government, local boards of education, professional subject matter and professional associations, individual schools, and local communities all impact on what is taught.

Skills such as reading, writing, arithmetic, and problem solving are part of the curriculum. The curriculum also includes basic information about our history, health, and a whole range of other subject matter that is important to our lives and perpetuates the priorities of society.

INSTRUCTION

Instruction is about *how* content, skills, and problem solving are taught and learned.

What many teachers refer to as discipline problems actually stem from instruction. *Behavior problems are at a minimum when instruction is effective.* A lesson is most effective when (1) it is made interesting, meaningful, relevant, or useful; (2) the lesson involves thinking; and (3) students are actively involved. This means planning instruction in ways that students *want to learn.* Glasser makes the point: "It does no good to push a student who does not want to learn any more than it does to get tough with a worker who is looking for another job." (Glasser, *Choice Theory in the Classroom,* p. 74)

This chapter gives an overview of basic instructional considerations using the components of the acronym "LIMES," which refers to *L*eft-right brain hemisphericity, *I*ntelligences, *M*odalities of learning, *E*motions, and *S*tyles. This is followed by a discussion of lesson planning, levels of intellect, instructional questions, a group questioning strategy, and choosing key words to frame questions. A short discussion of imaging, stories, metacognition, and the senses follows. The chapter concludes with additional principles for aiding recall, laser learning, and three seminal shifts regarding instruction. The overriding theme of the chapter is to offer multiple connections to the brain so students have multiple ways of knowing in order to increase the odds of understanding, application, and transference.

Left-Right Brain Hemisphericity (The "L" in LIMES)

We start with the concept of *left*-right brain hemisphericity. (The terms "left brain" and "right brain" are meant as generic locations for easy reference. More specifically, the terms refer to the hemisphericity of the cerebral cortex. This area of the brain is the core location for cognitive learning.) Understanding how the brain functions is important to the design of effective teaching and learning experiences.

Brain hemisphericity originated when medical practitioners were trying to stop epilepsy so that seizures in one side of the brain would not travel to the other side. This was accomplished by severing the corpus callosum, the thick cable of nerve fibers that connects the two cerebral hemispheres. A pioneer in this movement was Roger Sperry, who won the 1981 Nobel Prize in medicine for his work. Much has been learned in the intervening years, but the concept of hemisphericity remains useful and valid. The concept can help us in teaching and learning *as long as we use the two sides as a construct for understanding.* We should not pigeonhole behavior into either a left-brain or right-brain blueprint or fall into inaccurate assumptions and conclusions, such as making a relationship to handedness (lateral dominance) or intelligence. No relationship exists in either.

When we talk of brain hemisphericity, we are always talking about integrating both sides of the brain because the hemispheres of the brain are continually interacting. In fact, since the two hemispheres do not function independently, it is impossible to educate only one hemisphere in a normal brain. The reason is that the brain reduces information into parts while perceiving wholistically at the same time. For example, when we look at something that is in motion, numerous locations in the brain are activated to combine its form, dimension, perspective, color, and movement in order to see the object as a whole. Neuroscientists refer to this as operating in a "modular" fashion with autonomous systems devoted to different mental acts.

The left and right hemispheres of the brain have some distinctly different functions, but both sides are involved in nearly every human activity. For example, both sides work together to integrate words for proper speech intonation. The left side produces the correct speech, and the right side mediates the feelings attached to it. Words produced only with the left side will be intelligible but will sound flat or indifferent. Conversely, if only the right side is involved, then the language will sound like gibberish although the feelings accompanying them might be recognizable.

Another example of both hemispheres of the brain working together pertains to memory. The formation of memories involving words is concentrated in the left hemisphere of the brain, but visual memories stimulate greater activity in the right hemisphere. Specialization in a part of the brain does not mean exclusivity. In fact, hemispheric dominance runs the gamut from neutral (no preference) to strongly left or right. However, most people do have a dominant hemisphere that affects personality, abilities, and learning modalities.

In most people, the left cerebral hemisphere is the hemisphere of logic. It controls analytical and verbal intelligence. It is methodical, sensible, and processes sequentially. The right cerebral hemisphere controls spatial and artistic skills. It is intuitive, processes randomly, and involves feelings, expressiveness, and creativity.

The functioning of brain hemispheres can be categorized as follows:

Left Hemisphere of the Brain	Right Hemisphere of the Brain
• Analytical and methodical	Creative and expressive
• Deals with the sensible	Deals with fantasy and the imaginative
• Logical	Intuitive
• Processes information linearly	Processes randomly and wholistically
• Stimulated by function	Stimulated by appearance
• Detailed, orderly, likes instructions	Spontaneous, goes with the flow
• Sequence is important	Context is important
• Deals with time	Deals with space
• Interprets through words, symbols	Interprets through pictures, letters, graphs, charts
• Responsible for verbal expression	Responsible for gestures and facial movements
• Spoken, written language	Tone of voice
• Reading	Seeing or experiencing
• Recognizes letters, words, numbers	Recognizes faces, places, objects, music
• Deals with inputs one at a time	Integrates many inputs at once
• Parts first, then whole	Whole first, then parts
• Structure, predictability	Open-ended, surprises
• Main center for language	Main center for nonverbal ideation

Mindmapping

Challenge, complexity, and *novelty* stimulate the brain, light up both hemispheres, grab attention, and lead to greater learning and memory. The key point to remember is to plan for experiences so *the brain learns.* For example, the activity of plotting words *and* graphics integrates both sides of the brain and increases learning.

This type of activity is referred to as mindmapping, concept mapping, graphic organizing, "webbing," or clustering.

Here is a mindmap of this book up to this point.

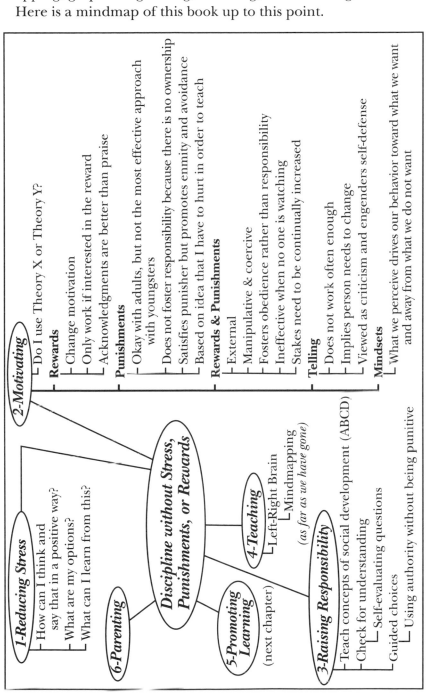

Variations include drawings or icons (in place of words) and use of colors.

In addition to traditional outlining, which is linear, use this type of visual organizing to string relationships in a less sequential, more visual manner. Information organized into wholistic conceptual frameworks is more easily remembered and understood than bits of discrete information.

At about grade three or four, teaching often moves from using activities, many of which appeal to the right hemisphere of the brain, to almost exclusively using methods and activities that appeal to the left hemisphere of the brain. The result is that many right-brained students, who need more creative and visual work (not to be confused with reading, which is a special skill), are nurtured less by schooling processes and move toward becoming at-risk students.

Intelligences (The "I" in LIMES)

Students are smart in ways other than those measured by intelligence quotient (IQ) tests. These tests measure essentially the same characteristics that Alfred Binet devised at the turn of the 20th century to predict which French children would succeed or fail in school: memory, vocabulary, spatial thinking, and the ability to draw analogies and solve puzzles.

In 1983, Howard Gardner's *Frames of Mind: The Theory of Multiple Intelligences* was published. Gardner listed seven intelligences, has since added an eighth, and indicated that there may be even more. (Gardner, 1993, 1997) Two fundamental propositions are central to Gardner's theory: (1) Intelligence is not fixed. Every time something is learned, the brain changes, and we have the ability to develop the intellectual capacity of our students. (2) Intelligence is not unitary. There are many ways to be smart, which Gardner refers to as *kinds of minds.*

The concept of multiple intelligences (MI) has had a profound influence on how we think about teaching. Emphasis shifts from "how smart students are" to "ways that students can be smart." This means teaching in many ways to provide varied learning experiences beyond the typical linguistic and logical ones predominantly used in American classrooms beyond the primary grades.

According to Gardner, intelligence must relate to those competencies that are valued in the world. School matters, but only insofar as it yields something that can be used once students leave school. (Gardner, 1997, p. 12) "An intelligence is the ability to solve problems, or to create products, that are valued within one or more cultural settings." (Gardner, 1993, p. *x*)

The eight (8) intellegences are categorized as follows:

Verbal-linguistic	*word smart*
Logical-mathematical	*logic/number smart*
Visual-spatial	*picture smart*
Musical-rhythmic	*music smart*
Body-kinesthetic	*body smart*
Interpersonal	*people smart*
Intrapersonal	*self smart*
Naturalist	*nature smart*

Here are the eight intelligences at a glance:

- *Verbal-linguistic* - This is the most commonly shared and crucial competence of the human species. It allows us to comprehend the meaning of words in verbal and written form. It also allows us to follow the rules of grammar and syntax and appreciate the sounds, rhythms, and inflection of words. Students show they are *word smart* when they are good at reading, writing, spelling, speaking, telling stories, and playing with words. They learn best through verbal presentations, reading, writing, and discussing.

- *Logical-mathematical* - This is the area of math-science. This intelligence allows us to work with objects, assess their qualities, and assign numbered symbols. It allows us to order, align, and sequence in the world around us. Students show they are *logic/ number smart* when they are good with numbers, sequencing, synthesizing, evaluating, and solving math problems easily. They often learn best through logic.

- *Visual-spatial* - The prime function of this intelligence is to form images and perceive the world accurately. It is linked to verbal intelligence in that the mind stores and recalls its information in pictures, which may then be verbalized. Imaging is a valuable asset in recall and in problem solving. Students show they are *picture smart* when they have good artistic capabilities, an eye for detail and color, spatial awareness, can manipulate perceptions mentally, and enjoy painting, drawing, and sculpturing. They visualize easily and are good with spatial relations. They learn best through imagery, films, videos, and visual aids.

- *Musical-rhythmic* - One of the earliest intelligences to appear, its core functions deal with rhythm, music, tone, pitch, and patterns. Of all the intelligences, the consciousness or mood altering effect of music and rhythm on the brain is the greatest. When words are combined with melody and rhythm, as in song, they are easier to recall. Music has the ability to inspire, to excite, to express joy and sorrow; it also has the ability to calm and soothe. Students show they are *music smart* when they have the ability to communicate or gain meaning from music; listen to music frequently; play an instrument or sing; and are sensitive to pitch, timbre, timing, tone, and rhythm. Students using their music smarts often think in rhythms, melodies, or lyrics. They like to sing, hum, chant, rap, read, or create music. They learn best through music or lyrics and when music is part of the lesson.

- *Body-kinesthetic* - The main characteristic of this intelligence is to use the body for expressive purposes. Involving the body in any learning event increases the neural activity of the brain and increases the chances for information to be stored in the muscles of the body. Students show they are *body smart* when they unite body and mind for physical performance, have good motor skills, use their bodies to communicate, are good at dancing or athletics, and use the body in skilled ways. They are coordinated; use gestures and body language; and enjoy acting, role-playing, dancing, or athletics. Students using their body smarts think in movements, gestures, and body language. They often learn best when there is movement or when the content is presented in a "hands-on" form.

- *Interpersonal* - This intelligence gives us the ability to communicate verbally and nonverbally with other people. It is the capacity to perceive emotions, moods, motivation, and intentions. It also allows us to empathize with another person.

Students show they are *people smart* when they make and maintain friends easily; are sensitive to the feelings, moods, and motives of others; are good mediators, leaders, and organizers; put themselves in the role of the other; and see things from the other's perspective. They often learn best when they interact with other people over subject content or skills.

- *Intrapersonal* - This intelligence involves knowledge of the internal aspects of oneself, such as feelings and emotional responses. Self-image and personal identity are part of intrapersonal intelligence. It also gives us our capacity to see wholeness and unity, to discern patterns as they relate to self, and see connection with large orders of things or higher states of consciousness. Students show they are *self smart* when they have access to their own feelings, strengths, ideas, values, and beliefs; set and meet goals; and enjoy private time to think and reflect. They know themselves well and have the ability to use that information when making decisions. They often learn best when they are given time to formulate their ideas and reflect on their learning.

- *Naturalist* - This intelligence describes the ability to recognize flora and fauna and classify like objects. Students show they are *nature smart* when they have keen observation skills, an ability to make distinctions, and to form classes among natural objects. They have an awareness of the natural world and phenomena, and discriminate among animals, insects, birds, rocks, plants, trees, flowers, stars, planets, or even some non-natural items like cars, airplanes, shoes, or hairstyles. They enjoy gardening or caring for animals. They often learn best when the content is sorted and classified and is related to the real world.

Using the theory of multiple intelligences can have a very positive effect on learning. Learners forget a great deal of what is taught, but the problem may be a reliance on only one intelligence. By appealing to several intelligences, we can enhance long-term memory. Attending to students' intelligences accommodates more learners and gives students a greater repertoire of problem-solving tools. Another reason to include several intelligences when planning activities is to aid students in building self-esteem. This occurs when students identify an area in which they have a natural competence. Knowledge about one's own intelligences helps in this regard.

Thomas Armstrong suggests that one way to ascertain students' most highly developed intelligence is to observe how they *misbehave* in class. The strongly linguistic student will be talking out of turn, the highly spatial student will be doodling and daydreaming, the interpersonally inclined student will be socializing, and the body-kinesthetic student will be fidgeting. These intelligence-specific behaviors can be thought of as a cry for help—a diagnostic indicator of how students need to be taught. (Armstrong, 1994)

Another good indicator of proclivities is to observe how students spend their free time. Highly linguistic students might gravitate toward books, social students toward group games and gossip, spatial students toward drawing, and body-kinesthetic students toward hands-on activities.

Two caveats regarding multiple intelligences need to be made clear: (1) Do not design lessons for each intelligence. Planning such lessons misinterprets the brilliance of the concept. The approach should be to *plan activities that incorporate as many intelligences as are purposeful*—rather than preparing lessons for each intelligence. (2) It is nonsensical and far too demanding to plan on teaching something seven or eight ways. The point of multiple intelligence theory is to realize that any important topic can be taught in more than one way. The maxim to remember about multiple intelligences is *the more ways we teach, the more students we reach.*

Modalities of Learning (The "M" in LIMES)

The *modalities* refer to visual and print, auditory, kinesthetic and tactile, olfactory, and gustatory learning. Whereas the intelligences tell us how people are smart, learning modalities explain how people learn.

Information comes to us through our senses of sight-*visual,* hearing-*auditory,* touching-*tactual or tactile,* taste-*gustatory,* and smell-*olfactory.* Home economics, science, and some fine arts activities employ the senses of taste and smell. But the visual, auditory, and tactual senses are used in the preponderance of lessons. In practice, the tactual sense is expanded to imply any body movement (kinesthetic). Although print is usually considered visual (for the blind it is tactile), *interpreting print requires other skills.*

The brain learns in many ways at once. As we grow and engage in various activities, some senses develop more than others, but none grows in isolation. The concept can be likened to use of the right and left hand. Although we use both, we prefer one to the other. Similarly, we do not have a single, dominant lifelong learning mode. We learn our first language through sound, but many adults find it easier to learn vocabulary of a second language by seeing words visually as objects or in print.

Visually-oriented people prefer seeing instructions. They form mental pictures, scenes, and even words by projecting them with the mind's eye. Auditory people prefer an oral briefing. They recall things that have been said, music, and other sounds. Kinesthetically-oriented people like to get physically involved and get their hands on the activity and often are the first to try things.

During teacher presentations, visual and verbal cues can help tap into various learning modalities. The following lists offer some suggestions:

Visual learners

> like to see things in writing
>
> picture in their minds
>
> organize by pictures
>
> like colors
>
> like to take notes
>
> like flash cards
>
> enjoy mindmapping and graphic organizers
>
> want to be shown how to do something rather than be told how to do it
>
> match clothes and colors
>
> enjoy looking at a drawing or diagram rather than hearing an explanation.

The following examples of *verbal connectors* both indicate and cue into a visual style:

> "You can see the situation."
>
> "See what I mean?"
>
> "It appears that...."

"In your mind's eye…."

"Show me what you mean."

"Do you get the picture?"

"Is it becoming clear?"

"This looks good."

"Here is a bird's eye view."

Auditory learners

need to hear themselves talk

learn by repeating

read out loud

study out loud

often request to have directions repeated

like oral directions

sub-vocalize when reading

like the sound of their own voice

remember directions better if they repeat them to a neighbor

The following examples of *aural connectors* both indicate and cue into an auditory style:

"I hear what you are saying."

"Does that sound reasonable?"

"That rings true."

"I hear you loud and clear."

"Does it sound right?"

"We're on the same wavelength."

"I remember it word for word."

"That rings a bell with me."

"I'm trying to hear you but you're going too fast."

We often assume auditory learners can learn just by listening. It is important to note that auditory learners need to *hear themselves*. They learn by verbal repeating. An aural learner who is not cued beforehand may listen and then turn to a neighbor and say, "What did he say?" This is particularly true regarding home assignments. Before giving students an assignment, cue them ahead of time by simply saying, "In a moment I'm going to give the home assignment." Also, after giving the assignment, have students turn to a learning buddy and repeat what was said.

Kinesthetic/tactile learners

> like manipulates
>
> enjoy flash cards—as long as they can hold them
>
> need movement
>
> use lots of hand gestures
>
> tend to have shorter attention spans
>
> tend to be leg and arm movers
>
> create energy to stay focused even though their movement itself does not teach anything

The following examples of *kinesthetic/tactile connectors* both indicate and cue into a kinesthetic/tactile style:

> "I've got a handle on that."
>
> "I can really get a hold of that information."
>
> "This helps me grasp the issue."
>
> "Raise your hand if you get a feeling for her point."
>
> "Get a grip on this point."
>
> "Hold on a second."
>
> "Can you put your finger on it?"
>
> "Does it touch you?"

Whereas colors and visuals can be used for visual learners and lyrics and rhythm can be used for auditory learners, finding movement for kinesthetic learners in the classroom can be far more challenging. Spelling words, for example, can be put on posters around the room. Students go to the various locations where the posters are, say a word out loud, and even draw the word with their hands through the air. The same procedure can apply to vocabulary, multiplication tables, geography, or other subject areas.

A fine line often exists between kinesthetic students and those labeled with Attention Deficit Hyperactivity Disorder (ADHD). The latter student will wiggle no matter what. A kinesthetic learner will only wiggle while he is concentrating. Kinesthetic learners will ask more often than others to go to the bathroom, sharpen pencils, and get out of their seats. Just allowing them to stand helps. Also, they will wait longer to ask questions or to ask for help.

A student's modality of learning can often be ascertained by observation. Visual learners usually follow the teacher with their eyes. Aural learners repeat out loud and want things repeated. Kinesthetic learners like to move while learning. Providing choices allows students to choose the modes that best suit them.

We need to recognize our own learning styles because we have a tendency to teach the way we learn. A teacher whose learning modality is highly visual will have a natural tendency to use visual activities, often to the exclusion of activities directed toward other modalities.

Emotions (The "E" in LIMES)

Achieving change is emotional as well as intellectual. Emotions can enhance the learning process or interfere with it.

Our emotional system drives our attention, which drives learning and memory. (Sylwester) Specifically, how a person "feels" about a situation determines the amount of attention he or she devotes to it. Students need to feel an emotional connection to their tasks, their peers, their teachers, and their school. For an increasing number of students, school is a place where making emotional connections is more important than anything else. This is especially true for so many adolescents, where a feeling of belonging almost overshadows all other needs. As indicated in Chapter 4 in the section *Reducing Anonymity,* this need is often the most important factor that keeps kids in school.

We generally focus on cognition when we teach, and we tend to avoid the emotions. Yet, students must feel physically and emotionally secure before they can process information. Threats are counterproductive because they stimulate emotions that interfere with higher-order thinking skills. Armstrong calls negative emotions such as humiliation, shame, guilt, fear, and anger "paralyzing experiences." (Armstrong, 1994) When students are anxious, the emotions interfere with thinking and disrupt the learning process. In short, negative emotions are counterproductive to learning.

Some knowledge of how emotions and thinking are intertwined is important because in every encounter there is an emotional subtext.

Wlthin a few moments of seeing or hearing something, we react. There is a very subtle, and sometimes not so subtle, liking or disliking. The brain evolved this way for survival. In case of a dire threat, we needed an immediate response. Not much time was allowed for a rational decision. "I'll get it or it may get me." The emotional mind still reacts before the thinking mind. Sensory signals from the eye or ear travel to the thalamus. The thalamus acts as a relay station for information and branches to both the neocortex, the thinking or cognitive part of the brain, and to the amygdala. The amygdala is an almond-shaped ganglion (mass of nerve tissues) perched above the brain stem adjoining the temporal lobe. The amygdala stores our emotions, especially fear and aggression. It is our emotional memory since the time we were infants. But there is one long neuron connection from the amygdala to the gastrointestines. That is why you may have a feeling that seems like it emanates from the pit of your stomach. It does. The branching allows the amygdala (emotions) to respond before the neocortex (thinking) because the circuit to the amygdala is smaller and shorter. This explains why we get angry before we think. This threat-response is great for escaping from predators, but not for learning. The short-term impact of this brain response includes impaired spatial episodic memory, weakened ability to prioritize, and greater likelihood of repeated behaviors that impinge on learning.

The brain biologically is going to pay attention and remember longer those things that have strong emotion, either negative or positive. Since emotional climate is critical for learning, we need to invest the first few minutes of every class in activities that allow students to get into a positive learning state and make the lesson "enjoyable" to the learner.

The implication for the classroom is to add emotional hooks to what we are teaching. The art of this craft is to create experiences, rather than just present information. For example, a high school history class is reading about immigration to the country in the early part of the 20th century. The textbook contains a graph showing great numbers coming from Eastern Europe. A simulation could give students some idea of what the experience was like for these people, who were mostly very poor, and who traveled across the Atlantic Ocean on ships as steerage. A group of students huddles sitting on the floor in one corner of the classroom. Crowded together, they move their upper bodies back and forth to simulate not only the movement of the ship but also how people were seasick for much of the voyage. No wonder they were elated to see the Statue of Liberty in the calmer waters of New York Harbor! When we add emotion to learning experiences to make them more meaningful and exciting, the brain deems the information more important, and retention is increased. (Wolfe and Brandt)

The human brain has a built-in attention preference for certain stimuli, such as novelty and pleasure. We can take advantage of the brain's preference for *novelty* by eliciting states of *curiosity, oddity, intrigue, suspense, anticipation, awe, confusion, surprise,* and *challenge.* We can increase *pleasure* by creating states of *anticipation, hope, security, fun, acceptance, success,* and *satisfaction.*

Knowing that we respond emotionally when fear and anxiety are involved should always be a classroom consideration. If a student feels helpless or incompetent, anxiety sets in and impedes learning. Conversely, when students are encouraged and challenged without coercion or fear of failure, they feel the likelihood of becoming more competent.

To move towards competence, students need to learn to accept feedback, *whether positive or negative,* without any emotional connotation or judgment. They need to learn to treat failure as an opportunity, not a disaster. Failure gives information one would not otherwise have. The approach is to see failure as a guide and not allow an emotional rush to swamp them. But we have done a funny thing with failure. Instead of keeping it as a lookout, we have too often given it the helm. Failure is a natural part of any learning. *You cannot learn and be perfect at the same time,* as indicated in Chapter 4 in the section *Reducing Perfectionism.* This phenomenon can be observed by watching very young children before they put on their belief systems. They take one shaky step and fall down; they take another step and plop. Without emotional freight, babies know instinctively that failure is a signal to try another way. If failure is feared, learning will never be optimal. If failure is used as a guide, not an accuser, success will be swifter.

Styles (The "S" in LIMES)

Styles refer to modes of behavior and communication. They have little to do with intelligences, abilities, or aptitudes.

No style is good or bad, right or wrong. Neither is one style better or worse than another; they are just different. For example, perhaps you have sometimes wondered why it seems so difficult to communicate with some people and why at other times you instantaneously hit it off with someone you have just met. The answer can be found in our styles.

Carl Jung, the Swiss psychiatrist who founded analytic psychology, was the first to develop the concept of behaviorial styles. Jung articulated a theory of personality behavior types, which he believed are genetically determined. They can be discerned by watching young children and discovering how they process experiences in different ways. Jung postulated that every individual develops a primacy in one of four major behavioral functions: intuiting, thinking, feeling, and sensing.

Over the years a number of inventories have been developed using Jung's "forced-choice" approach. If you have ever taken such an inventory, you might have had difficulty making choices between two opposites because the answers are not mutually exclusive. That is, one choice may be more representative but not to the complete exclusion of the other. Therefore, any inventory that uses a forced-choice approach is an artificial attempt to categorize and describe. If we keep this in mind and do not pigeonhole people by the results of such an inventory, the general concept can be useful.

From the many instruments now available using this forced-choice approach, four behavioral styles seem to emerge. To help understand this approach to styles, visualize a directional scale with a *thinker* in the north, a *feeler* in the south, a *doer* in the west, and a *relater* in the east.

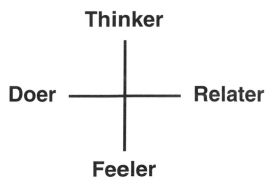

A *thinker* (north) analyzes and can be described as logical and structured, and as someone who *processes cognitively*. Jung describes a person in this category as processing analytically and inferentially. A *feeler* (south) can be described as personalized, spontaneous, emotional, and animated. Jung describes a person in this category as one who *processes subjectively*. A *doer* (west) is *orientated toward results* and can be described as assertive and directed, while a *relater* (east) is *into relationships*. Since directions are not limited to the ordinates of north, south, east, or west, thinking north *and* west, south *and* east, etc., is more useful. For example, my styles are predominantly in the thinker and doer quadrants. I am cognitive and project-oriented. My wife's are in the thinker and relater quadrants. She is a writer and desires interactions with others. Our daughter is predominantly in the feeler and relater quadrants. She is guided by her feelings and has a great desire to be with people. Knowing our daughter's styles allows my wife and me to be much more understanding of her. A parent who is aware of styles has a decided advantage in relating to the child. The same holds true for a husband and wife. Just knowing that my wife needs time to relate allows me to respond more successfully to my impulse of "getting on with the task." Being aware of styles enhances communications. Alessandra and O'Connor refer to this awareness as the *Platinum Rule:* "Do unto others as they would like done unto them." Relate to other people according to *their* styles.

In a classroom, a teacher whose own style is predominantly that of a thinker will have a propensity to plan fewer activities that tap into feelings, sentiment, or excitement. Similarly, a teacher who is predominantly a doer may have a tendency to plan too few activities where students interrelate. Knowing about behavioral and communication styles allows the teacher to plan activities that afford opportunities to appeal to all styles. This is especially important for at-risk students. Many students who drop out of school are "feelers," those who process subjectively. *If they feel school is not successful for them, why continue?*

To summarize, the "LIMES" acronym assists in remembering that some students are sequential learners and others need to see the whole picture (*l*eft-right brain). Every student can be smart in some way (*i*ntelligences). Some need to hear themselves while others need to move or touch (*m*odalities of learning). Anxiety should be reduced and feelings of enjoyment increased (*emotions*). Finally, learning can be enhanced by considering behavior and communication patterns (*styles*).

It is critical to remember that lessons are not planned around each entity. The purpose is to be *aware of them* so that when lessons are planned and implemented, learning will be enhanced and understanding of student differences will be increased.

Lesson Planning

Madeline Hunter's lesson-planning model is very useful in considering teaching and learning. Unfortunately, over the years her model has come under some criticism mainly because of faulty interpretation. The model has been incorrectly perceived as an inflexible recipe or cookbook approach. That is, if all the ingredients are not included and used in sequence, then the model is not being followed.

This is *not* how the model was supposed to work. Madeline Hunter saw the model as flexible and open-ended. The steps should be *considered* when planning a lesson. Having considered them, teachers should select, abandon, or judiciously include any or all of the steps.

Anticipate

1 **Mental Set** - Break Preoccupation/Get Attention.

- Link past experiences or future plans and interests to the lesson.

- Engage curiosity.

2 **Objective** - Give the intended objective of the lesson.

- Explain the purpose, meaning, and/or use of the lesson.

Participate

3 **Teach the lesson** - Facilitate the learning.

- Bear in mind (LIMES) left-right brain considerations, intelligences, modalities of learning, emotional considerations, and styles of behavior and communication to involve students.

4 **Check for understanding** - Obtain feedback.

- Check that students have learned what you have taught.

5 **Practice** - Apply.

- Give students an opportunity to practice the lesson, first independently and then with learning partners.

Reflect
6 **Closure** - Reflect/Reinforce.

- Have students articulate and share what they have learned.

- Think, pair, and share.

7 **What next** - Plan for long-term memory.

- Through inquiry and example, relate how the learning is meaningful, useful, relevant, or interesting. Have students use a learning log to record, "What did I learn?" and "What do I need to work on?"

Organizing the steps into the three categories of *anticipation, participation*, and *reflection* assists in both planning and implementation. This categorizing serves to remind us of the importance of reducing anxiety and increasing novelty when a lesson is introduced (anticipation). It also helps to focus on what the *students* will be doing to learn (participation). Likewise, reflection at the conclusion of a lesson aids long-term memory. Traditionally, not much time of a lesson has been devoted to reflection because the assumption has been that the teacher must be active in teaching. But it is in the processing time that learning becomes solidified. (Jensen, 1998, p. 47)

Levels of Intellect

A look at levels of intellect is useful, especially since the advent of media technology, where students are exposed to so much information, perhaps at the expense of higher levels of thinking.

Benjamin Bloom's taxonomy of educational objectives in the cognitive domain helps teachers and learners understand levels of thinking. (Bloom) The taxonomy categorizes higher-order thinking in ascending order, from the simplest to the most complex:

1. *Knowledge* - Remembering previously learned material (recall).

2. *Comprehension* - Grasping the meaning of material.

3. *Application* - Using learned material in new and concrete situations.

4. *Analysis* - Breaking down material into its component parts so that its organizational structure can be understood.

5. *Synthesis*- Putting parts together to form a new whole (creativity).

6. *Evaluation* - Judging the value of material for a given purpose.

At the lowest rung on the ladder, students can be asked to *recall* information. Second, if students can recount information in their own words, they probably *comprehend* it. If students can *apply* the information, they are at the third level. When students can *analyze* or examine components of the information, they have reached the fourth level. If students can combine or assemble information to draw a solid conclusion, they are at the *synthesis* level. Finally, when students make a judgment about the information expressing their opinion, they are at the *evaluation* level.

Levels from *application* upward require recall and comprehension. If students cannot recall and comprehend the information, they will not be able to apply it, analyze it, synthesize it, or make a considered evaluative judgment.

Following are two subject area examples.

Government

1. *Knowledge* - What students *remember.*
   What is the electoral college?

2. *Comprehension* - What students *restate* in their own words.
   How does the electoral college work?

3. *Application* - What information is to be *used* to solve the problem.
   Predict what would happen if the electoral college were to be eliminated.

4. *Analysis* - What is *broken down* into what parts.
   Differentiate between what the electoral college did before the 12th Amendment to the Constitution and its present role.

5. *Synthesis* - What two pieces of information are to be *combined.*
   How can the electoral college and the popular vote produce different results?

6. *Evaluation* - What students are to express an *opinion* about.

In your opinion, should the electoral college be retained or abolished? Defend your choice.

Literature

1. *Knowledge* - Describe one of the main characters in the story.

2. *Comprehension* - Compare characteristics between two main characters.

3. *Application* - Write a conversation between you and one of the characters.

4. *Analysis* - Explain how one of the main characters moves the plot forward.

5. *Synthesis* - Rewrite your own ending of the story for the main character.

6. *Evaluation* - Describe the author's message and how the main character fits into it.

Here are some key words to assist in planning and evaluation:

1. *Knowledge* (recall)

list	fill in
describe	identify
locate	recall
define	what
label	when
repeat	who
name	

2. *Comprehension*

paraphrase	translate
explain	interpret
discuss	summarize
compare	convert
review	how
match	why
give an example	

3. *Application*

apply	employ
construct	restructure
draw	predict
simulate	calculate
sketch	practice
demonstrate	how

4. *Analysis*	analyze	contrast
	classify	deduce
	dissect	categorize
	distinguish	separate
	differentiate	break down
	compare	subdivide
	infer	
5. *Synthesis*	compose	create
	combine	integrate
	design	formulate
	relate	assemble
	produce	rearrange
	put together	collect
6. *Evaluation*	judge	rate
	argue	debate
	assess	evaluate
	appraise	choose
	decide	defend
	criticize	support

Notice that the lower three levels—knowledge, comprehension, and application—describe a *convergent* thinking process whereby the learner recalls what is known and comprehended to solve a problem through application. In contrast, the upper three levels—analysis, synthesis, and evaluation—describe a *divergent* thinking process. These levels of processing result in new insights and discoveries that were not part of the original information.

Use of the taxonomy is especially pertinent today where so much information gathering becomes an end unto itself, as is the case with the expanding use of computers. For students to gain wisdom, higher-order thinking skills must be incorporated into instruction. Even students with learning difficulties can handle this successfully.

David Sousa offers some questions to stimulate higher-order thinking:

What would you have done?
What are some of the things you wondered about
    while this was happening?
What might happen next?

Why do you think this was the best choice?
What do you think might happen if...?
What do you think might have caused this?
Predict what will happen in the future.
How is it like...?
How is it different from...?
Give an example.
Where could we go for help on this?
Have we left out anything important?
In what other ways could this be done?
How many ways can you use this?
Do you agree? Why or why not?
What was the most important idea to you?
How would you change it?
What details can you add to give a clearer picture?
How can you test the theory?
How can you tell the difference between...and...?
(Sousa, 1995, p. 127)

A note of caution is necessary here. The brilliance of the taxonomy is that it helps to ensure that lessons are not exclusively aimed at only lower-level thinking. The government and literature examples were given to explain the concept—*not to expect each lesson to include all six levels of the taxonomy.*

Instructional Questions

Effective teachers ask effective questions because questions direct the thinking process.

The following will assist in more active thinking and increased student participation.

1. Ask "what" questions. Continually and repeatedly ask, "What if?" and "What else?" When students start thinking about answers to these questions, their mental images take on far more detail and their language takes on far more differentiation. In addition, they begin to "own" the information.

2. Use wait time to encourage thinking. Learn to be comfortable with silence. When you call on a student for a response, wait 10 seconds (not the usual 1-2 seconds) after your question. Responses will be longer, responses will be at higher intellectual levels, and students will demonstrate more confidence in their

answers. Also, this wait time will encourage students to offer a response instead of assuming another student will be called on.

3. Wait after an answer is given. Immediately following an answer, wait 5-10 seconds (not 1-2 seconds) before giving feedback or making another instructional move. This will both encourage other students to volunteer and model reflection on an answer.

4. Use levels of intellect. Instead of requesting only recall or information, ask questions that require higher-order thinking skills of analysis, synthesis, and evaluation. Students automatically will include lower intellectual levels in their answers.

5. Call the student's name *after* asking the question. When a student is called on before the question, other students do not pay as much attention or prepare a response. The exception may be for the student who is shy or has a disability and is not comfortable with "taking risks."

6. Do not repeat responses. When teachers do not repeat answers, students pay greater attention and show increased respect for their classmates' responses.

7. Pose, rather than ask, questions. Asking often implies a correct answer. Posing implies open-endedness, engenders dialogue, and invites students to think. Posing increases student involvement.

Group Questioning Strategy

Spencer Kagan of Kagan Cooperative Learning in San Clemente, California, believes that teachers often disempower themselves with the traditional approach to answering questions. All a student has to do is hold up a hand, and the lesson can be derailed with an off-the-wall question. This is a three-way lose situation. The teacher is disempowered because the question needs to be answered, the student may get a cursory or irritated response, and the class loses because it is time away from the class activity while the teacher deals with the question—which may be of no interest to the other students.

Another approach is to tell students to hold questions until inter-action time. When students work together as pairs and if one does not know the answer, then two students have the question. When students work in teams, the questioner asks the other team members.

Chances are one of the team members will know. If no one in the team knows, that means there is a team question since now a few people have the same question and the team has exhausted its resources. When all team members raise their hands, this signals to the teacher that the team needs help.

When using group questions, the teacher randomly chooses one member of the group to ask the question. This guards against a student's saying to the other members of the team, "I've got a question; so all of you put up your hands." In responding to the group's inquiry, the teacher has a few options. The question may be answered, thinking may be redirected, resources may be pointed out so the team can do their own research, or the question may be shared with the class. *The key is that the teacher is the filter for what goes on in the classroom.* Group questions are a three-way win because the students get a quality response, the teacher retains the agenda, and time is not wasted for the rest of the class.

Choosing Key Words to Frame Questions and Statements

Robert Greenleaf of Greenleaf Learning in Providence, Rhode Island, suggests paying particular attention to key words when asking questions. Specific words determine the levels for both thinking and group interaction. For example, key words in the three following questions evoke (even dictate) a predetermined, specific type of response.

The question, *"When was gold first discovered in California?"* evokes *"1848"* and may even conjure up James Marshall's discovering the gold nugget at Sutter's sawmill. Notice, however, that *"when"* and *"first"* in the question send a message that *only one correct answer is sought.* Once the answer is provided, there is no purpose in further deliberation. Also, a risk is involved. If the question were asked of the entire class, a student volunteering an incorrect answer would have been better off not participating.

A second question such as, *"What kinds of things do you think the pioneers heading for the promise of California gold would have brought with them?"* evokes a *multiplicity of responses.* A list of items would be engendered, such as water, food, clothes, shovels, pickaxes, and gunpowder. All responses are viable. The plurals, *"kinds"* and *"things,"* indicate that more than one response is necessary; thus learners continue to search for probable items. Students make use of their understanding (prior knowledge) of the time period and its technology and posit likely things the pioneers would have brought with them. In this case, students are encouraged to continue to search for additional responses, as the list is potentially extensive. Notice that little, if any, risk is involved in this processing to attempt additional answers.

A third question, *"How do you think the U.S. might have developed differently if gold had been discovered on the Gulf Coast instead of the West Coast?"* evokes a different type of response. *"Might"* and *"if"* indicate full license for the learner to explore possibilities, that developing ideas and relationships in one's thinking are sought. Minds stay engaged and connections are made. Also, the responses will be offered in more complete thoughts and full sentences, such as, "Fewer people would have gone west," "The people who discovered the gold would have become rich and bought most of the Caribbean," "It would have taken a lot longer for pioneers to move westward because there would have been less incentive," and "New Orleans would have been the economic center of the country instead of New York."

As key words in questions trigger very specific responses, key words in statements can also stimulate thinking. "Put your paper on your desk" requires only that the student process a simple direction. "The bell is about to ring. Think about what you need to do before you are ready to be excused," engenders much more complex, intellectual processing. Instead of simply following directions, students must determine what to do and then direct themselves to do it. Therefore, *choose words that mentally engage students.*

Imaging

Visualization of objects and events is a powerful way of storing information. (In contrast to *imagining*, which has no limits, *imaging* is specific and focused.)

We can even improve reading comprehension by encouraging students to make mental pictures as they read and use their own experiences. For example, students can mentally image the entrance to their residence—the first room they enter, then the kitchen, and then other rooms. This imaging encourages focusing and generates additional richness of detail. In this example, one can mentally stop in any room and visualize the furniture and decor. Using this technique, students can visualize or "peg" information in any location.

Any image can be created to enhance recall. For example, to learn Stephen Covey's seven habits of highly effective people (Covey) correctly and in proper order, I conjured up the following image.

Habit	Mental placement on my body
1. Be Proactive	head
2. Begin with the End in Mind	shoulders
3. Put First Things First	chest
4. Think Win/Win	belly
5. First Seek to Understand, ...Then to be Understood	hips
6. Synergize	back
7. Sharpen the Saw	thighs

By creating this visualization, I have immediate recall. In addition, it took less time to create the image than if I had attempted to memorize the list through repetition—and reinforcement takes but a matter of moments.

Conjuring up vivid images (right brain) while reading a book (left brain) encourages hemispheric integration and leads to improved memory and more efficient learning. If you think of engaging both sides of the brain, no matter what you are teaching, the learner builds up more hooks and cues to ensure long-term memory. The brain can keep on making connections and, therefore, grow throughout life. *Learning builds learning* because, as we continue to learn, the neural networks of the brain augment, creating ever-abundant connections.

In *How the Brain Learns,* David Sousa says:

> Imagery should become a regular part of classroom strategies as early as kindergarten. In the primary grades, the teacher should supply the images to ensure accuracy. Later, teachers should encourage students to form their own images. Research studies continue to attest to how the power of imagery aids in recalling word associations, visual arrays, prose learning, complex procedures, and motor learning. (1995, p. 96)

Here is a simple experiment you can do with your students. Find two similar reading selections. Have students read the first selection and then ask questions about the reading. Then take your students through a visualizing exercise. Use their bedroom as an example. Say, "As you read something that is important or that you wish to remember, make an image of it or describe it in two or three words and then place it on the bed. Place the next item in a different location and continue the procedure until the end of the reading selection." Have the students answer similar questions as they did before the imaging exercise. Explain to your students the reason for their improvement: the brain remembers experiences and images better than words.

Let your students also know that their memory can be improved when they think in images. Often the more unusual the image, the better the retention. A simple exercise proves the point. Envision a cow. The cow's name is Georgette. It's a Jersey cow. The cow is on the Empire State Building and is singing a couple of Christmas carols. Under the cow's chin is a ham. It's a Virginia ham. The cow is wearing yellow underwear. In the cow's hoof is a pencil. And the cow is making a connect-the-dots drawing of Marilyn Monroe who is walking down a road going to Mass.

You just named all original thirteen colonies: Georgia, New Jersey, New York (Empire State), the two Carolinas, Virginia, New Hampshire (ham), Delaware (underwear), "Pencilvania," Connecticut (connect the dots), Maryland, Rhode Island, and Massachusetts.

If you want to increase involvement and enhance recall even more, use oral repetition. The exercise would go as follows:

Envision a cow. The cow's name is Georgette.
What's the cow's name?

It's a Jersey cow.
What kind of a cow?

The cow is on the Empire State Building.
Where is the cow?

It's singing a couple of Christmas carols.
What is it singing?

Under its chin is a ham.
What's under its chin?

It's a Virginia ham.
What kind of ham?

The cow is wearing yellow underwear.
What's the cow wearing?

In its hoof is a pencil.
What's in its hoof?

And the cow is making a connect-the-dots drawing.
What kind of a drawing?

Of Marilyn Monroe.
Of whom?

Walking down a road.
Down a what?

Going to Mass.
Going where?

This visualization could be reinforced with a quick oral review. Ask the following questions, and have students repeat the word and the state the word represents.

What is the cow's name?

What kind of a cow is it?

Where is the cow?

Singing a couple of _____.

Under its chin is a _____.

What kind of a ham?

The cow is wearing _____.

In its hoof is a _____.

It is making what kind of a drawing?

Of?

Walking down a _____.

Going to _____.

An additional reinforcement would be to have students sketch a picture (on paper or by moving their hands in the air) and identify the parts of the picture using the names of the states.

"SAVER" is a simple acronym to remember when using imagery. "S" refers to *seeing* the image in the mind's eye. "A" refers to *associating* the Image to some *action*. "V" refers to *vivid*. The more colorful and clearly defined the image, the easier recall will be. "E" refers to *exaggerate*. The more extraordinary the better. "R" refers to *reviewing* the image periodically. Reviewing assists long-term retention.

Visualization should be encouraged regularly. It is a simple technique to improve performance in reading comprehension, vocabulary development, and other areas. Most important, because imaging increases comprehension and recall—two of the most tested skills in schooling—it gives students considerable confidence and faith in themselves.

Stories

Take every opportunity to simplify the written word so that information can be created in a picture or experience. One way to do this is to convey information in story form. When we use this approach to communication, we help create meaning and improve retention for the listener. Stories are retained longer than facts because they create visual images. Images touch emotions because they arouse sensations, which are remembered longer than facts.

When the history teacher was asked the secret for making the subject so interesting and students so enthused, the response was, "I can tell you in two words: Tell stories." An old storyteller's tale makes the point.

TRUTH walked around naked, and everyone shunned him.

STORY walked around in colored clothes, and everyone liked him.

TRUTH inquired of STORY, "What is it that you do that people like you?"

STORY lent TRUTH some colorful garb and interesting clothing.

Everyone began liking TRUTH.

Metacognition

Metacognition is awareness of one's own thinking. Arthur Costa, co-founder of the Institute for Intelligent Behavior in El Dorado Hills, California, Professor Emeritus at California State University, Sacramento, and former president of the Association for Supervision and Curriculum Development (ASCD), speaks and writes on the importance of this area.

Metacognition is essential for developing critical thinking skills. The objective of metacognition is to have the *learner* become aware of his own cognitive processes and to become involved in understanding what he is thinking as he proceeds. The student is reflecting to see whether or not what he is doing is working.

Reflect on whether or not you hear yourself talking to yourself while solving this problem: *How much is half of two plus two?*

When we hear ourselves thinking, we are metacogitating. But do not assume that every student does it. For example, a student works on and solves a problem, and the teacher says, "Tell us how you solved that problem." And the student says, "I don't know; I just did it." This shows a lack of metacognitive awareness.

Students often attempt to solve a problem or analyze a situation without thinking. The answer may be so obvious that they just say it. There are many situations that can be dealt with successfully in this way. However, a problem arises when this approach does not work because the task has become too complex. For students who are habituated to thinking at the perceptual level, and who have not developed cognitive tools, such problems appear to be "too much" for them to deal with, and they just give up. *The inability to take charge of one's own cognitive processes is a very large part of the at-risk/dropout problem—as well as of discipline problems.*

Although mastering subject matter is important, strategies to increase thinking power are equally important. Schooling today too often emphasizes "correct" answers and single solutions. But in so many situations, it is not how many answers one knows, but rather how one proceeds when one does not know, as when confronted with problems, dilemmas, enigmas, and situations to be addressed, the answers to which are not immediately known or readily available. This is becoming truer every day in the rapidly-changing information age.

When faced with a task, most of us just start doing what seems to be the proper thing, giving thought to what we do *only if it becomes necessary*. For example, when driving an automobile, we stop at a red light "automatically" because we have habituated the process. If we encounter a flashing red light, a situation that is not quite so common, we then start thinking. In school, the difference between those who succeed in doing the more complex tasks of cognition and those who do not is that successful students have learned to be conscious of what they are doing. They do not act impulsively or intuitively when it is inappropriate to do so.

As soon as a routine has been developed, the amount of thinking is reduced. This is the time to introduce a more difficult or complex task. Conscious thinking is forced back into play. This oscillation between a routine way of dealing with a task and the development of different approaches to deal with more complex tasks increases thinking power.

A good way to build awareness and improve thinking skills is to *have students talk about what is going on inside their heads when they are approaching a task,* instead of focusing on their getting the right answer. Practice with the intent of keeping the thinking process going—to sustain "openture" rather than coming to closure. Ask questions such as, "What was going on inside your head to come up with that answer?" "What was your strategy?" "How else could you have done that?" Talking about thinking begets more thinking. Teachers can model their own metacognition process to help students become more aware.

Still another approach is to ask questions such as, "Give me three reasons why this is the wrong choice." In answering such a question, students learn to make comparisons—one of the essential cognitive functions. In the process, students not only learn to develop criteria for making comparisons, they *become aware* that they are doing so.

Notice that asking questions, which encourages thinking and reinforces understanding, is more effective than the common approach of giving praise. Specific feedback is most useful. For example, rather than saying to a student, "That is a good job," the teacher would say, "You seem to be getting the hang of it, don't you think? Would you like to show me another example?" The student learns that he is gaining competence.

Rather than focusing on judging and ranking, the teacher becomes a mediator who helps students draw useful lessons from their own experiences. This includes understanding *why* success was attained or *why* there was a failure and what to do about it.

The Senses

A discussion of instruction would not be complete without mentioning the senses—the way humans receive all information. A snatch of a sensory memory and suddenly you are taken back to forgotten places, other faces. When golden oldies play, scores of long-forgotten words drift back into consciousness.

The more senses evoked while learning, the more anchors the student will have to hold that learning in memory. For example, adding colors could enhance the memory of the visioning exercise of Georgette, the Jersey cow on the Empire State Building. To realize the powerful effect of color, reflect on the one item the cow was using and see if you remember what it was as well as the color. Additional enhancement would occur if olfactory senses were used. Unlike other senses, smell speeds directly to the brain. Can you smell a banana? Can you smell coffee brewing in the morning? Using the same example, try smelling the tar of the freshly paved road Marilyn was using on her way to Mass.

Hearing, particularly music, hooks memory. Think of the tune "Twinkle, Twinkle Little Star," and the alphabet pops into mind. (Did you find yourself remembering a melody used in learning the alphabet? "ABCDEFG, HIJKLMNOP....") Music stimulates learning and retention. Studies in brain research suggest that the cells of the brain resonate to music. Some of the most beneficial effects are achieved by using music at a tempo of 60 beats per minute during quiet or study time. This tempo correlates with a relaxed heartbeat, causing the heart rate to slow and the body to relax, leaving the mind alert. Listening to the music of Mozart or 60-beat-per-minute baroque music (the largo or andante sections) in the background creates a refreshing and stimulating learning environment. Playing this type of music during reflection time enhances both the activity and recall. However, the rationale should be explained because some students prefer to study in quiet.

When kinesthetics are added, memory is enhanced even more. Here is an example combining arithmetic and rope jumping.

> Smart rope, smart rope, what's the trick
> to help me learn arithmetic?
> Denominator down—touch the ground
> Numerator top—give a hop.

The feet may trip, but weeks later the memory still does not.

It is worth noting that an attractive learning environment can heighten the senses. Secondary teachers can use the talents of their students to create as stimulating environments as are found in elementary classrooms.

Additional Suggestions for Aiding Recall and Memory

We tend to remember first impressions, that which is *repeated*, what strikes us as *outstanding*, what is *personal*, that which is *associated* with something we already know, and what was most *recent*. The acronym "PROPAR" assists in keeping the points in mind.

Primacy refers to the primary or first interaction. We remember our first impressions of people and experiences. This is the reason why the beginning of each classroom period is so important.

Repetition enhances recall. Anything that is repeated has a better chance of going to and remaining in long-term memory. Repetition during the lesson, and again in later lessons, aids recall. Distributive practice is more effective than elongated practice: practicing three times of short duration versus one time of a longer duration. Memory is especially enhanced when the repetition is done by the students—rather than only by the teacher—and when accompanied with some body movement.

We tend to remember anything that is *outstanding*, novel, different, or that catches our attention. We recall lasting impressions because they were out of the ordinary—be it a field trip, a special event, or a special manner in which the teacher is dressed or presents a lesson.

Similarly, we remember those things that are *personal* because they touch our emotions. We still remember a comment some teacher made because it encouraged us—or was disheartening.

Memory is enhanced when the brain *associates* something new with something already known or experienced. The introduction of a new skill or concept is a natural time to associate what will be learned with what students already know. Mnemonics, or memory associations, is an effective strategy to use. For instance, when teaching the planets in the order of moving out from the sun, use the sentence, "My Very Educated Mother Just Served Us Nine Pizzas." It helps remember Mercury, Venus, Earth, Mars, Jupiter, Saturn, Uranus, Neptune, and Pluto.

Recency refers to those things that were most recent (last). Recency is the reason why reflection time aids recall. In fact, often the best learning occurs during reflection time and is especially important for at-risk students. Reflection is best when it is both individual and shared. "Think, pair, share" is a useful strategy for reflection. For example, using this strategy, students first reflect individually by thinking of three things learned during the lesson. They then choose one of the three to describe to a learning partner (pair). Sharing takes place with the other in the pair, then in small groups or with the entire class.

Since recall is used so much for measuring success of schooling, here are a few additional points regarding the subject. Gestures serve to help people retrieve elusive words from their memory. (Begley, November 1998) People who are searching their "lexical memory" for a word often gesture in some way. The next time you are "fishing" for a particular word, notice how your hands or facial muscles become activated. Encourage gesturing when students have a memory blank. Another point has to do with eye movements. In a classroom when students are doing work or taking a test, the usual instructions are to look down at their own paper. Yet, recall is achieved best when it is accessed in the same way that it was stored. When visual learners take a test and look down, they may not be accessing information in the most efficient manner. After a test, when students are looking up, the visual memory comes flooding back. To improve examination performance, allow students to look up to access information in their memory.

Laser Learning

Laser learning refers to thinking and talking in short segments to increase retention.

Since the brain recalls in images and experiences, the learner first transforms key points into a few words to form a mental image. This is laser thinking. In order to get information to stick, the learner then "laser" talks by relating his image to another student—*in no more than thirty or forty-five seconds.* The short thinking and talking times generate just the right amount of stress to make learning most effective. This is a brain-chemical experience, not a social one. The process has nothing to do with the other person's listening or giving the learner feedback. It has to do with forcing the learner to think and say what he or she thinks he or she has just learned. For optimum benefit, this has to be done intermittently in short periods of time. It is only in the *saying* that the learner figures out what he gets or doesn't get. The strategy engenders the opportunity to self-correct.

The process needs to be explained to students. They need to understand that they will feel a little uncomfortable when they relate their learning to another person. They need to be told that when they think just miniscule things and put them into mental images, memory is increased because episodic pathways to memory are formed. (Sprenger). Students need to understand that they have to say it and hear themselves. It is in the saying that the brain's neurotransmitters get released. When the learner *states* what he has "learned," he realizes he has or does not "have it." You can see how this works by reviewing *The Raise Responsibility System*. Read the summary at the end of Chapter 3, then explain the program in one minute. You will see that only when the learner *says it* that he determines what needs to be reviewed more. Saying out loud what one has just learned is an excellent reflective strategy to improve learning. Again, the teacher's explanation of this process is necessary and assists students in becoming comfortable with the process.

Seminal Shifts

Three seminal shifts are important regarding instruction: (1) from changing others to self-change, (2) from a focus on teaching to one of learning, and (3) from calling on individual students to 100 percent student participation.

1. Shifting from a focus on changing students to a focus on self-change

Most people behave on the assumption that if something is not as they would like it to be, the change that is necessary is incumbent upon others. This specifically relates to instruction. If students are not performing as you would like, rather than expecting them to change, the question should be asked, "How can I, as the teacher, influence them to do what I would like them to do?"

2. Shifting from an instructional focus to a learning focus

Traditional teaching approaches have centered on getting and keeping student attention for most of the class time. According to Eric Jensen, the notion of continuously keeping the learner's attention is biologically and psychologically outdated. This is a model for control, rather than for learning. For optimal learning, the teacher need only have the attention of the student for a small amount of total time. Quality learning may begin by attracting the learner's attention with novelty, emotions, relevance, or curiosity. Then, once learners have had time to learn purposeful material in the way they do it best, it's time for integration, meaning, and memory. (Jensen, 1996, p. 37)

Cognitive research strongly affirms that we learn best when we are actively involved in interesting and challenging situations and when we talk about learning. (Sousa, 1998) Talking activates the brain's frontal lobe, which is necessary for understanding, meaning, and memory. Therefore, in most lessons, students should be actively engaged in activities other than sitting quietly and passively for long stretches of time. The brain simply learns best when it "does," rather than when it "absorbs." The old adage applies: *Students who do the talking and doing do the learning.* This is a way to close the learning gap, *the difference between what was taught and what was learned,* e.g., what was taught on Monday and what students remember on Tuesday. *Breaking Ranks* (with the status quo), the 1996 report of the National Association of Secondary School Principals, echoes this approach that students should take an active role in their learning rather than as passive recipients of information passed on by textbooks and lectures.

Two phrases always to keep in mind are *avoid boredom* and *avoid tedium.* Providing a variety of learning methods is the most effective approach to move from focusing on teaching to focusing on learning—to move from what is taught to what is caught. The more ways we teach, the more students we reach.

Consider the following statistics on learning. We retain 10% of what we read, 20% of what we hear, 30% of what we see, 50% of what we see and hear, 70% of what we say, and 90% of what we say and do. (Pike) An old Chinese proverb states the idea succinctly:

I hear and I forget. I see and I remember. I do and I understand.

Telling is not teaching, and listening is not learning. The best way to learn is to become a teacher—in part because staying active makes learning attractive. Learning occurs when the learner does work. This is one basis for cross-age tutoring. If you have large classes, teaching students to teach others should be considered, not only to reduce the teaching-learning ratio but also to increase personalization. Cooperative learning and think-pair-share activities can play an important role here. Pairing and sharing is especially effective because working with one other person poses little threat, prevents anonymity, and obtains high participation.

3. Shifting from calling on individual students (at the expense of not calling on others) to 100 percent student participation

Rather than ask the class a question and then have students raise their hands for attention (sometimes frantically at the primary levels and at the expense of those not called upon), *pose* a question, paying particular attention to choosing key words as discussed earlier in this chapter in the section *Choosing Keywords to Frame Questions and Statements*. Learning partners or groups then grapple with a response. Students quickly learn that the teacher is interested in everyone's involvement. Students who are correct still gain the internal satisfaction that comes from "being right."

A concluding comment: Use the maxim *Don't do things for students that they can do themselves*. Learning is an active, not a passive, process. A simple thought to keep in mind is, "Asking is the key to the target." Asking questions starts the thinking process. Smart questions activate the brain. A good question can be the most effective hook for engagement. Asking effective questions is so important that much of this book relies on honing this skill.

KEY POINTS

◆ When planning lessons, the acronym "LIMES" assists in keeping some key ideas in mind. The "L" refers to left-right brain hemisphericity to incorporate sequential as well as random organizing. The "I" refers to employing different types of intelligences. The "M" refers to varying activities by tapping into visual, aural, and kinesthetic modalities. The "E" refers to emotions that can either interfere or enhance learning. The "S" indicates that people have different learning styles and that a variety of activities needs to be incorporated in lessons.

◆ In addition to planning activities to hook students to the lesson, time should also be planned at the end of the lesson for reflection.

◆ Using levels of intellect ensures that students learn thinking and evaluating skills in addition to simply gaining information.

◆ Asking "what" questions, using wait time, calling on students after a question, not repeating responses, and posing questions all enhance participation and learning.

◆ Using group questioning strategies allows the teacher to have more control over the direction of a lesson.

◆ Choosing key words to frame questions enhances thinking.

◆ Imaging and visualization techniques promote retention.

◆ Stories clothe facts, thereby aiding retention.

◆ Metacognition—being aware of one's own thinking process— improves thinking skills.

◆ Using music, bright colors, and other approaches that appeal to the senses enhances learning.

◆ Laser learning—having students frequently think and share in short segments—increases retention and lets students discover what needs to be reviewed.

CLASSROOM MANAGEMENT

*Effective classroom management relies on
the use of procedures—not rules.*

Classroom management is about strategies to make instruction and learning efficient. *Good classroom management reduces behavior problems.*

ESTABLISHING PROCEDURES

Just as teachers, administrators, and other staff members know what to do when entering school, so should students know what to do when they enter a classroom. (Wong)

Students need to be inducted into the organization of the classroom. The way to do this is to teach procedures. For example, before having a classroom meeting, the first procedure is to quickly and quietly arrange the chairs in a circle. No meeting starts until this procedure is implemented successfully. Procedures should be taught before content. The aphorism *process precedes product* should be noted.

Procedure gives structure, which is especially important for at-risk students. The label "at-risk" has nothing to do with intelligence. It simply means these students are in danger of failing or dropping out of school. Often, the lives of at-risk students are chaotic, and the only part of their lives that is stable is school. The reason they are in danger is simply because they don't do their work. A prime reason why they don't do their work is that they lack structure, and procedures can establish that needed stability.

Too often, we assume that children know what we know and what we want them to do. This is especially true with procedures. Assume nothing—other than the fact that students may not be sure what is wanted.

TEACHING ROUTINES

Structure activities or arrange the environment to reduce or eliminate conflict.

In the elementary grades, this pertains to both indoor and outdoor activities. Establishing a "getting drinks" routine after vigorous playground activities is an example of an outdoor procedure. Children whose last names are in the first half of the alphabet will use the fountain by the restrooms. Those in the last half will walk to another designated drinking fountain. The person behind the drinker will slowly count to ten and then tap the drinker softly on the shoulder. Before initiating the procedure, have students experience it. Line up everyone for a dry run.

Reinforce the routine for lining up before entering the room at the start of the day. One teacher reminds her students that when they enter to put their backpacks away, sharpen pencils, place home assignments and lunch money on the desk, and begin their proofreading. Another does not allow students to bend her ear as they enter the classroom at the beginning of the school day, or after recess, or after lunch. Rather, she carefully watches how students enter and watches to see them start immediately on the assignment on the board or overhead projector. Then, once all are on task, she gives her attention to those who need it.

Professional judgment is required at all times to bring about optimal behavior. In the morning, it may be preferable to have students enter the room and start working immediately. After lunch or a morning break, allowing the students time to settle down may be more practical.

It is good to remember that with any new activity, such as a special game or a chance to touch a visiting pet, conflicts will occur—unless some management procedures have been established first.

ATTENTION MANAGEMENT

Too much time is often wasted regaining students' attention during or when ending an activity. Even the procedure of raising hands needs to be taught and practiced because it has three parts: prompt, focus, and signal. The *prompt* is when the teacher's hand is raised. Students who see the raised hand of the teacher *focus* on the teacher by raising their hands and stopping their activity. The *signal* means these students, whose attention is back with the teacher, signal other students still involved in the activity to give their attention to the teacher. Note that the responsibility for bringing back the attention of the entire class belongs to the students, not the teacher.

Telling students the routine will not suffice. Students need to practice seeing the teacher's hand raised, focusing by raising their hands, and then signaling others whose hands are not raised. The routine should be practiced until the teacher is satisfied with obtaining the attention of the entire class within a very few moments. Periodically, the routine may need to be practiced again.

Fun can also be incorporated for elementary grades, such as in getting students' attention by saying "FREEZE," where students instantaneously hold their positions whatever they may be doing at the moment. The position is released with "UNFREEZE." Another technique is to say, "Clap once if you can hear my voice." "Clap twice if you can hear my voice." The second round of putting hands together will gain everyone's attention.

Students in any grade level or class can always be asked for their suggestions. The key here is to establish at least one attention management routine so the attention of all students can be gained within a matter of moments.

SPONGE ACTIVITIES

When students enter the classroom, they should immediately become engaged in a learning experience. They may write in a journal, analyze a cartoon projected by an overhead projector, complete some assignment on the board, identify significant learning from yesterday's lesson, or some other useful activity that soaks up time while the teacher takes attendance or engages in some other routine. Nonactivity at the beginning of a period is a waste of time because the beginning of the period is an important learning time. (Sousa, 1995, p. 58)

REDUCING TARDIES

If tardiness is a problem in middle or high school, use something positive.

Give students an occasional one-question quiz at the start of the period. The question can cover home assignments, recently presented information, or anything that the teacher wants to reinforce. The quiz is for extra credit only; it can help a grade, but not hurt one. When the tardy bell rings, the responses are collected, or, if the school does not use bells, collect the quizzes two minutes into the period.

Starting class with an interesting or novel activity can also reduce tardies. All students, even high school seniors, enjoy listening to good stories. Start reading the story right at the official starting time of the class. Do not expect students to automatically appear on time the next day. However, you will have more success with many chronic latecomers if you do not bring attention to their late entering. Do not fret that your lack of attention to these students will encourage others to enter late. After a few days, most of your latecomers will arrive on time and in an orderly manner. If students are boisterous when entering the class, reading an interesting story will have more success in their entering in a quiet manner than any means of coercion. Stop and wait until they settle down; then continue. After a few days, their manners will change.

If a student continues to come late, personalize your relationship. Ask the student if coming to class late is really what the student *wants*. Then ask what the student is *doing* that prevents him from arriving on time. Contrasting what the student *wants* with what the student is *doing* leads to self-evaluation and the opening to develop a *plan*. The plan must originate with the student, although the teacher can certainly make suggestions. If the student continues to come late, have the student develop specific *procedures* to implement the plan. The key to success with this type of student is for the *student* to develop the plan, for the *student* to itemize specific procedures, and for the *student* to visualize specific activities—even to the point where the student visualizes walking into the class before the class starts.

A final point with chronic latecomers: Many of these students do not enjoy being late. They mentally punish themselves when they are late. Adding external punishment does little to help them solve their time-management problem. A contract with a consequence may alter behavior temporarily but will not be nearly so effective as personalizing your relationship with the student.

TAKING ATTENDANCE

Taking attendance should not subtract from learning time. While students are engaged in the sponge learning activity, take roll. In middle and high schools, have a student assist. In the class where the master absence list is developed, the helper takes out the cards (if the system uses them) that need to be sent to the office. During other periods, the helper checks the absence list and assists by completing any necessary forms while the teacher enters appropriate marks in the rollbook. Attendance is taken in less than one minute.

PASSING AND COLLECTING MATERIALS

Establishing routines for supplies and materials should be one of the first management decisions.

Use student assistants. For example, if the sponge activity is to write in journals, have two students volunteer to pass out the journals before the class starts. These students will arrive at class early because they have that responsibility. Students know where other students sit and can place the journals on the appropriate desks before most of the students enter.

When books or supplies are distributed and returned, establish a traffic pattern for collectors and distributors to ensure a smooth operation. For example, establishing a clockwise walking pattern in a crowded classroom prevents unnecessary physical contact.

HOME ASSIGNMENTS FOR ABSENTEES

At middle and high schools, when a student returns from an absence, one of the first orders of the day is to obtain any assignments that were missed. A simple procedure is to label a standard composition book for each period. When an assignment is given to the class, a student records it in the "assignment book." Then, when a student returns after an absence, the returning student obtains the missed assignment from that book. If any additional explanation is necessary, it can be given at an appropriate time during the period.

If students collaborate by using learning buddies, then the buddy can be responsible for informing the absent student. The assignment can be shared upon the absentee's return or, even better, by the buddy who informs the absentee by telephone or e-mail.

LENDING PENCILS

Beyond primary grades, where materials should be readily available, lending pencils is a constant activity. Getting pencils back can be challenging.

Teach the term "collateral." When borrowing a pencil, the student leaves a personal item, such as a quarter or a house key. Students do not forget to retrieve personal items of value. Certain students who are constantly borrowing from others are met with the response, "What's your collateral?"

SHARPENING PENCILS

Sharpening a pencil while the teacher is talking can be avoided with a simple procedure. When a student wants to sharpen a pencil, the student holds the pencil up as a communication signal. At a convenient time, nod—granting permission to go to the pencil sharpener.

Some elementary teachers restrict pencil sharpening to the beginning of the school day and after lunch. At any other time, they trade for a pencil in one of the pencil boxes around the room. Boxes are marked "sharp" or "dull." Students put their dull pencils in a "dull" box in order to take a pencil from a "sharp" box.

USE OF SUPPLIES

Let students know that they need to make their supplies last. Unless students are taught and practice some procedures, the supplies will be depleted well before expected. Coloring pens are a case in point. Students need to practice listening for the cap to snap on the pen. Otherwise, pens will dry out sooner than expected.

TEACHER ASSISTANCE TO A GROUP

When students are working in groups, the teacher needs some indication of which teams need assistance.

When students are working collaboratively, the use of colored cups allows the teacher to prioritize attention according to student need. Each group has three cups (available at any party store). The cups are placed upside down, each inside the other. When the green cup is showing, no assistance is needed. When the yellow cup is showing, the group has a question. When the red cup is showing, the group needs help.

INDIVIDUAL TEACHER ASSISTANCE

The best way to learn is to teach. Make it a policy that a student who has a question asks two other students for assistance before requesting help from the teacher. The first question the teacher asks the student who needs help is, "Whom did you ask for assistance." Aside from reinforcing the procedure, this also helps the teacher know if others have the same or a similar question.

INSTRUCTIONAL FEEDBACK

During a lesson, feedback from students lets the teacher know how successfully the lesson is going.

A simple technique is to have students point their thumbs up if they understand and thumbs down if they don't. For elementary students, another strategy is to use small cards of different colors. For example, when the teacher says, "Show me if you agree or disagree," students who do not agree raise a red card and students who do agree raise a blue card. Active participation makes students accountable and is more effective than calling on one student at a time to answer a question.

Another technique is to follow up a student's answer by asking the class, "Who agrees?" "Who disagrees?" Then follow up with, "Why do you disagree?"

Students who are not successful during guided practice time can be placed in a small group(s) for tutorial work with the teacher, while the other students can continue with independent work or another assignment.

CRUMPLING PAPERS—A PET PEEVE

When a student crumples papers while others are concentrating, the sound has a tendency to break preoccupation. The crinkling may be even more upsetting when it occurs as the teacher is talking. Showing students how to fold hot dogs and hamburgers can halt these unwelcome sounds. A paper folded vertically (left to right) is a hot dog. A paper folded horizontally (top to bottom) is a hamburger. Students have a choice of folding patterns when they want to discard a paper. Folding papers into hot dogs and hamburgers takes up no desk space because something else can be placed on top of it.

DISMISSAL PROCEDURES FOR MIDDLE AND HIGH SCHOOLS

The *teacher*, rather than an automated sound system, should dismiss students.

Depending upon the grade level and class, the dismissal may be by rows, sections, or in unison. Before dismissal, however, the teacher has the responsibility to ensure that the students leave behind them a classroom ready for the next class. Incoming students have a right to enter a clean and well-organized classroom.

This can be accomplished by assigning students various projects to be done toward the end of the period. Even though a teacher may be absorbed with the lesson or with individual students and forget that dismissal time is approaching, the student helpers become reminders when they start clean-up procedures. Carrying around the wastepaper basket, collecting materials, stacking materials, and placing the desks in order are done before dismissal in a well-managed classroom.

Remember reflection time. A few minutes before dismissal is an excellent time for students to reflect. A simple activity is to choose one learning from the lesson and share it with a learning buddy.

KEY POINTS

◆ The key to effective classroom management is establishing procedures.

◆ Structure activities or arrange the environment to reduce or eliminate conflict.

◆ Establish some prompt to regain attention when you want to address the class.

◆ When students enter the classroom, they should immediately become engaged in a meaningful learning experience.

◆ Taking attendance should not subtract from learning time. Take roll while students are engaged in a learning activity.

◆ Establish routines for supplies and materials as one of the first management decisions.

◆ Teach the term "collateral" and use it when lending pencils.

◆ The teacher, rather than an automated sound system, should dismiss students.

HOME ASSIGNMENTS

Showing how the home assignment is in the
students' own best interests
is the most effective approach.

Home assignments are an extension of instruction. They are related to teaching and learning, not to discipline in the sense of classroom disruptions or social irresponsibility.

PURPOSE

Home assignments provide opportunities to practice and improve skills or gain further knowledge or understanding. Home assignments also teach lessons that cannot be measured, such as self-discipline, perseverance, and time management. Home assignments teach how to begin a task, complete it, and be responsible for the outcome.

CONSIDERATIONS

Especially at the elementary grades, home assignments need to be tempered with considerations for other demands on young people's time. Home assignments have modest influence on achievement in the early grades. When the amount and number of assignments become overwhelming, negative attitudes about school and learning result. Assignments should be short, interesting, and easy to complete *by the students*. Leave the more demanding work for the classroom.

More than 100 studies have shown that it is not until middle school that home assignments really begin to pay off. (Begley, March 1998, p. 51)

ASSIGNING

In order to make home assignments attractive, offer the choice of two assignments. Be sure students understand the purpose of the assignments. Periodically, have a short discussion of the benefits. Ask for input from students. Explain what you believe students will learn or accomplish from an assignment, and then ask for suggestions.

Home assignments should be focused. For example, rather than asking students to write about an open-ended theme from a novel that the class is reading, ask them to pick one character and explain why that character behaved in a particular way.

SCAFFOLDING

Assigning a chapter to read before it is discussed in class is almost useless. The practice works only if the teacher does some pre-teaching by providing a cognitive map—an organizing scheme or scaffold. A scaffold is a frame built before constructing something. Building a scaffold for students makes it easier for them to make sense of what is being read. Give them clues about the chapter. Then, when they are motivated enough to read, they will enjoy the satisfaction of discovery.

Another approach is to teach students to preview or "multipass" by passing through the chapter looking for organizers before reading it. This scanning includes headings, subheadings, bold print and italics, chapter summary, pictures and graphs, objectives, chapter questions, and vocabulary words that are listed.

REDUCING THE CORRECTION OF HOME ASSIGNMENTS

Since we learn best by teaching, have students become teachers. For example, before the teacher checks any essay, at least two other people should check it. When final papers are submitted, they will be of higher quality and more enjoyable to read. Also, when papers are submitted, refrain from correcting them. Instead, make a comment such as, "You have a spelling error in this paragraph." "Check for noun-verb agreement in this sentence." Using abbreviations will save time: "✓ SP" and "✓ n-v agr." This "grappling" by the student encourages self-evaluation and self-correction.

Save time with arithmetic by selecting only five problems to correct, rather than checking all answers. The problems may be the last five or any five problems. When students submit their papers, correct only these pre-selected problems. Looking at only these will give you enough indication of whether or not more time needs to be invested in a review lesson with selected students.

Review *Collaborative Evaluation,* the last topic in the section *Collaboration—Rather than Competition—for Quality Learning* in Chapter 4.

KEY POINTS

◆ Home assignments are an extension of instruction. They are related to teaching and learning, not to discipline as it applies to inappropriate behavior.

◆ Evaluate the importance and necessity of each home assignment.

◆ Hold a quick discussion of what will be gained by the assignment.

◆ Point out what key things to look for before giving a reading assignment.

CONCLUSION

Anyone can lead one to the classroom,
but only a teacher can lead one to learn.

Curriculum, instruction, classroom management, and discipline are four separate entities. Curriculum has to do with *what* is taught, instruction with *how* the curriculum is taught and learned, and classroom management with how instruction is made *efficient.* Discipline has to do with *student* behavior. Whereas curriculum, instruction, and classroom management are the teacher's responsibility, *discipline is the student's responsibility.*

When a student disrupts the lesson, the teacher must determine from which category the problem emanates. Is the *curriculum* lacking in interest, relevancy, enjoyment, or usefulness? Is the *instruction* interactive and engaging to students? Is *classroom management* efficient? Or, is the student lacking *self-discipline?* Answers to these questions help point to the most effective resolution of the problem.

6

PARENTING

TIPS FOR PARENTS

An acorn is capable of becoming a mighty oak,
but it will never become a giant redwood—
no matter how much you push it.
Discover your child's nature and then nurture that nature.
–Jim Cathcart

Being a parent can be as frustrating and stressful as it is rewarding and joyful. Parenting is often fraught with emotional baggage and habits left over from our own childhoods. Yet, it is possible to break free of such habits and offer our children guidance without guilt or blame. When we plant flowers and they do not grow as we would like, we don't blame them, we look for reasons why the flowers are not doing well. Yet, when we have problems with our children, we too often blame them—along with criticizing and nagging them. But if we know how to influence them, they will mature, which is what we want. This does not mean we can change their nature, but we can certainly nourish them to become responsible and contributing members of society. The challenge for many parents today is one of being neither overly strict nor overly permissive. This chapter focuses on how to accomplish both.

PRACTICE POSITIVITY

One of the most effective ways to influence and to reduce stress for both parent and child is to communicate using positive messages. Just think for a moment of your reaction when someone made a positive statement about you. On the other hand, think about your emotions when someone said something that you interpreted as criticism or blame. People do better when they feel better, not worse. Yet, we often ignore this common-sense approach and send negative messages because we allow our impulses to direct what we do.

The first step to reducing stress is simply to become aware of the number of times you state something negatively that could be stated positively. For example, suppose you have an adolescent who would like to visit her friend on a school night. You are concerned that home assignments be completed first. When your child asks, "Can I go to Hillary's house?" your response may likely be, "Not until you finish your home assignments." If you practice the mental habit of positivity, your response would be something like, "Sure, you can go—as soon as your assignments are finished" or simply, "When you are satisfied with your assignments." Two very important principles are at work here. In the latter two statements, the responsibility is clearly on the young person, where it belongs, and, in addition, you have conveyed a message of trust. Notice that the responses, whether stated negatively or positively, are basically the same. That is, the home assignments will be completed before the youngster visits the friend. However, how the message is received is dramatically different.

Here is another example where positivity is used and where the responsibility is placed on the youngster. It is natural for a parent to admonish a young child before the child leaves for school. The parent may say, "Don't forget your lunch," or "Don't forget to take your key." A more effective approach to accomplish the same objective is to say, "Check your list." This approach not only eliminates nagging, but it puts the responsibility on the youngster, who has made the list perhaps with your assistance. Lists can be made for school-related assignments and materials, appropriate dress pertaining to inclement weather, or other situations that the child can check before leaving.

Stating ideas in positive terms not only reduces stress, it also builds trust, avoids conflicts in interactions, and increases the amount of satisfaction and contentment. Consider the woman who reduced her aggravation every time her husband or two children dropped their dirty clothes on the floor instead of putting them in the hamper. The situation became unfair to the others as well because the sight of the dropped clothes so bothered her that she indiscriminately blew up at all members of the family. She then asked herself, "How could I turn this into a positive situation for me as well as for them?" She told her family that whenever any clothes were found on the floor, she would pick them up, as she would do anyway, but the culprit owed her a five-minute backrub, collectable whenever she wanted it and done lovingly. The result not only freed the air of a lot of negativity, but she received a number of loving backrubs. Also, fewer clothes began appearing on the floor.

John Goddard, perhaps the world's most famous lecturer on travel adventures, relates how his father handled situations. When John was eight years old, he told his father he wanted to be a fireman. His father did not tell him that he could fall off the fire truck as it turned around a corner or how dangerous fire fighting is. When John was ten, he told his father that he wanted to be a policeman. His father did not tell him that police work is a dangerous profession, that he might get hurt, and that it required rigorous training. Instead, his father told him that he would look fine in a blue uniform with copper buttons. His parents never fed him any negatives. The lesson Goddard makes is that when parents look at and talk to children, they should *empower them, rather than instill fears.*

Another way to communicate in a positive manner is to comment on the youngster's action, rather than on the youngster himself. Separating the deed from the doer is one of the most important attributes of *The Raise Responsibility System.* The adult does not identify the young person's action; instead, the youngster himself identifies a level of social development. Doing so automatically separates the act from the actor and causes the young person to reflect and accept responsibility. No embarrassment is involved and no dignity is lost. A major advantage of the approach is total acceptance from the parent, rather than conditional acceptance. The message communicated is that the child is always accepted, but collaboration is necessary so everyone can be satisfied with the child's actions.

This concept of separating the person from an action, that is, separating love from behavior, applies well to giving a money allowance. A prime purpose for giving an allowance is to engage youngsters in making decisions regarding saving, spending, and charity. This is totally different from family obligations. If a parent is not satisfied with behavior or how chores are done, these should be dealt with separately, rather than by turning the allowance into a reward that is contingent on pleasing the parent.

Focusing on stating thoughts and desires in positive terms is challenging, but it is also fun. When people become aware of how often they state something negatively, they become amazed at the frequency. Just a little practice can turn what would have been a negative statement into a more positive one.

Chapter 1, *Reducing Stress,* offers additional suggestions on this topic.

OFFER CHOICES

Choices are a critical component of fostering responsibility and influencing behavior. The reason is that choice brings ownership; it fosters a sense of independence and also empowers. Offering options engages a youngster in cooperation and is much more effective than giving commands.

The choices can be limited, but the sooner a young person starts to make choices, to exercise decision making, the more responsible the youngster becomes. Of course, the choices must be ones that satisfy both parties. Suppose a youngster is asked to suggest a chore he will do. If the chore the youngster offers is not satisfactory, then the parent asks, "What else?" The same two words "What else?" "What else?" are repeated until both parties agree. Offering options, rather than imposing the chores, gives the ownership to the youngster. Later, if the youngster does not fulfill the chosen chore, rather than imposing a consequence, the consequence is *elicited* from the youngster. The two friendly words "What else?" are again used until there is agreement. Another approach regarding chores is for the parent to *add* choices. For example, if a youngster has two chores to perform and is not doing them, *add* three more so that five choices are available; the youngster then chooses two from the five. Empowering by *adding to* is a positive approach and is much more effective than threatening to remove a privilege for noncompliance, which is a negative approach.

I remember refusing to eat what my mother had given me for dinner as a youngster. This is a common way for a child to assert a desire for power. Forcing a child to eat is rather difficult and often results in the child's becoming more obstinate. My mother simply diffused the situation by asking, "Which are you going to eat first, your carrots or your peas?" Notice that in the process, the responsibility was placed on me, where it belonged.

A perennial challenge for parents has to do with the desire to be obeyed, in large part because we think that what we want is better for the youngster than what the youngster wants. Often, especially with older adolescents, parents would be well served to make the choice of *being kind, rather than of being right.* A father was seeking advice because he felt that he could not communicate with his seventeen-year-old son. The counselor asked, "Whose fault is that? Do you expect your son to communicate with you if you don't successfully communicate with him?" The counselor suggested that when the father gets home to go up to his son and say, "Son, I realize that I have not communicated the best that I can. Is it possible that you could be doing the same?" The counselor then challenged the man, "But I don't think you would have the courage to do it." Two months later, the man called and said that he had been trying to reach out, trying to communicate with his son, but had not been successful. Then came a Sunday morning when the son was in the kitchen chewing on a sandwich, and the father was in the bedroom chewing on his nails. Suddenly, the father walked into the kitchen and said, "Son, I realize that I have not communicated with you the best that I can. Is it possible that you could be doing the same?" The boy suddenly felt about ten feet tall; he lifted his father up and hugged him.

As adults can make choices to change behaviors, so can young people. Change is a product of a decision, and decisions are possible only when there are choices. Therefore, offering choices paves the way to change behavior. Remember that young people exercise choice without parents' permission. A powerful choice is to do nothing. Adults call this defiance. The most effective way to avoid this is for the adult to offer choices.

We have been brought up to believe that power corrupts and that absolute power corrupts absolutely. However, *powerlessness* also corrupts. When people feel a lack of power, the mission becomes one of gaining it. Even children have a natural desire to feel empowered. Offering options is an easy way to accomplish this. As long as a young person has a choice, the youngster does not lose— and not losing is more important than winning.

Chapter 1 offers additional suggestions on this topic.

ENCOURAGE REFLECTION

The underlying theory behind every strategy in this book is geared toward reflection. Reflection is simply the act of thinking about our relationships, our desires, and our behaviors. The purpose of reflection is to stimulate *internal motivation*, which is far more effective in changing behavior than anything that is imposed externally. Even though we may temporarily control others, we don't change them. Besides, controlling others is counterproductive to the very thing we want, which is having them *want* to change. The question then becomes one of how to influence others to change themselves. The most effective and powerful approach is to have them reflect.

My wife and I visited our cousins, and we accompanied them when they picked up their daughters. One was at a babysitter's while the other was at a friend's home. Before the children were picked up, the parents described their daughters. The six-year-old was a parent's dream. The three-and-a-half-year-old was a real challenge. The parents told us that the younger daughter had a difficult time sharing. In preschool, she would express her unhappiness by screaming out if she did not get what she wanted. The parents described her as being very manipulative.

When both girls were in the car, my wife and I announced that we had a gift for them but that the store only had one Versatile set left. (Versatiles are manipulatives that come in a long narrow container. They are tiles of different shapes with numbers on the reverse sides. The object is to match the designs to make certain patterns. When the tiles are turned over, the numbers appear in a certain order.) I asked the girls if they would mind sharing. They assured me that there would be no problem.

At the house, after showing the girls how the Versatiles were used, it was agreed that the younger daughter would have the first turn. It was also agreed that each would have two turns before sharing. The younger sister, after her allotted two turns, did not want to give the set to her sister. I reminded her of the agreement wherein each player was to receive two turns. She ignored my comment.

I asked myself, "What can I *ask*, not tell, to have her reflect on the agreement in order to have her take responsibility?" As she was playing with the set for the third time, I asked, "Was this your second try at your second game?" The youngster looked at me and then gave the set to her sister. Asking a reflective question was more successful than using coercive persuasion in any of its various forms.

Later, I shared some questioning techniques with the parents, ones that would prompt the challenging child to reflect and think about her actions. When I spoke to the father months later, he told me that his younger daughter was still very clever at winning but that she had stopped her outbursts when she did not get her way.

Sometimes we need to be happy with only a single step in the right direction. A single is not a home run, but it gets the player to first base and going in the desired direction. In the situation with my cousin's daughter, the child was not pleased that she gave up the set when she still wanted to play with it. I was not pleased that she did not share after her allotted second try. However, progress was made. I was satisfied with a step in the right direction.

Criticizing, complaining, and nagging are coercive, external approaches and are often stress-inducing. In addition, such approaches engender resistance rather than responsibility. Forcing responsibility is difficult and perhaps even impossible because, although responsibility can be assigned, it only becomes effective when voluntarily taken. *Awareness* and *ownership* always precede taking responsibility. That is the reason why asking effective questions is so successful in changing behavior. Questions direct the other person's thinking. It is the questioning process that starts the thinking process, both for the questioner as well as for the person answering. This is the reason why smart communicators ask smart questions. They not only hear the answers, but also the person asked hears his own answers. The person answering gains clarity.

Furthermore, the answers that are most effective for people are their own. People don't argue with their own statements. There is immediate ownership, and ownership is a critical component to self-evaluation and change.

It is because effective questioning directs thinking to self-evaluation that it is one of the most valuable skills to be cultivated when working with anyone, especially young people.

USE EFFECTIVE QUESTIONS

Here is an invaluable set of four questions that leads to a change in behavior:

(1) "What do you *want?*"

   Asking this question stimulates thinking and leads to reflection.

(2) "Is what you are *choosing to do* helping you get what you want?"

This question leads to evaluation of one's behavior.

(3) "If what you are choosing to do is not getting you what you want, then what is your *plan?*"

This question encourages the making of a plan. The plan may be made solely by the young person or with assistance, but it must be the youngster's plan, not the adult's.

(4) "What are your *procedures* to implement your plan?" Or, for a younger child, "What steps will you take to make your plan work?"

This question leads to mental imaging and specific steps that will be taken to carry out the plan. These implementation ideas can come about with the assistance of the parent, but, as with the previous question, should be elicited from the young person before the adult makes a suggestion. *"What else?"* is a good follow-up question to encourage more specificity.

A question that has a positive focus is more effective than one that invites a negative response. For example, "What is the best thing that happened today?" elicits a more positive response than, "What happened today?"

As emphasized in Chapter 1 in the section *The Importance of Reflection and Self-Evaluation,* the quality of the answers depends on the quality of the questions. The parents spent $500 to send the youngster to summer camp. Upon return, the parents ask, "How was camp?" The youngster responds, "O.K." That is all the parents receive for their camp expenditure. However, the youngster's response would have been completely different had the parents asked a more specific question: "What was the most enjoyable experience you had at camp?" This question leads the youngster to reflect and relive an enjoyable experience.

Persistence may be necessary, especially with adolescents. Be persistent and patient, as was done with a fifteen-year-old girl who had low self-esteem and a bad attitude. The parent knew about asking effective questions, so instead of the normal evening greeting, "How was your day?" the parent asked, "What was the best thing that happened to you today." The youngster replied, "Nothing. Get off my back!" The parent did not give up. The same question was asked several times over a period of weeks, getting the same negative response. Weeks later, the daughter came in for breakfast and said, "I already know what is the best thing that will happen to me today." The parent was startled by this uncharacteristic expression but asked, "What is it?" The teenager replied with a big smile, "I woke up thinking about the best thing that will happen to me today."

Following are some questions particularly effective with young people:

- What have you done to get what you want?
- What can you do to improve the situation?
- What are you doing that is working?
- How would you describe the way you want it to turn out?
- What were you able to do today better than in the past?
- To what do you attribute your doing better today?
- What did you learn about doing it that you can apply to other areas?
- What was special for you about what you did?
- What was most pleasing for you today?
- What would you like to look forward to for tomorrow?
- What do you most appreciate?
- What plans do you have for the future?
- What would motivate you to use your plan?
- What do you see as your next step?
- How can I help you?
- On a scale of 1 to 10, how have things been in the past 3 days? What would it take to make a 10?

I was seated on an airplane next to an active young boy whose mother was having a challenging time with him. During the course of the flight, the young boy took the phone out of its security case from the back of the seat in front of him and started to play with it. I leaned over to him and asked, "What would happen if you broke the phone?" Without a moment's hesitation, the youngster replaced the phone. The question that I asked led to quick reflection. Rather than aiming at obedience by telling the youngster what to do, I aimed at responsibility. Telling the boy what to do may have led to the same result, but I doubt if it would have been nearly so effective or have led to such a rapid response.

Asking effective questions is a skill and requires practice. Thinking about a skill is not practicing the skill. Thinking is necessary for focus, but only the actual asking of questions in real situations is practicing the skill. We learn to do something by doing it—not by *thinking* it or *trying* to do it. Trying to stand is not standing. You either stand or you don't. Asking a person to try to take a $5.00 bill from your hand will result in this awareness. If the person takes the bill, the person did not *try*; the person actually did it. If the person just *tried* to take the money, it would still be in your hand.

It is almost impossible to raise a child without criticizing. One way to reduce criticism is to turn it into questions. Asking, "If you were to do that over again, what would you do differently?" will get the message across without bringing aggravation to the parent and negative feelings to the child.

As parents, we can also reflect by the questions we ask ourselves, such as, "Am I proud of the way I interacted with my child?" "Would I be offended if someone interacted with me as I interacted with my child?" "What is my plan for next time?"

LISTEN TO LEARN

If I were limited to one recommendation that would improve relationships between parent and child, especially with teenagers, it would be *listen to learn.* Listening and valuing young people's feelings and ideas is what promotes the ability of parents to effectively communicate with them.

Listen to learn means not inserting one's opinion and not judging what the youngster says *while the youngster is speaking.* Parents have a natural tendency to approve or disapprove of young people's statements. Parents' first reaction is to evaluate from their own point of view and then approve or disapprove of what the youngster says. This is listening autobiographically. The tendency to make evaluations is common in almost all conversations, but it is much more intense when feelings are involved. An easy strategy for replacing this tendency of listening autobiographically is to cultivate the habit of listening to learn.

Listening in anticipation of what a child will say is also a habit to be broken. Listening in anticipation encourages interruptions. A child wants to be acknowledged and does not wish to feel that you know what he is about to say. A parent who listens well acknowledges the youngster's feelings and opinions. In addition, listening well can be a model for adolescents, who often do not listen well.

"Zip the lip" is extremely difficult for a parent, but it is the surest way to improve communication and understanding. *No great insight ever enters the mind through an open mouth.* It is important to let young people know that a parent is willing to listen, even though it may not result in agreement. A simple, "Talk to me about it" is an effective start toward dialogue. Just use the most effective sales principle: *Inquiry precedes advocacy.*

LIMIT LECTURING AND TELLING

Parents fear that children will not make responsible decisions, so lecturing begins. This implies that the parents do not have faith in their children's decision-making abilities. After awhile, children lose faith in themselves, in their own inner knowing. If young people do not have faith in themselves, then the parents' faith in them decreases even more, and the lecturing begins again.

Even well-intentioned lectures convey the subtle, negative message that what the youngster has done is wrong or not good enough. This often results in defensiveness and resistance, especially with adolescents. If telling worked, young people would do exactly what they were told. Trying to persuade adolescents by using reason often has little effect; they know they are right. In addition, the youngster sees this as, "My parents are trying to control me again!" An adage when dealing with young people is not to say more than thirteen words at a time, and with a teenager, make it twelve.

Since young people are sensitive about being told what to do, yet parental help is perfectly appropriate, think of suggestions as questions: "What do you think about...?" "Have you thought of...?" "Would you consider...?"

A habit is most easily changed by replacing it with another. When there is a temptation to tell, redirect it by thinking of the question, "Will the results be better if I tell or ask?" Another approach is to follow Harry S Truman's approach: "I have found the best way to give advice to your children is to find out what they want, and then advise them to do it."

CHECK ASSUMPTIONS

Some of the decisions we make are based on inaccurate assumptions. We may know exactly what we are thinking and what we mean, but the child may have a completely different perspective.

In a Calvin and Hobbs comic strip, Calvin says to his mom, "I'm hungry. Can I have a snack?" His mom says, "Sure. Help yourself." In the next scene, Calvin is walking through the living room carrying a big cookie jar, one cookie in his hand and another cookie in his mouth. He hears his mom say, "You can have an apple or an orange from the fridge." Calvin stands there and thinks, "Even though we are both speaking English, we are not speaking the same language." Calvin's definition of a snack is a cookie. His mother's definition of a snack is an apple or orange.

A father is walking through the forest with his three-year-old daughter. As they are walking, he repeatedly tells her to stay on the path. The little girl is walking all around. She looks at this tree, that bush, meanders here and there. He continually says, "Stay on the path. I told you to stay on the path." Eventually, he gets so angry with her that he pulls her over, shakes her a bit, and shouts, "I told you to stay on the path!" The little girl looks up at him with tears in her eyes and says, "Daddy, what's a path?"

FOCUS ON THE IMPORTANT

Choose your battles. While clashes may be unavoidable, it is not necessary to get pulled into every skirmish. An effective strategy here is to ponder the answer to the question, "Will this matter a week from now?"

Youngsters explore and try out different roles. These can be irritating and bewildering. As painful as it may be to watch, it is one way that young people learn to function on their own. As a rule of thumb, *only make a fuss about those issues that are harmful to the youngster or others, or are irreversible.* Wearing baggy pants or an "outrageous" hat at thirteen may not be very serious; getting a large tatoo on your arm with controversial language is serious. Situations that involve safety or that are illegal or immoral are non-negotiable.

ASK FOR ASSISTANCE

As no one can place knowledge or wisdom into the head of another, so no one can make another person responsible. Although responsibility can be delegated, it does not become effective until taken. A much-overlooked opportunity is for young people to help parents. In former generations, the parents were the center of the household and children were expected to assist in the running of that household. Very often in today's family, the emphasis is on giving to children, rather than on the children doing the giving.

An effective way for parents to gain respect and assistance is to refrain from doing some favors for their youngsters and let their youngsters perform services for them. A simple way to do this is for the parent to express a need, giving the child an opportunity to help. Children (and adults) grow by giving. Some examples are, "I need quiet time," "I need you to help me put the groceries away," or "I need your help with dinner." Machiavelli made the point: *People are by nature as much bound by the benefits they confer as by those they receive.*

A request for assistance is easy to hear. This approach is proactive and is more effective than a reactive approach that criticizes, blames, or complains, such as, "You should have helped me with the groceries."

RECOGNIZE IMPLICIT MESSAGES

Parents deliver explicit messages unaware of sending implicit ones. "Explicit" refers to the actual words stated. "Implicit" refers to what is learned by inference. For example, tickets for a movie theater are more expensive for a thirteen-year-old than for a twelve-year-old. The parent wants to save money so the thirteen-year-old daughter is told to state her age as twelve. The explicit message is that saving money is desirable; however, the implicit message is that being dishonest is acceptable.

The teenager tells the parent, "I'm going out tonight; I may be late and I may drink at the party." The parent says, "You're grounded!" The explicit message to the offspring is very clear; yet, so is the implicit message: "I don't trust you."

Here is another instance of the parent's sending one message, but the result from the implicit message is counterproductive. The eighteen-year-old calls her parent and says she drank a little too much and she wants to be picked up. This is a very responsible thing to do. However, the parent becomes angry with the daughter. On the drive home, the parent relentlessly chastises her daughter, who concludes, "I'm not going to tell my parent next time."

If parents get angry and forbid young people to do certain things, they can put their heads in the sand believing their prohibition is going to be effective. However, in more cases than we would like, offspring will do what they want anyway; they just won't talk about it to their parents. In such situations, the parents *have lost the opportunity to influence their children*—to tell them how they see the situation, to share what they did when younger, and to share their parental feelings about the situation.

Parents always need to be aware of implicit messages. When parents become upset and yell at children, the implicit message taught is that when upset, yelling is acceptable. The same goes for hitting. The parents, usually without realizing it, are teaching the youngster to deal with upsetting situations by losing control and even striking out.

FOSTER RESPONSIBILITY

Fostering responsibility should start at a very young age. A young child sits in the highchair and drinks his milk. When he is finished, he throws the bottle away. He hears the "thump" sound and likes it. He enjoys flexing his muscles. When the mother picks up the bottle, the infant is getting a message that he, to a certain extent, can control his mother. The mother decides that she is not going to let her child behave this way. The mother does not threaten or punish; she simply makes sure her hand is ready when the baby finishes the milk. She then removes the bottle and cleans his face while talking to him. The mother begins to teach her son responsible behavior at a very young age.

Very young people cannot be left to their own devices. It is a parent's responsibility to protect the child. For example, if a child runs into the street, a parent can pick up the child and put her on the sidewalk. The parent can talk to the child about the dangers of cars but needs not make the child feel blameworthy for her innocent act. Rather than focusing on what the child did wrong, a wiser approach is to have the youngster develop a plan and procedure to prevent a reoccurrence.

As children grow older, parents often resort to rules. Especially with teenagers, this invites a problem because when rules and prohibitions are established, they are seen as restrictions. Teenagers, who are asserting their independence, view restrictions as controlling. Rebellion is not their focus; rather, their focus is on finding and asserting their identity. Instead of establishing restrictions, parents can help by communicating expectations, which are much more positive. Using self-evaluative questions and entering into dialogue with teenagers is much more effective than imposing restrictions.

The media plays a significant role in the lives of youth. Young people have rights, know them, and articulate them in their parents' faces. However, rights need not be at the expense of responsibility. Treating young people with respect and dignity fosters responsibility. This is especially important during the adolescent years when parents (and youth) are under such stress. By these years, much of what parents want can only be negotiated. Parents can no longer physically control youngsters, just as they can no longer control their children's exposure to outside influences or what their children do when not in their presence.

When responsibility has been fostered, parents are always "with" young people. "What is the right thing to do?" "Do I really want this?" "Am I being manipulated?" "What would my parents think?" are constantly thoughts on their children's minds. When parents have been negotiating with children, and the children understand the difference between internal and external motivation (a prime focus of *The Raise Responsibility System*), young people find it much easier to make responsible choices.

EXHIBIT PERSONAL RESPONSIBILITY

As explained in the discussion on motivation earlier in this book, we act and communicate from the beliefs we hold. These beliefs are often not clear to us. For example, the parent praises the youngster by saying, "I am so proud of you." The implicit message the parent sends is that if the child really loved the parent, the child would always do things that make the parent proud. To a certain extent, the parent is saying that the youngster is responsible for the parent's feelings. The message sent is, "If you really loved me you would make me happy." The same message is implied when the parent makes comments like, "You're making me angry," "You're making me upset," or "You're making me sick." Comments like these place the responsibility for how the parent feels on the child. (This logic was discussed more fully in Chapter 1 in the section *The Empowerment of Choice* in the topic *Choice-Response Thinking*.)

When a parent gets upset, stimulated by a child's action, the thinking process often appears to be, "I am upset, and it is the child's fault." In these cases, the parent is not taking personal responsibility for his or her own response. The parent should be thinking, "I'm upset; how can I best handle the situation?" Instead, the parent is putting the responsibility for his or her feelings on the youngster.

Similarly, it is easy to turn this around and believe that if other people are responsible for our feelings, then we are responsible for other people's feelings. For instance, the parent feels the caretaker role and accepts responsibility for making the child happy and puts his or her own desires aside. This approach is neither good for the parent nor for the growing child. For example, when the child asks the parent to do something and the parent gives herself or himself up to do it, the parent, sooner or later, feels some anger or resentment. Just as important is the implicit learning. It teaches that the child need not value what the parent wants—that the child comes first.

The child not only learns to be manipulative *but also becomes more demanding of the parent's time.* It would be better for the parent sometimes to say, "I'll do that with you later," or "I need some time alone. You need to play by yourself now." Children learn that they can indeed make themselves happy. Of course, any parent will often put his or her child first—but not to the point of dependency, and less and less as the child grows more able to take responsibility.

It is the nature of childhood to test during this transition period between being cared for and caring for oneself. A youngster will attempt to manipulate by yelling and screaming. If the parent always gives in to the manipulation, the implicit message is that the child should use the approach again because of its success. Young people can become very good at having others take responsibility for them.

The approach of demonstrating personal responsibility is one of the hardest to implement, but the benefit is most worthwhile because the parent is role-modeling personal, responsible behavior. Needless to say, at first a child will not like it. But after a while, the youngster realizes more satisfaction by taking personal responsibility than by relying on someone else for his or her happiness. When the parent says to the child, "I have to take care of you because you can't do it for yourself," and the child goes along with it, the child's self-esteem is compromised. However, when the parent says, "I am here for you if you need me, but I have faith that you can make yourself happy," the child learns to behave in a more autonomous, responsible way.

MAINTAIN STANDARDS

The British poet Samuel Taylor Coleridge was visited by an admirer one day. During the conversation, the subject came around to children. The visitor stated that he believed children should be given free rein to think and act and learn at an early age to make their own decisions—the only way they can grow into their full potential. Coleridge invited the visitor outside to see his flower garden. The visitor took one look and exclaimed that it was nothing but a yard full of weeds. Coleridge retorted that the garden used to be filled with roses, but this year he thought that he would let the garden grow as it willed without tending to it, and that this mess was the result.

At times children, and especially adolescents, will not like what is required of them and will act as if they do not like their parents. During this time in youngsters' lives, being a parent takes precedence over being a friend. Remarks such as, "You don't understand," or "I'm the only one who has to," or "I'll die if you don't let me," are attempts to have the parent relent and say, "Yes," when the parent knows it is really best to say, "No." In these situations, the parent should focus on what is best for the youngster *in the long run*. However, in the process, the child needs to understand the reasons for the decision. A simple technique to employ when a "No" needs to be given is to place the challenge on the youngster by simply saying, "Convince me." The challenge encourages reflection and responsible thinking. This is especially important with teenagers, who want to feel right even when they are wrong.

Just as our democratic system of government needs to be learned by each generation, so do the morals, values, and ethics upon which democracy rests. In a practical sense, this means that *behaviors take precedence over feelings*. The young boy in the park goes up to a smaller boy and pushes him down, hurting the smaller boy. The mother runs to the pusher, her son, and asks, "What made you feel so bad to do a thing like that?" Even if the boy could articulate the reason, it is no excuse for what he did. Rather than feelings or excuses, *the behavior should be addressed.* Developing a sense of right and wrong takes precedence over natural impulses.

Treating young people with respect and dignity is the most effective way for a parent to receive respect in return. Parents get offended when children treat them discourteously but often fail to recognize when they themselves are not respecting their children. For example, a parent who goes through a teenager's possessions without permission is showing disrespect. Parents would get angry if the teenager went through their possessions without permission. Of course, teens owe parents the courtesy of informing them as to their whereabouts and how they can be reached. If respect and courtesy are linked and applied, much of the rule making that our children believe is the parents' way of controlling them can be eliminated.

USE AUTHORITY WITHOUT BEING PUNITIVE

The keys to the success of using authority without being punitive are in using positive communications, empowerment of choice, and reflection. These practices instill the mindset that the objective is to raise responsibility, rather than to punish. Punishment fosters evasion of responsibility and also has the disadvantage of increasing the distance between parents and children. A far more effective approach than punishment is to treat the situation as a teaching and learning opportunity. Elicit from the youngster what the youngster can do to ensure that the situation will not be repeated. In this way, the young person creates and maintains ownership. The implicit message is that a person is responsible for his actions and that inappropriate action is being remedied. This approach uses irresponsible behavior as an opportunity for growth.

If an elicited consequence is not appropriate or acceptable, "What else?" is asked until there is agreement on the consequence. Any consequence should fulfill three requirements:

1. The consequence should be related to the incident.

2. The consequence should be reasonable.

3. The consequence should be related to growth.

The teenage girl slams her bedroom door repeatedly. The father tells the daughter that the slamming really bothers him. The daughter agrees not to slam the door, but the behavior continues. The father tells his daughter that if she develops a procedure it would be easier for her to direct her impulse, and he communicates that he has confidence she can do this. He attempts to assist: "When walking into the bedroom," he says, "pause, turn around, then close the door." The daughter visualizes the procedure. The father invites her to suggest a better procedure or to alter his. After a few moments, they agree. However, the father now wants to be prepared to use authority, just in case the situation is repeated. So the father asks, "What could be done if it occurs again?" "What else?" "What else?" The daughter understands that the door will be removed if the slamming continues. It does. The father takes a hammer and screwdriver, taps the hinge bolts upward, removes them and the door, and puts the door in the garage. The father informs his daughter that he knows how much she desires her privacy and that he prefers to leave the door on its hinges. He tells his daughter that the door will be replaced as soon as she comes up with a more effective plan for not slamming it.

While using authority, the father approached the situation with a strategy. First, he was positive by showing faith in her and even helping her establish a procedure. Second, he helped her become aware of her choices. Third, he encouraged reflection just in case the situation was to be repeated. Finally, he followed through but still invited his daughter to make a new plan.

LET THE YOUNGSTER LEAD

If a youngster is critical of the way a parent does things, a good strategy is to let the youngster plan an activity. Assistance can be given by providing a few guidelines and a budget. This strategy will not necessarily ensure that everyone has a great time, but it eliminates much of the complaining.

A forgetful or unreliable child can also lead by being in charge of a message center, such as a "Things to Remember" board (on or near the refrigerator, of course). Things that are important, such as appointments and activities, are on the board and are read each day. "I didn't know" is not an acceptable excuse. The youngster can post messages on the board. The strategy also ensures that the youngster in charge of the board will not "forget" what is on it.

TEACH PROCEDURES TO DEAL WITH IMPULSES

Impulses, emotions, and even behavior reflexes emanate from within ourselves, even though something outside of us may have caused the stimulation. As with dreams, emanations may "pop up" without any deliberate thinking. Although the bad news is that these eruptions cannot be entirely prevented, the good news is that they can be diminished by our response to them—even to the point that they no longer direct our behavior. Our choice of how we respond to the impulse, urge, or reflex affects its frequency and strength. For example, a youngster gets angry. Unless the youngster consciously chooses to respond to the anger in a constructive way, the emotion will continue to erupt and may even increase in frequency and duration. Learning a *procedure* is the most practical way to deal with destructive thoughts, negative emotions, or inappropriate behaviors.

The most effective approach is to first recognize and teach that, *whatever the internal emanation,* the person still has a choice of responses. Here is a simple strategy for younger children. A small drawing of a traffic signal is made or purchased and the colors of the signal filled in. With older children, just a mental image of a traffic signal will do.

The RED on the top indicates to STOP and breathe *out.* When in a highly emotional state, breathing is shallow. Exhale the remaining breath. Then while slowly inhaling *with a long gasping breath,* the youngster visualizes the YELLOW of the traffic signal. During this *gasping* breathing, the jaw is opened—releasing tension—and the person is prevented from becoming emotionally hijacked. During this second phase, options are considered by asking, "What is the smartest way to handle this situation?" The GREEN of the signal indicates to go with the wisest decision. (A longer discussion of this approach is found in Chapter 4 in the section *Challenges: Impulse and Anger Management.*)

This procedure must be continually practiced until it becomes habitual. The next time the youngster allows emotions to direct his behavior, the first action should be to hold up a signal. (A few signals can be scattered around in various places for quick grabbing.)

Consequences mean nothing to a person in a highly emotional state. Using a prompt is more successful than threatening or punishing—and is less stressful on both parties.

Even very young people can learn that, although emotions and thoughts cannot be stopped from erupting, *growth and maturation come according to how people respond to them.* The more an emanation like anger is responded to with a procedure such as described above, the less its frequency and intensity become.

INTERVENE IN SIBLING SQUABBLES

Positive sibling relationships can be a source of strength for life, whereas unresolved early conflicts can create wounds that never quite heal.

When an older child is hitting his baby sister, of course the parent needs to intervene immediately and make it clear that hurting others is not acceptable. The same is true for verbal abuse between siblings, which leaves one or both constantly angry or with depleted confidence. Treating the word "hate" like a forbidden swear word and not allowing "shut up" between siblings are simple examples. Without access to this sort of incendiary language, fighting becomes less frequent. A "no hitting, no hurting" expectation can be established so the youngsters will know that they are to work out their problems peacefully.

Parents need not intervene in every children's quarrel. However, parents should intervene directly whenever an argument turns violent or threatens to do so. Most children hate fighting—even when they are winning. They do it because they do not have the tools for dealing with their frustrations. Fighters should be separated to cool off. An effective technique is to have them sit down until each gives the other permission to get up. *This technique diminishes anger more speedily than if the children are separated completely.* Parents can then listen to both parties while the youngsters come up with a solution.

Another approach is to have each sibling write down his or her side of the story. This will provide for a cooling-off period. When the parent looks at the two stories, each will be different. The charge is then given for the siblings to present an ending that both can live with. A variation is to have them write their individual stories and then read each other's. Then have them create a plan they both can agree on, even an impractical one. Anger dissipates even more as they come up with zany endings.

The strategy in Chapter 4 in the section *Conflict Resolution: Solving Circles* definitely should be reviewed.

BE AWARE OF GENDER DIFFERENCES

One of the most important parental teachings is that being different is not being wrong. Understanding differences is crucial in our diverse, civil society. Understanding differences includes how males and females operate.

Generally, girls will sit and discuss feelings rather easily. Boys usually will not. In order to get boys to express feelings, engage them in some activity, such as throwing a baseball, playing basketball, or taking a walk.

Boys have a very strong desire to feel competent. Telling a boy what to do interferes with his desire for competency, which is why boys so often react negatively even when they know a parent is correct.

Understanding the differences between parents is also helpful. Whereas a mother has a desire to protect a boy and prevent him from doing something because he may get hurt, a father may say, "Let him do it. That is how he will learn." A father is more likely to think that as long as an activity is *not life-threatening, unhealthy,* or *morally wrong,* it should be allowed. For example, a father is more willing to allow boys to engage in rough and tumble play.

This "boy-play" is natural and different from what we normally think of as negatively aggressive behavior, such as bullying. The sooner the parent intervenes when a youngster bullies, the better. Bullies tend to grow into, not out of, their behavior.

USE ACKNOWLEDGMENTS MORE THAN PRAISE

After conducting a seminar in Washington, D.C., I received a letter from one of the participants, a principal in Alexandria, Virginia. She wrote:

> Your comment about acknowledgments versus praise really hit a chord with me. My eleven-year-old daughter had done something terrific and I launched into my usual, "Oh, Honey, Mommy's so proud of you." Well, she stopped me mid-gush, put her hand on her hips and implored, "Mom, please stop!

Whenever you do that, you make me feel like you're surprised that I can do things—like I'm not capable!"

The mother was using praise in an attempt to reward her daughter. Although the mother's intentions were honorable, the complimentary message was not congruent with the implicit message, which questioned the child's competency.

Praise, such as the kind the mother used, has its price. With older children, it can be demeaning. With young children, it encourages them to do what parents want them to do in order to make the adult happy. A statement like, "I'm so proud of you because you're such a good boy" implies that the boy is O.K. only when he is good, and that when the boy is not good, he is not O.K. Praise is also like candy; once you start giving it, stopping is difficult because the child wants it constantly.

The Virginia mother has since started to acknowledge her daughter's actions *without* constant reference to her own motherly pride. Acknowledgment simply identifies ownership and responsibility for the achievement, which has a more powerful effect for developing self-esteem.

Self-esteem has to do with (internal) feelings of competency. In this sense, people empower themselves. When the focus is on the action, then reflection and feelings of competency thrive because of the satisfaction engendered. Much of the flawed self-esteem movement is based upon an external approach, as if someone else can pass out self-esteem.

My concern with the self-esteem movement is that it encourages approaches that address the *person*, rather than the *action*. For example, rather than saying, "I'm proud of you for getting such a good grade," simply saying, "Well done!" is more meaningful and sends a more empowering message. Saying, "I see you made your bed" fosters feelings of self-competence. In contrast, saying, "I'm so proud of you for making your bed," encourages making decisions to please the parent.

Acknowledgment accomplishes the intent of praise but without the disadvantages. It fosters feelings of being worthwhile, without relying on the approval of others. The long-range effect is to engender self-confidence and self-reliance, rather than dependence on others for feelings of one's self-worth.

Young children generally want to behave in ways that please their parents. However, we really want our children to learn to do the right thing, not because someone is dangling a carrot in front of them, but because it is the right thing to do. When people do the right thing—when they make good decisions, when they behave in a responsible manner—they feel good. They learn to value themselves. Developing responsibility—rather than obedience to please—is more advantageous for both children and parents. The children gain confidence and the parents promote responsibility. Parents who foster this approach give children a precious gift that is treasured for a lifetime.

An easy way to distinguish between praise and acknowledgment is to consider whether the comment would be made to an adult. If the comment would not be made to an adult, then it is probably patronizing praise.

As Ralph Waldo Emerson so aptly put it, "The reward for a thing well done is to have done it."

HONOR HOME ASSIGNMENTS

Home assignments teach two lessons. The most obvious reason for home assignments is to provide opportunities to practice and improve skills or to gain further knowledge or understanding. Practice is essential for skill mastery. Gaining knowledge and understanding is not limited to class time.

Home assignments also teach other lessons: responsibility, self-discipline, independence, perseverance, and time management. Home assignments teach how to begin a task, complete it, and be responsible for the outcome.

When a home assignment is difficult and the young person begins to struggle, parents want to help, and they should—up to a point. When the helping has reached the point where the youngster knows how to do the assignment, then the parent should back away; otherwise, the rescuing and over-involvement result in a gradual dependence on others.

Home assignments should be something done on a regular basis. A time that can be used regularly is most effective. Selecting a time that is earlier is preferable to a time that is later. Young people are generally fresher and more alert in the late afternoon or early evening than they are later on.

We choose our attitude when doing any activity, and this includes home assignments. Assuming that the parent will also be involved in some worthwhile activity while the youngster tends to home assignments, the parent can make a positive comment that both have responsibilities. Also, an encouraging comment, such as, "What do you expect to learn or reinforce from this assignment?" is preferable to one that is negative or nagging, such as "Have you finished your assignment?" Negative comments only encourage doing the assignment in order to get away from the negativity. This often results in the youngster's doing the assignment but then forgetting to take it to school. The motivation in such cases is not the assignment, but rather getting away from the nagging.

WORK SMARTER RATHER THAN HARDER

Do not do things for young people that they can do for themselves. Performing tasks engenders responsibility.

Once a task has been performed, the objective should be to focus on progress—rather than on perfection. If the activity does not meet parental expectations, something positive can be found on which to comment. This is far more effective than comments that foster guilt or a sense of failure. A positive approach prompts an incentive for the task—in contrast to criticizing, which provides a disincentive.

A specific time of day for required activities should be chosen. When structured and organized, tasks are more easily undertaken. When establishing routines, timing should be considered, such as whether or not the child is tired or hungry.

Offering help to start an activity is a good technique. Younger children prefer starting tasks with others rather than in isolation. After the youngster is involved, then withdraw, saying something like, "I'm sure you have the skills to do the rest without my help."

Any task should be age appropriate. "Tidy your desk," is more manageable and not as discouraging as, "Clean your room." In addition, once the desk is cleaned, the other may naturally follow.

It is important to recognize when a child is overtired, ill, or overwhelmed by expectations. These may be causes for being cranky or uncooperative. Similarly, if a child's favorite activity or television program is interrupted, the youngster should not be expected to be very cooperative.

Especially with an adolescent, the "state of mind" needs to be considered. A typical example is a parent's demand on a youngster's time. The son has not taken out the trash or completed some other chore. He is watching television. The parent gets after him. The poor timing is met with a negative reaction. A more successful approach would be to ask to see the son at the end of the television program or wait until he is upright, preferably in motion. Once on his feet and moving, the young man will be in a state of mind much more receptive to taking out the trash. In addition, the implicit message will not be that what the parent wants is more important than what the youngster wants. A key phrase to remember is "Under duress, they do less."

NURTURE YOUR CHILD'S NATURE

If an acorn is planted in good soil, is fertilized, and receives adequate water, the acorn will grow and may wind up becoming a giant oak tree. However, if a giant redwood is desired but an acorn is germinated and planted, that acorn will still grow up to be an oak.

Young people are not clones of their parents. Some are continually engaging in thought, while others are driven by how they feel. Some are constantly engaged in activities, while others are constantly looking for relationships. Being mindful of the child's nature can have a dramatic effect on relationships. The key consideration here is to work with youngsters according to *their* make-up. Simply remembering that each child is different, and not a duplicate of parents, can reduce stress and enhance relationships.

REAP THE JOY

A joy of parenting is watching a child develop and mature. Possessiveness has been a hallmark of parenting for hundreds of generations. Today, parents can no longer consider children their possessions. Children have rights and are watched over by the general society. An indication of this is the fine line drawn between punishment and child abuse.

Perhaps the paramount desire of parents has to do with simultaneously giving roots and wings. Parents model, foster values, and teach by what they say and do. They provide the shelter, clothing, affection, and security so necessary for a healthy environment. All of these provide roots. Parents also give wings and hope that the direction of flight will be toward responsible living. Perhaps the combination of roots and wings was most eloquently expressed in 1932 by Kahlil Gibran in *The Prophet.*

> *Your children are not your children.*
> *They are the sons and daughters of Life's longing*
>   *for itself.*
> *They come through you but not from you,*
> *And though they are with you yet they belong not to*
>   *you.*
>
> *You may give them your love but not your thoughts,*
> *For they have their own thoughts.*
> *You may house their bodies but not their souls,*
> *For their souls dwell in the house of tomorrow, which*
>   *you cannot visit, not even in your dreams.*
> *You may strive to be like them, but seek not to make*
>   *them like you.*
> *For life goes not backward nor tarries with yesterday.*
>
> *You are the bows from which your children as living*
>   *arrows are sent forth.*
> *The archer sees the mark upon the path of the*
>   *infinite, and He bends you with His might that*
> *His arrows may go swift and far.*
> *Let your bending in the archer's hand be for*
>   *gladness;*
> *For even as He loves the arrow that flies, so He loves also*
>   *the bow that is stable.*

KEY POINTS

◆ Practice positivity. One of the most effective ways to influence children and reduce stress is to communicate using positive messages.

◆ Offer choices. Choice brings ownership and empowers. Offering options engages a youngster in cooperation and is much more effective than giving commands.

◆ Encourage reflection. The purpose of reflection is to stimulate internal motivation.

◆ Use effective questions. Effective questions direct thinking to self-evaluation. This process brings awareness and clarity, both for the questioner and for the person answering.

◆ Listen to learn. Listening to and valuing young people's feelings and ideas are what promote the ability of parents to effectively communicate with them.

◆ Limit lecturing and telling. Although the intention may be to share and save youngsters from a frustrating experience, the message is often perceived as criticism. Lectures convey the message that what the youngster has done is wrong or not good enough. This often results in defensiveness and resistance.

◆ Check assumptions. We may know exactly what we are thinking and what we mean, but the child may have a completely different perspective.

◆ Focus on the important. Choose your battles. While clashes may be unavoidable, it is not necessary to get pulled into every skirmish.

◆ Ask for assistance. People become responsible by giving and putting forth effort; give young people opportunities to help you.

◆ Recognize implicit messages. "Implicit" refers to what is learned without our intentions. When parents become upset and yell at children, the implicit message is that when upset, yelling is acceptable.

◆ Foster responsibility. Parents can best view the adolescent years as a quest for identity. Conflicts can be avoided by using reflective questions and negotiating through dialogue, rather than by using coercion.

◆ Demonstrate personal responsibility. Accept responsibility for allowing a situation or stimulus to upset you; do not blame the child. The parent should be thinking, "I'm upset; how can I best handle the situation?"

◆ Maintain standards. Sometimes maintaining standards takes a higher priority than that of parental popularity.

◆ Use authority without being punitive. Rather than imposing a punishment, a much more effective approach to changing behavior is to elicit a consequence from the youngster. Then the young person has ownership of it.

◆ Let the youngster lead. Have the youngster plan an activity. Assistance can be given by providing a few guidelines and a budget.

◆ Teach procedures for dealing with impulses. Recognize that people have choices regarding their responses to impulses.

◆ Intervene in sibling squabbles. Parents need not intervene in every children's quarrel, but should intervene whenever an argument turns violent or threatens to do so.

◆ Be aware of gender differences. Engage boys in an activity before expecting them to express their feelings. Boys have strong desires to feel competent, and "telling" a boy what to do interferes with this.

◆ Use acknowledgments more than praise. Acknowledgment simply identifies ownership and responsibility for the achievement.

◆ Honor home assignments. They provide opportunities to practice and improve skills and teach other lessons such as responsibility, self-discipline, independence, perseverance, and time management. Assist only to the point where the youngster can do the assignment himself.

◆ Work smarter rather than harder. Do not do things for young people that they can do for themselves. Focus on progress, rather than on perfection.

◆ Nurture your child's nature. Simply remembering that each child is different, and not a duplicate of parents, can reduce stress and enhance relationships.

◆ Reap the joy. A joy of parenting is watching a child develop and mature while simultaneously giving the child roots and wings.

SUMMARY

The world is a looking glass
and gives to every man the reflection of his own face.
Frown at it and it, in turn, will look sourly at you;
laugh at it, and with it, and it is a jolly, kind companion.
–William Makepeace Thackeray

As emphasized throughout this book, optimism pays. Listen to your self-talk. As you can upset yourself with negative self-talk, so you have the capability to talk yourself into a positive state. Be kind to yourself. Be like the monkey who eats only the healthy part of the banana.

No empowerment is more effective than self-empowerment. Because being positive is so enabling, it is best to displace thoughts and communications that are destructive. Continually ask how what you want to communicate can be put in a positive way. For example, saying, "You are bad tempered," has the same meaning as, "You need to work on controlling your temper." However, the first *labels* the person, whereas the second *enables* the person.

People change more by building on their strengths and aptitudes than by working on their weaknesses. This does not mean that an area of weakness should not be worked on, but it does mean that a parent's emphasis should be on what the child can do, rather than what the child cannot do. The simple belief that something can be done is the spark that ignites the brain to act.

Listen to how you communicate with your children. Listen to the tone of your voice. It communicates your emotions. Be aware of your body language. Facial expressions, body stance, and gestures communicate your message as much as the words you actually say.

Separate the young person from the behavior. If a child is not acting responsibly, acknowledge the action, but do not call the child irresponsible. Label the behavior, rather than the person. "Do you consider that the responsible thing to do?" or "That was not worthy of you," are better than "You are irresponsible." Of course, having the child do the labeling is even more effective.

The whole problem with *telling*, rather than *asking*, must be kept in mind constantly because so often parents tell a youngster what the parent would do in a similar situation. Unfortunately, a common message is that what the youngster does is not good enough, or certainly not as good as what the parent suggests. A simple solution to this dilemma is for the parent to ask the youngster reflective questions.

Three ways to impair relationships are to criticize, blame, and complain. Rather than using these negative approaches, ask a self-evaluative, reflective question in order to involve the child in a non-threatening way.

No one likes to be cornered, literally or figuratively. Having no choices encourages resistance because of the feeling of being trapped. When a child has no options, the result is not only resistance but also resentment.

Refrain from arguing. It only fuels hostility and diminishes healthy communications. Arguments rarely focus on solutions, and reasoning with someone who is upset is futile. One approach is to simply hold up your hand, palm out, making the "stop" sign, or signal "time out" with hands overhead like a referee. Also, avoid attempting to talk young people out of their feelings. Young people have the right to feel hurt, upset, and disappointed. Their reactions should be acknowledged without being condoned. The acknowledgment itself can diffuse anger mightily.

Deal in the present. The past cannot be changed. When it is re-lived, it becomes the present and builds frustration.

Avoid doing things for young people that they can do themselves. Accept the fact that growth comes through struggle. Babying children keeps them dependent and hinders their development.

Focus on treating children as if they are who, how, and what you would like them to be. Treating people as if they are responsible increases the chances of their becoming so.

EPILOGUE

BUSINESS:
A POOR MODEL FOR LEARNING

There is no such thing as an immaculate perception.
What you see depends upon what you thought before you looked.
—Myron Tribus

Government, business, and even education leaders often compare schooling to business. Schools are referred to as workplaces, students are referred to as customers, and performance is measured by accountability. Equating young people's learning with what adults do to make money is a false equation. Using a business model for learning is a practice that has been described by the comic strip character Dagwood Bumstead: "You know, that makes a lot of sense if you don't think about it."

THE PURPOSES OF SCHOOL AND BUSINESS ARE DIFFERENT

The basic purpose of business is to survive. Even in graduate business courses that teach that one purpose of business is to serve, the fact remains that if there is no profit, the business will eventually fail.

Survival is not a factor in schooling. Society finds ways—be they public, private, or a combination thereof—to educate its young. The purpose of schooling is to promote understanding, make meaning, and perpetuate and improve society. Preparing students to live successful lives certainly includes some of the necessary skills and characteristics essential in business. However, the fact that some of the same skills are used does not mean that the skills taught in school are taught *for* purposes of business.

THE PRODUCT IS DIFFERENT

Businesses produce *products*. The product may be tangible or intangible and in the form of information, services, or goods.

Learning is a *process*, not a product. Even if students were to be considered products, the product would be their education. Schools educate and businesses train. The term "training" is not often used when referring to K–12 education. Schools do not train for specific information dissemination as do businesses, nor are students trained to provide services to others, nor are they trained to produce goods for use or for consumption. Training is used for areas that are vocational in nature.

In a business transaction, the customer is clearly identified. This is not the case in education. The customer consists of parents (especially in this age of school choice), the society at large (since students are members), other institutions of learning (where students often need to qualify), and future employers. In business, *only* the customer needs *live with the product*; however, the people who live with the results of schooling are the parents and others with whom the learner interacts.

Business can control the components of its product—what will go into making a product. Schools do not have this luxury; they (at least the public schools) have no discretionary power to determine or control the "raw materials." Besides, students are not assembled according to well-established specifications. Schools must individualize education for many students.

Business has the opportunity and even the obligation for recalls. No such possibility exists for schools. Clearly, comparing the building of people to building products is a faulty comparison.

THE PEOPLE ARE DIFFERENT

Students are young people and, as such, are different from adults. When juvenile courts were established, the legal system acknowledged that childhood is different from adulthood. Vast amounts of psychological, social, developmental, medical, and brain research have demonstrated that children and youth are different from adults. Few parents—whether in government, business, or education—would ever consider treating their own eight-year-old as an eighteen-year-old.

THE TASKS ARE DIFFERENT

The nature of the work differs. Business has to do with providing a product or service to others. Schooling has to do with personal and social growth. A review of the chapter on teaching clearly demonstrates that the nature of learning differs from the nature of producing.

FUNDING AND COMPENSATION ARE DIFFERENT

In business, the person who pays derives the benefit. This is not the case in education. The person who is most directly involved— the learner—does not pay for education. In addition, even though businesses and other agencies contribute to the support of schools, the primary revenue source for public education is the general society—not private funds.

Also, and this may not be apparent to those who equate learning with business, *money is a satisfier—not a motivator.* Giving a person more money rarely produces more work. Money does not usually make a person work harder. Take yourself as an example. If you were given more money, would you work harder than you work now? If a chief executive officer (CEO) of a business were given more compensation, do you think he or she would work harder? Money is compensation, and unless a person is being paid by piecework or is on commission, money will not often motivate him to work harder.

Students do not receive money for learning. Besides, giving money for learning would be a mistake. External rewards alter motivation and diminish creativity, two of the most powerful incentives for learning.

In business, if a worker does not perform satisfactorily, the employment, along with the compensation, is removed. Public schools do not fire students or prevent their continued attendance.

THE SUCCESS FACTOR IS DIFFERENT

In business, success on the job often requires initiative, flexibility, and teamwork. No defense is given here for not employing similar approaches in schools. However, that is not currently the case in most schools. Schooling is administered in a competitive manner. Grades, rankings, and other evaluation techniques are largely based on pitting students against each other and militate against initiative, flexibility, and teamwork.

Outcomes in the business world can be objectively measured. Units manufactured and sold, the number of customers returning, and the number of retained clients can all be objectively measured. This is not the case in learning; outcomes cannot be objectively measured. Even if they could be, the evaluation instruments currently available could indicate only an insignificant amount of learning that had been acquired—either in quality or quantity.

In this regard, businesses do not set up evaluation instruments that mandate only a fifty percent (50%) success factor. It is interesting to note that educational leaders follow the ideas of business and government leaders. But these leaders would never consider evaluating the success of workers on any kind of an instrument where, by design, half would fall below the average. Yet, this is what schools do when standardized tests are administered. Not only do half of the students fall below the average, so do half of the schools. No other institution would operate in this way—a poignant, and unfortunate, further differentiation.

THE PROCEDURES AND TIME FACTORS ARE DIFFERENT

A manager who oversees employees, an administrator who is accountable for a project or department, or a business executive who is responsible for the success and survival of the business operate differently from a teacher. The teacher's charge is to impart information, foster comprehension, develop communication skills, and build behavior to promote a civil society. Therefore, a slow learner is treated differently from a fast learner. Various activities are assigned according to the students' skills and abilities. Because schools aim at attending to students' needs, flexibility of time is incorporated. In contrast to schools, business uses procedures that focus on production and are usually under strict time constraints.

Finally, business primarily deals in the present. Schools deal primarily with the future.

CONCLUSION

Learning is learning; it is not business. Comparing learning to business is not only a poor metaphor, it is a false one. Just because business and learning share attributes of efforts and skills, it is unwise to compare them for the reasons listed. We would be well served to call attention to and refute the comparison whenever made.

BIBLIOGRAPHY

Alessandra, Tony, and Michael O'Connor. *The Platinum Rule*. New York: Warner Books, 1996.

Alexander, F. M. *The Use of the Self*. Great Britain: Guernsey, Channel Islands: Guernsey Press, Ltd., 1985.

Armstrong, Thomas. *ADD/ADHD Alternatives in the Classroom*. Alexandria, VA: Association for Supervision and Curriculum Development, 1999.

_____. *Awakening Genius in the Classroom*. Alexandria, VA: Association for Supervision and Curriculum Development, 1998.

_____. *Multiple Intelligences in the Classroom*. Alexandria, VA: Association for Supervision and Curriculum Development, 1994.

Begley, Sharon. "Homework Doesn't Help," *Newsweek* (March 30, 1998).

_____. "Mind: Living Hand to Mouth: New Research Shows that Gestures Often Help Speakers Access Words from Their Memory Bank," *Newsweek* (November 2, 1998).

Bellanca, James. "Teaching for Intelligence: In Search of Best Practices," *Phi Delta Kappan* (May 1998).

Bloom, Benjamin S., and others, eds. *Taxonomy of Educational Objectives: Cognitive Domain*. New York: David McKay Co. Inc., 1956.

Bluestein, Jane. *21st Century Discipline: Teaching Students Responsibility and Self-Control*. Jefferson City, MO: Scholastic, Inc., 1988.

Bracey, Gerald W. *Setting the Record Straight: Responses to Misconceptions about Public Education in the United States*. Alexandria, VA: Association for Supervision and Curriculum Development, 1977.

Bromley, Karen, Linda Irwin-DeVitis, and Marcia Modlo. *Graphic Organizers: Visual Strategies for Active Learning*. New York: Scholastic Professional Books, 1995.

Bruner, Jerome. *Going Beyond the Information Given.* New York: Norton, 1973.

_____. *The Process of Education.* Cambridge: Harvard University Press, 1961.

California State Department of Education. *Toward A State Of Esteem: The Final Report of the California Task Force to Promote Self-esteem and Personal and Social Responsibility.* Sacramento, CA: California State Department of Education, 1990.

California State Department of Education, Sacramento County Office of Education, and California Partnership in Character Education. *Building Communities & Schools of Character.* Mechanism for Change Conference: Character Education, March 11, 1999.

Canfield, Jack, and Mark Viktor Hansen. *The Aladdin Factor.* New York: Berkley Books, 1995.

Canfield, Jack, and Harold Wells. *100 Ways to Enhance Self-Concept in the Classroom.* Boston: Allyn and Beacon, 1994.

Capell, Dianne. Personal correspondence to Marvin Marshall. January 7, 1999.

Cathcart, Jim. *The Acorn Principle.* New York: St. Martin's Griffin, 1999.

Chase, Bob. "Trial by Fire: Are We Setting Up New Teachers to Fail?" *Education Week* (November 18, 1998): 17.

_____. "Stigmatizing Success," *Education Week* (January 20, 1999): 37.

Clark, Richard E. Personal correspondence to Marvin Marshall. September 3, 1995.

Coleman, James S. *The Adolescent Society: The Social Life of the Teenager and Its Impact on Education.* New York: Free Press of Glencoe, 1961.

Covey, Stephen. *The Seven Habits of Highly Effective People.* New York: Simon & Schuster, 1990.

Crawford, Donna, Richard Bodine, and Robert Hoglund. *The School for Quality Learning.* Champagne, IL: Research Press, 1993.

Cummings, Carol. *Winning Strategies for Classroom Management.* Alexandria, VA: Association for Supervision and Curriculum Development, 2000.

Danzig, Robert. *Cooperating School Districts 2000 Character Education Conference.* St. Louis, MO: July 13, 2000. (Available on audio cassette tape CE0002)

D'Arcangelo, Marcia. "The Brains Behind the Brain," *Educational Leadership* 56, no. 3 (November 1998): 20–25.

Deci, Edward L., and Richard Flaste. *Why We Do What We Do: Understanding Self-Motivation.* New York: Penguin Books, 1995.

Deming, W. Edwards. "A Day with Dr. Deming," sponsored by the Chief of Naval Operations, December 21, 1991, and published by the Chief of Naval Operations, The Pentagon, Room 4E522, Washington, D.C. 20350-2000.

———. *Out of the Crisis.* Cambridge: Massachusetts Institute of Technology, 1986.

———. *The New Economics for Industry, Government, and Education.* Cambridge: Massachusetts Institute of Technology, 1993.

Dewey, John. *Experience & Education.* New York: Macmillan, 1958.

Dickinson, Amy. "Bully Pulpit," *Time* (August 30, 1999): 76.

Dill, Vicky Schreiber. *A Peaceable School: Cultivating a Culture of Nonviolence.* Bloomington, IN: Phi Delta Kappa Educational Foundation, 1998.

Dougherty, John W. *Four Philosophies that Shape the Middle School.* Bloomington, IN: Phi Delta Kappa Educational Foundation, 1997.

DuFour, Rick. "Functioning as Learning Communities Enables Schools to Focus on Student Achievement," *Journal of Staff Development.* Oxford, OH: National Staff Development Council (Spring 1997).

Elam, Stanley. *How America Views Its Public Schools: The PDK/Gallop Polls, 1964–1994.* Bloomington, IN: Phi Delta Kappa International Foundation, 1995.

Elias, Marilyn. "3 Studies, 1 Result: School Bullying Worsening," *USA Today* (August 23, 1999).

Ellis, Albert. "Rational Emotive Behavior Therapy as an Integral Control of Psychology," *International Journal of Reality Therapy*. Boston, MA: Northeastern University (Fall 1999).

Ellis, Albert, and Catherine MacLaren. *Rational Emotive Behavior Therapy: A Therapist's Guide*. San Luis Obispo, CA: Impact Publishers, 1998.

Farivar, Sydney. "Research Review: Citizenship Education," *Social Studies Review*. Millbrae, CA: Journal of the California Council for the Social Studies (Spring 1996).

Fouse, Beth, and Suzanne Brians. *A Primer on Attention Deficit Disorder*. Bloomington, IN: Phi Delta Kappa Educational Foundation, 1993.

Frankl, Viktor E. *Man's Search for Meaning*. New York: Washington Square Press, 1968.

Fuetsch, Michele. "Program Aims to Keep Teachers from Quitting," *Los Angeles Times* (June 3, 1993): J1.

Fulghum, Robert. *All I Really Need to Know I Learned in Kindergarten*. New York: Villard Books, 1989.

Gardner, Howard. "A Prescription for Peace," *Time* (January 25, 1999): 62–63.

_____. *Frames of Mind: The Theory of Multiple Intelligences*. New York: Basic Books, 1993.

_____. "The First Seven . . . and the Eighth," *Educational Leadership* 55, no. 1 (1997): 8–13.

Gauld, Joseph. "Why American Education is Failing: A Plea for Intrinsic, Rather than Extrinsic Forms of Motivation," *Education Week* (April 29, 1997): 41.

Gaustad, Joan. "Characteristics Associated with Student Discipline Problems," *ERIC Digest* 78. Reported in *Thrust for Educational Leadership*. Burlingame, CA: The Association of California School Administrators (October 1994).

Gelb, Michael J. *Body Learning*. New York: Henry Holt and Company, 1994.

_____. *Thinking for a Change*. New York: Harmony Books, 1995.

Gibran, Kahlil. *The Prophet*. New York: Alfred A. Knopf, 1996.

Glasser, William. "A New Look at School Failure and School Success," *Phi Delta Kappan* (April 1997).

_____. *Choice Theory: A New Psychology of Personal Freedom*. New York: HarperCollins, 1998.

_____. *Choice Theory in the Classroom*. New York: Harper & Row, 1998.

_____. *Every Student Can Succeed*. San Diego, CA: Black Forest Press, 2000.

_____. *The Quality School*. New York: HarperCollins, 1992, 1998.

_____. *The Quality School Teacher*. New York: HarperCollins, 1993, 1998.

_____. *Schools without Failure*. New York: Harper & Row, 1969.

_____. *The Identity Society*. New York: Harper & Row, 1975.

Goldstein, Sam, and Michael Goldstein. *A Teacher's Guide: Attention-Deficit Hyperactivity Disorder in Children*. Salt Lake City: Neurology Learning and Behavior Center, 1995.

Goleman, Daniel. *Emotional Intelligence*. New York: Bantam Books, 1995.

Gootman, Marilyn. *The Caring Teacher's Guide to Discipline: Helping Young Students Learn Self-Control, Responsibility, and Respect*. Thousand Oaks, CA: Corwin Press, 1997.

Gray, John. *Men Are from Mars, Women Are from Venus*. New York: HarperCollins, 1992.

Grote, Richard C. *Discipline without Punishment*. Kansas City, MO: American Management Association, 1995.

Halford, Joan Montgomery. "Easing the Way for New Teachers," *Educational Leadership* 55, 5 (February, 1998): 33–36.

Harris, Judith Rich. *The Nurture Assumption: Why Children Turn Out the Way They Do – Parents Matter Less than You Think and Peers Matter More.* New York: The Free Press, 1998.

Healy, Jane M. "The 'Meme' That Ate Childhood," *Education Week* (October 7, 1998): 56.

Helmstetter, Shad. *Choices.* New York: Simon & Schuster, 1989.

Hicks, Jerry. *Los Angeles Times* (October 30, 1997).

Hill, Napoleon. *Think and Grow Rich.* North Hollywood, CA: Wilshire Book Co., 1996.

Hunter, Madeline. *Discipline That Develops Self-Discipline.* Thousand Oaks, CA: Corwin Press, 1967.

_____. *Motivation Theory for Teachers.* Thousand Oaks, CA: Corwin Press, 1990.

Jameson, Marnell. "Bully for Them," *Los Angeles Times* (March 9, 1997).

Jamison, Kaleel. *The Nibble Theory and the Kernel of Power.* Mahwah, NJ: Paulist Press, 1989.

Jensen, Eric. *Completing the Puzzle: A Brain-Based Approach to Learning.* Del Mar, CA: Turning Point Publishing, 1996.

_____. *SuperTeaching.* Del Mar, CA: Turning Point Publishing, 1995.

_____. *Teaching with the Brain in Mind.* Alexandria, VA: Association for Supervision and Curriculum Development, 1998.

Kennedy, John F. *Profiles in Courage.* New York: Black Dog & Leventhal, 1955, 1984.

Kohn, Alfie. *Beyond Discipline: From Compliance to Community.* Alexandria, VA: Association for Supervision and Curriculum Development, 1996.

_____. "How Not to Teach Values: A Critical Look at Character Education," *Phi Delta Kappan* (February 1997).

_____. *Punished by Rewards.* Boston: Houghton Mifflin, 1993.

_____. "Students Don't 'Work'—They Learn," *Education Week* (September 3, 1997).

_____. "The Author Responds," *Phi Delta Kappan* (May 1997).

_____. *What to Look for in a Classroom.* San Francisco: Jossey-Bass, 1998.

Langdon, Carol. "The Third Phi Delta Kappa Poll of Teachers' Attitudes Toward the Public Schools," *Phi Delta Kappan* (November 1996).

Lickona, Thomas. *Educating for Character: How Our Schools Can Teach Respect and Responsibility.* New York: Bantam Books, 1991.

MacDonald, Glynn. *Alexander Technique.* Great Britain: Hodder & Stoughton, 1994.

Manges, Charles D., and Stanley E. Wigle. "Quality Schools and Constructivist Teaching," *Journal of Reality Therapy.* Boston, MA: Northeastern University (Spring 1997): 47.

Margulies, Nancy. *Mapping Inner Space: Learning and Teaching Mindmapping.* Tucson, AZ: Zephyr, 1991.

Marshall, Marvin. "Ensuring Social Responsibility," *Thrust for Educational Leadership.* Burlingame, CA: The Association of California School Administrators (January 1994).

_____. "Evaluation: A Tool for Better Relationships," *Thrust for Educational Leadership.* Burlingame, CA: The Association of California School Administrators (November/December 1997).

_____. "Fostering Social Responsibility and Handling Disruptive Classroom Behavior," *NASSP Bulletin.* Reston, VA: The National Association of Secondary School Principals (March 1998).

_____. *Fostering Social Responsibility.* Bloomington, IN: Phi Delta Kappa Educational Foundation, 1998.

_____. "Rethinking Our Thinking on Discipline: Empower—Rather than Overpower," *Education Week* (May 27, 1998): 32, 36.

_____. "Using Teacher Evaluation to Change School Culture," *NASSP Bulletin.* Reston, VA: The National Association of Secondary School Principals (October 1998).

Marshall, Marvin, and Sherry Posnick-Goodwin. "Behaving for All the Right Reasons," *California Educator.* Burlingame, CA: California Teachers Association (April 1998).

Maslow, Abraham H. *Motivation and Personality.* New York: Addison Wesley Longman, Third Edition, 1987.

McGregor, Douglas. *The Human Side of Enterprise.* New York: McGraw-Hill, 1960.

Meduna, Mary J., and Stanley E. Wigle. "Do They Work and What Are the Consequences of Their Use? Two Questions to Ask about External Motivators," *International Journal of Reality Therapy* XVII, No. 1 (Fall 1997): 42–45.

Mulrine, Anna. "A Common Thread? Once Bullied, Now Bullies—with Guns," *U.S. News & World Report* (May 3, 1999).

National Association of Secondary School Principals (NASSP). *Breaking Ranks: Changing an American Institution.* Reston, VA: National Association of Secondary School Principals, 1996.

National PTA. *Discipline: A Parent's Guide.* Chicago: National Congress of Parents and Teachers, 1993.

Nelsen, Jane, Lynn Lott, and Stephen Glenn. *Positive Discipline in the Classroom: How to Effectively Use Class Meetings.* Rocklin, CA: Prima Publishing, 1993.

Oakley, Ed, and Doug Krug. *Enlightened Leadership.* New York: Simon & Schuster, 1993.

Peale, Norman Vincent. *The Power of Positive Thinking.* Pawling, NY: Peale Center for Christian Living, 1978.

Phi Delta Kappa. *Handbook for Developing Schools with Good Discipline.* Bloomington, IN: Phi Delta Kappa, 1982.

Pike, Robert W. *Creative Training Techniques Handbook.* Minneapolis, MN: Lakewood Books, 1994.

Prager, Dennis. *Happiness Is a Serious Problem.* New York: Regan Books (HarperCollins), 1998.

Pryer, Karen. *Don't Shoot the Dog.* New York: Simon & Schuster, 1984.

Raffini, James P. *150 Ways to Increase Intrinsic Motivation in the Classroom*. Boston: Allyn & Bacon, 1996.

Rasch, Bradley W. "Consequence: A Forgotten Concept," *Phi Delta Kappan* (March 1997): 575–576.

Raywid, Mary Anne, and Libby Oshiyama. "Musings in the Wake of Columbine: What Can Schools Do?" *Phi Delta Kappan* (February 2000): 444–449.

Reavis, George H., and Carter V. Good Lee. *An Educational Platform for the Public Schools*. Bloomington, IN: Phi Delta Kappa Educational Foundation, Facsimile Edition, 1996.

Reynolds, Gardner. "Some Thoughts on Peer Pressure." Paper submitted to Marvin Marshall. Loredo, Texas (October 1996).

Ruenzel, David. "Gold Star Junkies," *Teacher Magazine* (February 2000): 25–29.

Sagor, Richard. *At-Risk Students: Reaching and Teaching Them*. Swampscott, MA: Watersun Publishing Company, 1993.

Salk, Lee. *Familyhood: Nurturing the Values that Matter*. New York: Simon & Schuster, 1992.

Scoresby, A. Lynn. *Teaching Moral Development*. Oram, UT: Knowledge Gain Publications, 1996.

Secretary's Commission on Achieving Necessary Skills. *Teaching the SCANS Competencies*. Washington, D.C.: United States Department of Labor, 1993.

Senge, Peter M. *The Fifth Discipline: The Art and Practice of the Learning Organization*. New York: Doubleday, 1990.

Shore, Rebecca. *Creating a Positive School Climate*. Mt. Kisco, NY: Plan for Social Excellence, 1997.

Simon, Sidney B. *Negative Criticism*. Chesterfield, PA: Values Press, 1978.

Sousa, David A. "Brain Research Can Help Principals Reform Secondary Schools," *NASSP Bulletin*. Reston, VA: The National Association of Secondary School Principals (May 1998): 21–28.

_____. *How the Brain Learns.* Reston, VA: National Association of Secondary School Principals, 1995.

Sprenger, Marilee. *Learning and Memory: The Brain in Action.* Alexandria, VA: Association for Supervision and Curriculum Development, 1999.

Sullo, Robert A. *Inspiring Quality in Your School: From Theory to Practice.* Washington, D.C.: National Education Association, 1997.

Sutton, James D. *If My Kid's So Nice... Why's He Driving ME Crazy?* Pleasanton, TX: Friendly Oaks Publications, 1997.

Sylwester, Robert. *A Celebration of Neurons: An Educator's Guide to the Brain.* Alexandria, VA: Association for Supervision and Curriculum Development, 1995.

Tamara, Henry. "Principals Urge Broad Changes in High Schools," *USA Today* (February 22, 1996).

Time Magazine (November 2, 1992): 57.

Time Magazine (April 28, 1997): 28.

Tracy, Louise Felton. *Grounded for Life?! Stop Blowing Your Fuse and Start Communicating with Your Teenager.* Seattle, WA: Parenting Press, 1994.

Tribus, Myron. Personal communication to Marvin Marshall. June 27, 1997.

Urban, Hal. *Life's Greatest Lessons: 20 Things I Want My Kids to Know.* Redwood City, CA: Great Lessons Press, 2000.

U.S. News & World Report, "A Generation of Stone Killers: What Makes Childhood Kids Do What They Do" (January 17, 1994): 33.

Van der Meer, and Ad Dudink. *The Brain Pack: An Interactive, Three-Dimensional Exploration of the Mysteries of the Mind.* Philadelphia, PA: Running Press Book Publishers, 1996.

Van Ness, Ross. *Raising Self-Esteem of Learners.* Bloomington, IN: Phi Delta Kappa Educational Foundation, 1995.

Viadero, Debra. "Research: Bullies Beware," *Education Week* (May 26, 1997): 19–21. www.charactercounts.org/backgrnd.htm

Wolfe, Pat, and Ron Brandt. "What Do We Know from Brain Research?" *Educational Leadership* 56, no. 3 (November 1998): 8–13.

Wong, Harry K., and Rosemary Wong. *The First Days of School.* Sunnyvale, CA: Harry K. Wong Publications, 1991.

Wubbolding, Robert. *Employee Motivation.* Knoxville, TN: SPC Press, 1995.

_____. *Understanding Reality Therapy: A Metaphorical Approach.* New York: Harper Perennial, 1991.

_____. *Reality Therapy for the 21st Century.* Philadelphia: Brunner-Routledge, 2000.

Wycoff, Joyce. *Mindmapping: Your Personal Guide to Exploring Creativity and Problem Solving.* New York: Berkley Books, 1991.

Zahorik, John A. *Constructivist Teaching.* Bloomington, IN: Phi Delta Kappa Educational Foundation, 1995.

APPENDIX

THE RAISE RESPONSIBILITY SYSTEM

A NEW APPROACH

1. The program starts with a seminal shift by focusing on *fostering responsibility rather than compliance.* The usual approach is to aim at compliance or obedience, which too often results in resistance and even rebellion. This is especially the case with adolescents. When responsibility is raised, compliance and obedience become natural by-products.

2. *The Raise Responsibility System* is proactive. The stage is set for dealing with disruptive behavior *before* such behavior occurs. This is in contrast to a reactive strategy of dealing with disruptive behavior after it occurs.

3. In contrast to the usual approach of telling students what to do, a *guiding approach* is used because improvement is most effective using reflection and self-evaluation.

4. The teacher moves into *a stress-reducing* mode when handling disruptive behavior, rather than the usual stressful state that develops when a student disrupts a lesson.

5. *Constructivist* teaching—where students create their own examples to develop meaning—is used because this approach is most effective when emphasizing thinking, understanding, and self-control. For this reason, the strategy can be used at any grade level.

6. A *deductive* approach is used. Four concepts are taught first—before specifics. This is in contrast to the more common inductive approach of first teaching the specifics in order to arrive at general concepts.

7. The student identifies a *level* of development rather than a specific behavior. This strategy *separates a good person from bad behavior,* the doer from the deed, the actor from the act. This eliminates the need for the student to be defensive, a major block to acknowledging responsibility for one's actions.

8. Learning the levels of development has the natural effect of encouraging young people to *think about their goals,* rather than just their roles when influenced by peer pressure.

9. Students learn the difference between internal and external motivation. Understanding motivation has a *self-evaluative* aspect. Just understanding the difference can significantly change behavior.

10. The program fosters *internal* motivation, so students *develop a desire* to be responsible and act appropriately. This is in contrast to the usual approach where the motivation to change comes from an external source.

11. Discipline is viewed and treated as a *responsibility of the student,* rather than as a responsibility of the teacher. If any record keeping is involved, *the student,* not the teacher, *does the work.*

12. The program can be used at *any grade level* and in *any subject area* because students describe what each level of development would be like as it applies to their classroom. In this way, the levels become classroom-specific.

13. *Choice-response thinking* is continually emphasized because our choices direct our lives.

14. Young people *become empowered* to react in positive ways, which prevents victimhood thinking.

15. *Rewards for expected behaviors are not used.* Rewards can be fine acknowledgments. Rewards can also serve as excellent incentives—if the person is interested in the reward. But when rewards are used to manipulate behavior, they become the focus. They encourage young people to think, "What's in it for me?" and lead them to think that society will reward them for appropriate behavior. In addition, rewards do not satisfy the critical question, "How effective are rewards when no one is around?"

16. *Punishments are not used.* Punishments are based on the idea that a youngster has to be harmed in order to learn. People act better when they feel better, not worse. Punishments satisfy the punisher but have little long-lasting effect on the punished because, once the punishment has been served, the youngster feels free of any further responsibility. In addition, punishments for young people are counterproductive because they adversely affect relationships.

17. A classroom disruption is viewed as a *teaching opportunity* for raising responsibility. When a student acts inappropriately, the teacher uses the opportunity as a teachable moment, the same as when a student makes an academic mistake.

18. Although disruptive behavior has traditionally been dealt with privately, this strategy allows the guidance to take place in a *whole-class setting.*

19. *Class time is not wasted* when the teacher attends to a disruption. During the short guidance interchange, the entire class is reinforcing the levels of development.

20. The classroom maintains a *safe, positive learning environment* at all times—even when a student demonstrates irresponsible behavior. The reason is that *coercion is not used.*

21. The strategy establishes a noncoercive classroom that is the foundation for *promoting learning.* When *The Raise Responsibility System* is used in a classroom, the atmosphere of the classroom changes. When the program is used school-wide, the culture of the school changes.

Instructional Model
The Raise Responsibility System

The system is based on the following instructional model:
- **(1) Teaching the levels**
- **(2) Checking for understanding**
- **(3) Guided choices**

(1) Teaching the levels

Four levels of development are taught:
- **(A) A**narchy (absence of order)
- **(B) B**ully*ing* (breaks laws and makes own standards)
  [Note verb form.] Obeys only when enforcer shows more authority

- **(C) C**onformity (conforms to expected standards)
  ***Ex**ternal motivation (stimulated externally)*
- **(D) D**emocracy (develops self-discipline and demonstrates responsibility)
  ***In**ternal motivation*

(2) Checking for understanding

Disruptions are handled by <u>checking for understanding</u>.

The purpose is for the disrupting student to *recognize* and *acknowledge* the developmental level of the action.

Recognizing the level is necessary in order to accept responsibility.

The key to raising responsibility is (1) <u>teaching the levels</u> and (2) <u>checking for understanding</u>.

The vast majority of situations are handled using this basic learning approach of teaching and then checking.

(3) Guided choices

<u>Guided choices</u> are used for students who have acknowledged disruptive behavior and continue their irresponsibility.

Authority without being punitive is used in these situations.

<u>Guided choices</u> stop the disruption and give the student a responsibility-producing activity.

FORMS

Levels of Development

D <u>D</u>emocracy

<> Highest level of development

- Develops self-discipline
- Displays civility and sense of community
- Does good because it is the right thing to do
- <u>Demonstrates responsibility because it is essential for democracy</u>

The motivation is <u>internal</u>.

C <u>C</u>onformity

<> Appropriate and acceptable level of behavior

- Complies
- Cooperates
- Conforms to expected standards

The motivation is <u>external</u>.

B <u>B</u>ullying

<> Neither appropriate nor acceptable level of classroom behavior

- Bosses others
- Bothers others
- Breaks laws and makes own rules and standards

Obeys only when confronted with more authority

A <u>A</u>narchy

<> Lowest level of behavior

- Absence of order
- Aimless and chaotic
- Absence of government

Anarchy is the fundamental enemy of civilization.

> **The difference between levels C and D is often in the *<u>motivation</u>*, rather than the action.**

Sample Letter to Parents
The Raise Responsibility System

Dear Parents:

Our classroom houses a small society. Each student is a citizen who acts in accordance with expected standards of behavior.

With this in mind, rewards are not given for expected behavior— just as society does not give rewards for behaving properly. Also, irresponsible behavior is seen as an opportunity for growth, rather than for punishment.

Our approach encourages students to exercise self-discipline through reflection and self-evaluation. Students learn to control their own behavior, rather than always relying on the teacher for control.

We want our classroom to be encouraging and conducive to learning at all times. In this way, young people develop positive attitudes and behavioral skills that are so necessary for successful lives.

Sincerely,

Teacher

Essay
The Raise Responsibility System

<u>Describe clearly and fully</u>:

1. What **<u>did</u>** I do?

2. What **<u>can</u>** I do to prevent it from happening again?

3. What **<u>will</u>** I do?

- -

Note: The purpose of the essay is to:

(1) isolate the disrupting student, and

(2) give the student a responsibility-producing activity to have the student think about his/her disruption.

The key is for the student to describe—not for the teacher to tell.

Before the student leaves the classroom, two questions are asked:

Do you know why this form was given to you?

Do you think it is personal?

Self-Diagnostic Referral – Upper Elementary
The Raise Responsibility System

Name _____

Date _____

1. What happened?

2. On what level did you act?

3. Explain this level.

4. When you act on this level, how must the teacher treat you?

5. Is this how you want to be treated? Why or why not?

6. On what level should you act?

7. List at least one solution to the problem you could have used if youhad acted more responsibly.

Self-Diagnostic Referral
The Raise Responsibility System

Name (Print) ———————————————————————

Date ———— Period ————

1. Define the problem you created that resulted in your getting this assignment.

2. Tell on what developmental level you acted.

3. Explain this level.

4. Explain why you see yourself at this level.

5. When you act at this level, on what level must the teacher react to you ?

6. How must the teacher treat you on this level?

7. Is this how you want to be treated in the classroom?

8. Why or why not?

9. On what level should you have acted?

10. If you had acted on this level, how would the situation have been different?

11. **On the back** of this Self-Diagnostic Referral, list three (3) solutions to the problem you could have used if you would have acted more responsibly.

Parent Note
The Raise Responsibility System

Re: Period:

Dear Parent:

Self-Diagnostic Referrals are enclosed. The purpose of this type of referral is to help students understand their self-chosen behavior level and to become more socially responsible. The **first** referral is handled between the teacher and the student.

If a **second** referral is necessary, a copy of the **first** and **second** are sent home.

Please note that your child has chosen to act on a level that is not acceptable in my classroom. Please have your child explain this level to you.

If a **third** referral is necessary, a copy of all three are sent home, and future socially irresponsible behavior will be referred to the school office.

Please sign this note and have your child return it to me. Thank you.

_____

Teacher

_____

Parent Signature

Date:

Date due back:

Problem:

Grades 5–8 Sample Schedule of Implementation
The Raise Responsibility System

Day 1 (15 minutes)

Introduce levels A and B.

Day 2 (45 minutes)

Sponge – Students create examples of levels A and B.

Pass out the **Levels of Development** (form describing levels A, B, C, D).

Review levels A and B.

Discuss level C and <u>external motivation</u> (**especially peer pressure**).

Discuss level D and <u>internal motivation</u> (**especially responsibility and initiative**).

Divide students into groups.

  -Groups create three (3) **examples** of **classroom behavior** for each level (A, B, C, D).

  -Inform students that on the next day all members of the group will stand together during their presentation.

  -Each group chooses a leader who is responsible for coordinating the presentation/report of that group.

Groups then create three examples for each level.

HOME ASSIGNMENT: Students copy the following on the **reverse side of the** *Levels of Development* form for parent signature.

(Student's name)_____ has explained the *Levels of Development* to me and that levels A and B are not acceptable levels of classroom behavior.

  _____
           Parent signature

Day 3 (15 minutes)

Groups meet and choose <u>one</u> of their three examples from each level to report.

Groups share the one example from each level.

Substitute Teacher Information

The Raise Responsibility System

READ TO EACH CLASS AT THE START OF THE PERIOD.

This class understands levels of development. It is the basis of discipline in this classroom. A substitute teacher does not have to be versed in the system to use it.

It is the responsibility of the class members to maintain their own discipline. Students know that they choose the level of behavior they want.

If students behave and do the given assignment, they are on *Level C* or *Level D* and should not present a problem.

Level B students are the ones who defy your authority. My students know that they alone choose their level of behavior and that they must accept the responsibility for their choice. I need a list of the defiant students so they can carry out the assignment that goes along with their choice of behavior.

Please leave me a list of students *who chose to act on Level B.*

INDEX

NOTES

NOTES

NOTES

NOTES

NOTES

NOTES

For additional copies of
Discipline without Stress, Punishments, or Rewards
call the order line at Piper Press
800.606.6105
or order online at
www.DisciplineWithoutStress.com